NOT
without
incident

With every kind wish.

Henry L Podmore.

SELECTED
MEMOIRS
BY

HENRY L PODMORE

Catchrose Ltd.
Newcastle, Staffs.

First published in Great Britain 1991
by Catchrose Ltd.
Brampton Bridge House
Newcastle
Staffs.
ST5 1ED

ISBN 0 9517424 0 X

Typeset and printed by
Newcastle Instant Print
12 Queen Street
Newcastle
Staffs ST5 1ED

CONTENTS

	Illustrations	iv
	Preface	v
1.	Some Boyhood Incidents	1
2.	Diverse Recollections of a Science Undergraduate	7
3.	Early Motoring Incidents	11
4.	The Pre-war Years	18
5.	Life in the Royal Armoured Corps	25
6.	Some Experiences of an Officer Cadet	29
7.	Chemical Warfare Training	33
8.	More than a Mere Incident	39
9.	Further War Experiences	49
10.	One of War's Tragedies	55
11.	The Netherlands and the Approach to Germany	58
12.	The Accident	63
13.	Some Post-war Events in Germany	67
14.	Back to Business	78
15.	The Lands Tribunal and a Terrible Tragedy	86
16.	The Beirut Incident	91
17.	The Domain of Ultra-fine Grinding	96
18.	Overseas Marketing	100
19.	*Keramos II* and Some Early Incidents	121
20.	Coastwise in Brazil	127
21.	The Amazon Adventure	135
22.	North to the Caribbean	142
23.	The Unique San Blas Islands	148
24.	The Historic Panama Canal	154
25.	Darwin's Galápagos Islands	161
26.	The Marquesas and Tuamotu Atolls	166
27.	The Magic of Tahiti	170
28.	Island-hopping to Bora-Bora	181
29.	The Cook Islands to Fiji	186
30.	*Keramos II* in New Zealand	195
31.	To Sydney and a Rude Awakening	203
32.	The Great Barrier Reef	206
33.	Across the Timor Sea and Indian Ocean	211
34.	To the Land of the Pharohs	217
35.	The Final Lap	222
	Acknowledgements	225
	Bibliography	226

ILLUSTRATIONS

1.	The author's early introduction to sailing.	107
2.	Podmore China plaque.	107
3.	The author in the Normandy bridgehead.	107
4.	Members of the Belgian Resistance Movement	108
5.	A Warning for troops entering Germany.	108
6.	*Keramos I* in Paris.	109
7.	*Keramos II* under sail.	109
8.	Vibro-Energy mills processing alumina.	110
9.	The author taking a sextant sight.	110
10.	The statue of Christ, Rio de Janeiro.	111
11.	The yacht harbour, Rio de Janeiro.	111
12.	The three spirits of the Amazon.	111
13.	San Blas Island chief and family.	112
14.	A San Blas mola.	112
15.	The onset of a storm.	112
16.	Murray and sea lion pups, Galápagos.	113
17.	The Galápagos marine iguana.	113
18.	Galápagos cattle being loaded for shipment.	114
19.	The tomb of the last king of Tahiti.	114
20.	The island of Ua Pou in the Marguesas.	114
21.	Cook's Bay on the island of Moorea.	171
22.	The Kia Ora Village Hotel, Moorea.	171
23.	The Bora Bora lagoon.	172
24.	A Fijian *bure kalou*.	*172*
25.	Polynesian *tikis* and a cannibal fork.	172
26.	Roberton Island, New Zealand.	173
27.	A Rotorua geyser, New Zealand.	173
28.	The village of Rotorua, New Zealand	173
29.	The roofs of the Sydney Opera House.	174
30.	The Lindeman Island Hotel, Great Barrier Reef.	174
31.	The zircon lagoon on Stradbroke Island, Australia.	174
32.	The open-air cinema, Christmas Island.	175
33.	Direction Island in the Cocos Group.	175
34.	Guy and Nick with their catch.	176
35.	Collecting rain water during crossing of Indian Ocean.	176
36.	Nick making a Seychellois flag.	177
37.	The Vallée de Mai, island of Praslin, Seychelles.	177
38.	The market, Victoria, Seychelles.	178
39.	The legendry love nut.	178
40.	The Aga Khan's Porto Cervo.	178

PREFACE

It would seem that some people prefer a quiet, routine life, like a couple I once knew, who for more than twenty years went to the same small seaside resort for their annual holidays, and not only stayed at the same hotel each time, but insisted on having the same bedroom. Then there are people who crave adventure, but for whom it is denied by circumstances which impose a dull confined existence.

I happen to have been born with an inquisitive mind and an insatiable wanderlust, but have been fortunate, in as much as, events have fortuitously evolved to provide ample satisfaction for both idiosyncrasies – and as a result, life for me has certainly been "not without incident".

After sailing round the world, and subsequently retiring from an eventful business life, I used a little of the resulting spare time to edit some of the many photographs I had taken in distant lands and to incorporate the slides in audio-visual programmes – the dual projectors being controlled by a digital tape recording incorporating the commentary, music and sound effects. Some of those who saw these travelogues suggested that the content would provide suitable subject matter for an illustrated book. But when my preliminary drafts were seen, I was persuaded to widen the scope, so as to include incidents which have occurred throughout my life.

The resulting book is not a biography – as in many lives, some parts are perhaps best unsung – but a collection of anecdotes, strung together by just sufficient biographical information to provide necessary continuity.

Werrington   Henry L. Podmore
Stoke-on-Trent

October 1991

To the Family and friends
with whom I have shared
experiences that were
'not without incident'

1

SOME BOYHOOD INCIDENTS

I was born a couple of years before the outbreak of World War I. At that time, my father was the manager of the clay production department at the Royal Doulton pottery in Burslem, Stoke-on-Trent. Our home was nearby in the district of Porthill but shortly afterwards, we moved to a house at Newchapel, on the outskirts of the city. My mother, before her marriage, had been a nursing sister at one of the local hospitals.

I well remember the photograph being taken which is shown at Plate 1. After getting dressed in my smart uniform, mother took me to a photographer's studio in Burslem. On the way we passed a policeman, whom I saluted, and was much pleased when he returned the salute – while keeping a dead straight face. At the entrance to the studio, there was a row of grimy iron railings, along which I dragged my hand. Mother was naturally afraid that I would wipe my dirty hand down the front of my uniform, so before the photograph could be taken, Henry had to wash his hands – and get a very severe scolding.

On the outbreak of war, a requirement arose for very large quantities of porcelain insulators for use on the telephone lines between the trenches. At that time, they were being made manually – consequently, the process was slow and very labour intensive. Father was allotted the task of speeding up production and this he did by inventing a machine to make the insulators automatically.

Using plastic clay as the raw material, this ingenious machine shaped the exterior surface of the insulator and simultaneously formed the inner skirt. A screw thread was then cut inside the skirt, which enabled the insulator to be screwed onto the supporting steel bracket. The purpose of the skirt was to ensure a dry connection between the insulator and the metal support. These machines could produce about twenty insulators per minute and within a matter of months, a dozen or so units were in production.

Father was also made responsible for the conversion of part of the Royal Doulton workshops to facilitate the machining of steel shells for artillery ammunition. On completion of this assignment, management of the new activity was added to his other responsibilities.

I was the second child and as such, grew up with a sister. I vividly remember, when I was about four years old, pushing her into a very muddy duck-pond. I also remember, even more vividly, the consequences, which while not painful in any way, were nevertheless intended to make me appreciate to the full, that there is no future in pushing young ladies into ponds.

I also clearly remember the night when I was awakened by a distant droning noise and saw flickering lights on the curtains. I got out of bed and on opening the curtains, saw what I had previously heard people talking about – a German zeppelin. The lights were, no doubt, produced by searchlights and reflections from the airship's aluminised fabric. I ran to my parent's room and excitedly told them what I had seen, whereupon, mother's first reaction was to suggest that I had been having a nightmare and that I should go back to bed.

After I had described the zeppelin in greater detail, father became sufficiently interested to go to my room and take a look for himself, but of course, by that time, the zeppelin had moved out of sight. As a result, mother tucked me up in bed and told me to go to sleep and have no more stupid dreams.

The following morning, neighbours came round to our house and asked if we had seen the zeppelin. If I subsequently had nightmares – nobody ever talked about them.

One outcome of the air raids, was the introduction of lighting restrictions and on the very first night of the blackout, father was experimenting on his car in the garage. For some time he had been endeavouring to make the car run on paraffin, as petrol was severely rationed. On this particular night, he was working by the light of a candle inside a glass jam-jar, when somehow it ignited the fuel, and within seconds, the car was ablaze. To prevent the house being burned down, he pushed the car out of the garage and I well remember the horror with which I watched the fierce flames, leaping thirty feet or more, into the all pervading blackness of the night.

Next morning, father and I surveyed the charred and twisted wreckage. The heat must have been immense because the glass windscreen had melted and was hanging down like icicles. I asked father what he intended to do with the wreck and without hesitation, he said that he would rebuild it as a lorry, for which there was then a good demand – and this he did. Because many of the required parts were unobtainable, he had to make them from the most suitable material he could find. I remember him spending many hours cutting and filing the teeth on a gear-wheel, which he fashioned from a piece of thick steel plate.

During my childhood, I was afflicted by almost every possible illness and when I contracted double pneumonia, I was not expected to live. Apparently, I just made it, but from then on, I was always regarded and treated as a delicate child.

2

The vicar at the nearby church – the Revd J. G. Hamlet – had previously been a teacher at Wrekin College. He had gained a degree in mathematics at Oxford and still retained an active interest in teaching this and several other subjects. As a result, he would spend a few hours during the week, giving private tuition to students working for various examinations. He also had a class for a few young children who were not yet of school age and when I was about four years old, I was very fortunate in being able to join this class. My association with this remarkable gentleman developed into a friendship, which was to have a great influence throughout my student life.

By the end of the war, father had several other inventions to his credit, in addition to the insulator machine and soon the royalties from the patents far exceeded his salary from Doulton. Consequently, he decided to invest in two small watermills near to Stone – a few miles from the Potteries. The mills were used to calcine and grind cow bones for the production of bone china and prepare glaze for the pottery industry.

This activity and the fact that he wished to become more closely involved in the management of the family pottery – Podmore China Co – resulted in him leaving Royal Doulton and starting to work on his own account. Within a year, he purchased the large mill at Consall, which had been idle throughout the war. This mill was powered by three of the largest waterwheels in Britain and two water turbines. All were in urgent need of repair and consequently, he set about the tremendous task of rebuilding them and installing new plant and equipment. The mill had originally been built to grind corn, but when Josiah Wedgewood introduced white earthenware, it had been adapted to the calcining and grinding of flint pebbles; the product then being transported to the Wedgewood works in Hanley, by pack mules.

The nearby Consall Hall had also been unoccupied during the war, and was to be later acquired and refurbished for use as our residence.

By now, I had a brother. For a short period my sister and I went to the local village school but subsequently, travelled each day by train to Leek, where we attended the respective High Schools. Until the age of thirteen thereabouts, I continued to be regarded as a delicate child. My school work was poor, but in due course, the syllabus changed to include general science and in place of the tiresome arithmetic, we had geometry, algebra and trigonometry – subjects which laid greater stress on reasoning and deduction. As a result, my position in class rapidly improved.

At about the same time, I found that I could kick a ball equally well with either foot and this led to an interest in soccer. I studied the rules and tactics of the game and was soon playing in the school second eleven. My health improved dramatically and no longer was I to be regarded as a weakling. The following season I played in the first eleven and was elected team captain.

The man who taught chemistry and physics (Mr. A. D. Price – but known to the boys as "Taffy"), happened to be exceptionally good at his job. He had the ability to hold the class enthralled, while he carried out instructive experiments, accompanied by an interesting and always amusing commentary. Without a doubt, "Taffy" was largely responsible for my becoming passionately interested in his two subjects. At home, I fitted out a laboratory and for my birthday and Christmas presents, I always requested apparatus and chemicals, so that in due course, it became quite well equipped.

Explosives fascinated me and as November the fifth approached, I would be busy making fireworks of various types. The "bangers" consisted of pieces of gas-piping measuring up to about four feet in length, which were rammed with gunpowder and ignited by a time fuse. Their performance, as might be expected, was highly unpredictable, because most of them would rise skywards and whiz around, before exploding and scattering shrapnel to the ground – one did not have to be told to take cover!

Literature on the making of explosives was not easy to come by but in one book, I found information on a mixture containing potassium chlorate, which would explode on slight impact. This greatly intrigued me, so I began to work out a method of mixing powders, without involving any risk of impact. In due course, I felt sufficiently confident to have a go at mixing the actual constituents of the explosive. The remaining problem was to produce the detonating impact by remote control – and the more remote the better! The method I eventually decided upon, involved placing about a pound of the highly dangerous mixture on the concrete yard, in front of our garage, and above which was a hay loft. I then proposed to take several pebbles up into the loft and position myself so that I could put my arm through an open window and release a pebble from a point directly above the explosive. After quickly withdrawing my arm – I would then hit the hay! The first time I tried it, the pebble missed, but not so the second, for there was an almighty bang and tiles from the roof clattered down onto the yard.

When I looked through the window, I was dismayed to see father's car making an emergency stop, just short of the garage. Father had obviously heard the explosion and seen the tiles and other bits and pieces falling to the ground. When he got out of the car, he must instinctively have suspected the cause of the commotion, because he immediateley called, "Henry". I thought I might as well face the music there and then, so I slowly made my way to where father was, by this time, examining a wide gaping crack right across the concrete yard.

He greeted me with the words, "Well, and what was all that about?" I played for time by giving him a wordy account of the experiment, after which I expected his wroth – if nothing more – to fall upon me, but true to his enquiring nature, he merely said, "Yes, but how on earth did you manage to mix the materials without killing yourself?"

In a book on pottery, I read how the famous *Rouge Flambé* was produced. Apparently, the glaze containing copper oxide, had to be fired under reducing conditions. In my laboratory, I had a small kiln and the necessary materials – so, why not make some of the very valuable *Rouge Flambé*? Accordingly, I prepared a small vase and applied the necessary glaze. This was then placed in the kiln, which I planned to fire under reducing conditions by passing through it, a stream of hydrogen. I realised that the kiln would have to be purged of air, otherwise when the temperature was raised, the hydrogen and air mixture would explode.

All went according to plan during the early stages, but when the pyrometer registered a temperature of about $1080°C$, I could not resist the temptation to open, very slightly, the spy-hole on the kiln door, in order to see if the black glaze had changed to the fabulous ruby red. I can't remember what I saw, because on opening the spy-hole, air must have entered the kiln to produce a terrific explosion. What I do remember, was mother lifting the kiln door off my chest, as I lay slumped against the opposite wall of my laboratory. A short time previously, mother had given birth to a daughter and after the explosion, she was heard to admit to a fear that having just gained a daughter, she was about to lose a son.

The sixth form at school was divided into an 'arts section' and a 'science section'. Naturally, I saw myself destined for the latter. I did not despise the arts, in fact, the first prize I managed to gain at school was for drawing, but I began to give almost all my time to the study of science, resulting in other subjects being sadly neglected – that is, until one day when I began to see things in a somewhat different light.

Father had invited to the house an eminent scientist and I was allowed to join them for afternoon tea. During the conversation, father asked our guest what subject he believed opened up most potential for a scientific career. Of course, I hoped he would say 'chemistry' or failing that, 'physics' – but he didn't. He said there was little point in developing ideas in any subject, unless they could be clearly communicated and discussed in a way which would arouse interest and ultimately lead to further development. Hence, the most important subject must be one's own native language.

So from that day on, I decided not to neglect the study of 'English'. In fact, when in due course, I found myself in the sixth form science section, I entered for the school essay prize. This had invariably been won by a boy in the arts section, but one of the optional titles, *The Development of the Incandescent Lamp*, rather intrigued me. Accordingly, I researched the subject in various libraries, and in due course submitted my essay, which to the surprise of many, including myself, was considered worthy of the prize.

While in the sixth form, the Revd George Hamlet encouraged me to work for the University Matriculation Examination, which I succeeded in passing with a distinction in chemistry.

2
DIVERSE RECOLLECTIONS
OF A SCIENCE UNDERGRADUATE

During my first year at the University of Birmingham, I read chemistry, physics, pure and applied maths, and German.

The 'freshers' who were interested in association football, were invited to participate in a practice match, and the following week, I was very surprised to find that I had been selected to play for the University second eleven – and even more surprised a week later, to learn that I had been chosen to play in the first eleven. Thereafter, I played regularly for the University against other universities and also against some of the local league teams, including Aston Villa, Birmingham City and West Bromwich Albion.

As captain of the University table-tennis team, I was fortunate in having an opportunity to frequently visit the then British champion – Adrian Haydon. At his home, on the outskirts of Birmingham, he had a large table-tennis room, in which I spent many enjoyable hours. Sometimes, Adrian, while at the table, would also be keeping an eye on his young daughter, Ann, who was to become Ann Jones – the Wimbledon Tennis champion. Other famous exponents of the game whom I met and played against included Zabados and Bellak (World Doubles champions) and also the great Victor Barna who was World Singles champion for several years.

The various research activities at the University greatly interested me. One day, I was introduced to a physics research student, named Watson Watt, who told me that he was trying to make radio signals bounce off brick walls. He later took his equipment, including the specially modified cathode ray tubes, over to Daventry in order to further his research with the aid of the powerful signals from the BBC transmitter. During the course of these experiments, he occasionally saw a ghost signal pass across his screen, and then it occurred to him that these mysterious signals were only observed when an aircraft was passing overhead. His calculations showed that the powerful radio signals were being reflected by the aircraft and recorded on his equipment. Watson Watt had, in fact, invented what was subsequently to become known as radar and which was to play such a significant role in World War II.

In the Chemistry Department, I came to know well another research worker – Maurice Stacey – who was endeavouring to synthesise ascorbic acid (vitamin C). On one occasion when I visited him, he showed me a flask containing a thick syrupy liquid and told me that he was sure it contained vitamin C, but until he could get the product into a pure state by crystallisation, he was unable to verify the molecular structure by X-ray analysis. He said he had spent weeks trying to make the liquid crystallise by centrifuging, rapid cooling and seeding with various types of crystals, but all to no avail. The man was clearly becoming despondent.

The next time I saw Maurice was on the first day of term after the Easter vacation and he was overcome with excitement. It transpired that before the vacation, he had put the flask containing the obdurate liquid in a locker and then gone home to ponder on what he might do next, in order to make it crystallise. However, on returning and taking the flask from the locker, he was amazed and overjoyed to find that it contained gleaming white crystals. These were subsequently shown to be vitamin C, and it was the start of a brilliant academic career for Maurice. During the war, while in the USA, he directed research work on chemical separation processes for essential constituents of the atom bomb and after the war, returned to Birmingham to become the Professor of Chemistry.

My final year was devoted entirely to chemistry, with much of the time being spent in the laboratories. The professor of Chemistry at that time was W.N.Howarth F.R.S. (later Sir Norman Howarth), who was making a great name for himself by researching the structure of complex carbohydrates. On his visits to the senior laboratories he would discuss work with the students in considerable detail and greatly encourage individual enterprise. He was a stickler for tidy work, and would walk past and ignore any student who had an untidy work bench.

The Final examinations involved working on many three and four hour papers in the Great Hall and even longer periods in the laboratories. During the Finals, we had a heat-wave and in one of the practical exams, the product of a required reaction was a blood-red azo dye. Perspiring hands mopped perspiring brows and soon hands, faces, hair and clothing all took on this intense coloration. The examination atmosphere was tense enough, but to see everyone apparently dripping in blood, did nothing to calm our frayed nerves.

The most dreaded part of the Finals, however, was without doubt, the oral exam. – particularly when we learned that the examiner was to be Professor Robinson, from the University of Manchester. He was known to be a brilliant chemist, but as an examiner, he had a fearsome reputation among students. He expected very high standards and had little time for those who failed to measure up to his exalted expectations. Accordingly, I decided to become familiar with his work, by reading many of his research papers. On the eventful day, we had a long practical examination during which the Professor approached each student in turn. When, in due course, he came to the boy working next to me, I could overhear the conversation, which did nothing at all to allay my worst fears.

When he came over to me, he asked what I was doing. Whereupon, I took courage in both hands and said, "I have just commenced a reaction similar to the one you used in the third stage of your synthesis of the blue colouring matter, as found in the cornflower. . . . . . .". He immediately interrupted my carefully prepared spiel with, "You say it is similar – how does it differ?" But fortunately, before I could try to answer, he began to tell me about this brilliant synthesis. I listened attentively and every now and then, interjected with an apt comment or question to keep his discourse going. After about twenty minutes, during which I had not answered a single question, he patted me on the shoulder and said, "You will be alright". And with that he moved away, to leave me breathing the biggest ever sigh of relief.

While I was attending the University, my elder sister was also in Birmingham, following a nursing career at the Queen's Hospital. From time to time our parents would visit us and together we would go to the theatre or some other place of entertainment. On one such occasion, we decided to go to the Ice Rink, to see an ice-hockey match between the local team and a visiting Canadian team. This proved to be such a great attraction that we were unable to get four seats, all together; the best we could do, was to get two together, for mother and father and two singles, which were some distance away. The match developed into a very bad tempered affair. At one point, a player was penalised and in anger, he hit the puck off the rink and right into the audience. This caused some obvious commotion, but in due course play was resumed

At the end of the match, I joined up with mother and father and together we made our way to where we had left my sister – but she was not to be found anywhere. Soon all the people had departed and as we still had not found her, we approached the management to ascertain if they could throw any light on the mystery. We described the girl and immediately someone said, "That could be the lady who was taken to hospital". They then told us that when the puck was driven into the audience, it had struck a young lady on the forehead and rendered her unconscious. We now had to find to which hospital she had been taken and make our way there. Eventually we located her; she was still

9

unconscious and very poorly. After several weeks she was allowed home, but it was quite some time before she was well again. The management disclaimed all responsibility for injury sustained by spectators and as a result, our attempts to obtain some measure of compensation failed completely.

After coming down from Birmingham in 1936 with an Honours Degree in Chemistry, I joined my father in the family business. By this time, the scope of the company activities had considerably widened, to include – in addition to the grinding of minerals – the preparation of glazes, colours and a range of compounded clays. As a part time student, I studied ceramics at the local Technical College, which later became the Stoke-on-Trent Polytechnic.

My duties now called for a fair amount of travelling, so I parted with £50, to become the proud owner of a second-hand Riley Nine.

3

EARLY MOTORING INCIDENTS

Shortly before we moved to Consall, I was given for my birthday, a gleaming red pedal-car. Each day, I would venture a little farther afield and in particular to an incline on the pavement, where during descents the car could attain maximum speed. Many people stopped to admire my proud possession and some of the local children would ask if they could have a ride; to which request I would invariably agree.

One day, a boy who had on previous occasions driven my car, asked if he could have a go down the incline. I naturally consented, whereupon he said, "Stay here, while I go up the hill and then watch me come down, very fast". I saw him take the car up the hill and round the slight bend at the top, then waited for him to come speeding down – but he didn't. After a while, I decided to go up the hill to ascertain the problem, but neither the boy, nor the car, were to be found anywhere. I looked all around and asked people if they had seen a boy with a red car, but my enquiries came to naught. Heartbroken, I returned home to tearfully relate my loss, which father reported to the police.

A few days later, a policeman called and told us that my car had been found at a nearby house. He went on to say that it would be necessary for me to identify the boy, after which we could repossess the car. Accordingly, father and I went with the constable and soon I saw once again my car – and the boy. As we left the house with the car, I asked father what would happen to the boy. Father, no doubt wishing to take advantage of the occasion to impress upon me the fact that there is no future in stealing, said, "The police will deal with him – no doubt he will have to go to prison". I remember being very upset and wanting to go back to the house, in order to tell the policeman that I wished to forgive the poor boy.

This true story and others not so true, concerning the little red car, became many years later, favourite bedtime story subjects for each of our young children. The climax to the true story always featured the fact that there is no future in stealing, but the punishment dealt out to the boy, always stopped well short of going to prison.

One of our former local Members of Parliament, Harold Hales (the man who presented the Hale's Trophy for the fastest liner crossing of the Atlantic), was said to be the first man in North Staffordshire to own a motor car, when he bought a two cylinder Benz, around 1900. In that case, father must also have been a pioneer motorist locally, by virtue of his owning a very early two cylinder Wolseley. I never knew that particular car, but I do remember father's second Wolseley, which had large brass headlamps connected to an acetylene generator on the runningboard.

As soon as it was possible to purchase lorries after World War I, father decided to obtain one for use at the pottery. It was to be a two ton Halley – painted red. Each day, I would enquire if it had been delivered and the answer was always, "no" – until the day came, when I was told, "It is going to be delivered tomorrow". On the following day, I eagerly awaited father's return from work, so that I could learn all about the bright red Halley, but when he eventually arrived, it was obvious that he was far from happy. "Wasn't it delivered?", I asked. "Yes it was", came the gruff reply and then – "They sent it with a woman driver and on entering the works she couldn't stop the thing, with the result that it demolished the bottle oven. We now have an essential part of the works out of action and a completely useless lorry".

It was about this time that my brother was born. When I was taken into the room to see him for the first time, I was asked what I thought about him, whereupon I understand my only comment was, "He is as red as the Halley".

Father used to relate the most amazing motoring experiences and I must admit, there were times when I wondered to what extent they were really true, but as I became older, I often accompanied him and came to know that strange things did indeed happen, when he was at the wheel.

One day, we were returning home after dark, when the car began to falter. Father stopped to investigate and found the engine was very hot. He therefore removed the filler cap from the radiator, in order to check the water level; to enable him to see, he struck a match and brought it towards the filler pipe. Immediately, flames shot several feet into the air, setting his hair alight and badly burning his face. From that day, his hair always receded from his brow, while the eyebrows and eyelashes never properly grew again. It later transpired that the cylinder-head gasket had failed, so allowing petrol vapour to enter the radiator.

On another occasion, father told me that he was proposing to purchase a mill at Stretton, near to Burton-on-Trent and had arranged to meet the gentleman, with whom he was negotiating. He asked if I would like to go with him to see the mill and naturally I was happy to do so.

Father always drove pretty fast but on the narrow winding road beyond Uttoxeter, we were held up by a slower car and this caused him to become more and more frustrated, as it was imperative that he be in good time for the appointment. Eventually, we came to a comparatively straight section of the road where father put his foot down and swept past the offending car. Immediately, the driver of the overtaken car started to blow his horn and the passenger leaned out of a window and waved excitedly. Father said, "I don't know what's the matter with them, I overtook perfectly correctly, so they can stay where they are" and with that, he drove still faster to make up for lost time and to get away from the car that was now desperately trying to overtake us.

It became a real race, with both cars going far too fast for safety, until eventually, father decided to slow down and let the other car come past. As it did so, the passenger motioned us to stop – which we did. The other car also stopped and the driver jumped out and .rushed towards us, "I am awfully sorry" he said, "but when you overtook us, the spare wheel fell off the back of your car and we thought we should let you know". Father, whose opening words seemed likely to be "What the hell - -" now found himself thanking the man and apologising for putting him to so much trouble – and no little danger.

The outcome of all this was that we now had to turn round and go back about five miles to retrieve our wheel, which we found lying in a ditch. For the benefit of younger readers, perhaps it should be explained that at the time, the spare wheel was strapped onto the back of the car and it was not unknown for the straps to fail.

When hundreds of coal-fired bottle ovens were in operation, smog in and around the Potteries could be really terrible. On one occasion, father and I were caught, after dark, in such a fog and soon we became hopelessly lost. We found ourselves in a narrow country lane and as we rounded a bend, we heard a woman scream. Father immediately stopped the car, whereupon the woman dashed towards us and called out, "Oh thank goodness you stopped – I thought you were going in". Father asked, "In where?" After the woman had regained her composure, she said, "In the reservoir – come and see". We got out and there indeed, only a few feet in front of the car, was a sheet of water. The woman then went on to tell us that during the previous week, a car had gone into the reservoir at the same place and the four occupants had been drowned. Father feelingly thanked the providential woman and then carefully reversed the car away from the threatening water. After 'retracing our steps' and meandering for a few miles along narrow country lanes, we eventually found ourselves approaching Congleton.

As the following Sunday was a nice clear day, father suggested that we should go over to Congleton and take a look at the reservoir that had so nearly led to our demise. We drove round the town and made numerous enquiries; we studied the map and explored many country lanes – but we never did find that reservoir again.

Some years later father had another adventure in the fog. He had gone over to Chesterfield to visit some potteries and had taken mother with him. As they did not return at the expected time, I began to worry but eventually, received a telephone call from father. He told me they had been involved in an accident, but were both unharmed and would be returning home by taxi. In due course they arrived and father told me of their shattering experience.

I feel I cannot do better, than record the story as father related it and which went something like this: "After leaving Buxton and getting up onto the high ground, we ran into fog, which in places was so dense that Bert (Alberta) had to walk in front of the car to guide me. From time to time, I stopped so that she could get into the car for a rest. As we neared Leek, I had made such a stop and after Bert had rested, she got out to resume walking. I also got out and went up to a stone wall, to respond to a 'call of nature'. While I was so occupied, I suddenly realized that the car was moving – I ran and tried to catch up with it, as it rapidly gained speed down a steep incline – but it was impossible. I watched the tail-light disappear into the gloom, as we followed, walking down the road.

It was then that we saw two faint lights approaching – it was a pony and trap. As it passed us, the driver said, 'It's a nasty night mister', to which I agreed and then realized that the trap must have passed my car, as it hurtled down the ever steepening road – goodness knows what the man would have thought had he known there was nobody in it. By this time, I recognized that we were on the steep part of the Upper Hulme bank and approaching the village.

We could still hear the car, away in the distance, and soon there was an almighty crash. After a while, we came up to the public house and we could see where the stub axles of my car had scraped across the front wall of the building, before ploughing through a garden and then plunging over a rocky precipice. It took some time to get down to where the car had finally come to rest and where two men, with storm lanterns, were searching among the wreckage. I asked them what they were looking for, to which they replied, 'The driver'. I told them, 'You can stop looking, because I am – or at least was – the driver'".

At that time, the main road passed through the village of Upper Hulme and had a gradient of one in seven. The most likely explanation for the car moving away, was that the brakes would have become overheated, due to repeated application and during the short stop, may have cooled sufficiently to partially realease the hand brake.

For years after, one could still see the marks across the entrance to the public house. If anyone had been leaving, as the car swept by, the story would indeed have had a tragic ending. As might have been expected the car – a sturdy Rover – became a total write-off.

I often visited the Motor Show with father and found great interest in the cars, as well as in the clever sales talk. On one occasion, at the Rolls Royce stand, a man was looking in admiration at one of the shining monsters, when he was approached by an eager salesman. "What do you think of her?" was his introductory gambit. "She's terrific", replied the onlooker, "but unfortunately I shall never be able to afford such a car". The salesman asked what car the man owned and on receiving the information, he made a note of it, together with the price paid. He also noted similar information regarding four previous cars and then said, "So it would seem that over the past eleven years, you have expended on cars, a sum sufficient to have provided you with a Rolls Royce at the outset and this would have resulted in your enjoying the use of a real car, all the time". It was not until father asked me where the flaw was in the argument, that I began to doubt the logic.

During my student days many people smoked and I was often encouraged to do likewise. At university much time was spent in the laboratories, where smoking was not permitted and when not in the laboratories, I was under the watchful eye of the football coach, who frowned upon smoking. As a result, I did not get much opportunity to get hooked on the habit – but there was another reason. I had calculated that, if instead of buying twenty cigarettes a day, I were to invest the money, I would eventually have the means to buy a Rolls Royce – and this is what I did.

After the introduction of the motor car, dogs took a long time to develop traffic sense and continued to dash across the roads, just as they had previously done when they could easily avoid horse-drawn vehicles. Consequently, dogs presented a real motoring hazard and many were run over. One day, I was out with father, when four dogs bolted, one after the other, from a hole in a fence and attempted to pass in front of the car. As there was no possibility of stopping in time, we heard four bangs, and on going back, found that all four had been killed instantly.

On another occasion, we were going along one of the back streets in Stoke, when a dog dashed out of a doorway and straight under the car. We stopped and walked back to where the poor dog was lying motionless at the side of the road. Nearby, a man was leaning up against the wall of a house; he wore no coat and his thumbs were tucked behind his braces. Father approached him and asked if he knew who was the owner of the dog. "Yus, that bitch were moine", came the rough reply. Father expressed his sorrow for what had happened but made it quite clear that he was not at fault, as the dog had run straight into the car, making it quite impossible to avoid the stupid animal.

After further commiseration regarding the loss, father took a halfcrown from his pocket and suggested that the man should, "Get himself a drink". This brought forth a torrent of abuse which terminated with, "They cós kape they hafecran; that were a pedigray – only a wik since, oi gif foive quid fer er". Father was somewhat taken aback by this unexpected retort, but quickly joined battle with,"I am not buying your dog – simply offering you something to get a drink, as I am sorry you have lost your dog". The man was definitely determined to seek compensation for his loss, while father was equally determined not to be browbeaten. Thus the argument continued, with first one and then the other, appearing to get the upperhand. What the man lacked in debating skill, he more than made up for by the loudness of his outbursts and the use of a wide range of powerful expletives – many of which were new to me! After about ten minutes of this wordy contest, I was amazed to see the dog slowly lift up its head and then scamper back into the house. Immediately, the man thrust out his hand and said "Give us they hafecran". Father handed over the coin and as we walked back to the car, he said, "Let that be a lesson to you – never complete a business deal too quickly".

A local man, who had quite a reputation as a motorist, was Captain Unwin VC. The Victoria Cross had been awarded in recognition of his outstanding gallantry, while in command of the SS *River Clyde* in the legendary landing at Gallipoli, during World War I. Although badly injured himself, he had repeatedly dived into the water to rescue members of his crew and others.

The Captain owned a two-seater sports car, which he drove like a road racing car and as he had a business interest in the ceramic industry, he would occasionally call upon father at the Shelton works. At the entrance, there were two massive stone gate posts. On one of his visits, the Captain approached far too fast, the car skidded and hit one of the posts, so knocking out a large piece of stone. Father, on hearing the crash, rushed out to see if the Captain was injured – only to be met with, "This entrance is far too narrow; you should get that damned post moved back a bit". Father eyed the large piece of stone that had been dislodged and curtly countered with, "If you come on here again like that, I shall have no gate post to move back".

One day, father said he was going over to Wooton Lodge to disccuss some business with the Captain and asked if I would like to accompany him. On arriving at the stately home, the first thing I noticed was the famous car, now looking even more battered, and with various bits and pieces hanging limply down. We entered the imposing entrance hall, which had large oil paintings on the walls, together with the name plate off the SS *River Clyde*. But what attracted my immediate attention, was the beautiful young lady in a long white dress, who was seated at a spinet and producing the most delightful music. The setting was reminiscent of the opening sequence in a romantic film. The lady was the Captain's daughter and I was much pleased when she joined us for afternoon tea.

Father noticed a large rectangular patch on one of the walls, which indicated that an oil painting had recently been removed, so he asked the Captain what had happened to it. Whereupon the Captain tersely replied, "The damned Yanks have had her". Then, pointing to a large portrait of one of his ancestors, he added, "It will be his bloody turn next". The daughter looked at her father disdainfully, and very sweetly murmered, "Fa – ther".

Some time later a story was hitting the head-lines in the local newspapers. Apparently, the Captain, accompanied by a friend, was driving along a country lane near his residence, when he overtook the village parson. The Captain stopped and offered the man a lift, which was accepted. Thereupon, he opened up the raised dickey seat at the back of his car and helped the parson to climb into it. The Captain then drove off at his usual break-neck speed, which did not slacken when he came to a steeply hump-backed bridge – the car left the ground and the parson shot up into the air, over the roadside hedge, and landed abruptly in the adjoining field. It was only on arrival at the next village, where the Captain had arranged to deliver the poor man, that it was realized he had mysteriously disappeared. As can be imagined, the parson was very much put out by this incident – in more ways than one – and he subsequently sued for substantial damages, but happily, an amicable settlement of the affair was eventually reached.

I have previously mentioned that my first car was a Riley Nine – as were several subsequent cars. Before the war, I became an enthusiastic member of the Riley Motor Club, with a particular interest in rallying and attended many races where Riley Nine drivers such as Freddy Dixon and Percy McClure gained notable success. Since then I have owned many cars and driven in many parts of the world, but I cannot recall a single noteworthy incident as a driver.

4

THE PRE-WAR YEARS

My father always encouraged me to see things for myself and not simply accept the views and opinions of others – something I was always happy to do. So one day, I decided to attend a spiritualist meeting to see a séance. I was much intrigued by the phenomena but quickly came to the conclusion that some, at least, were contrived. I was not deceived by those based on scientific information, such as the mysterious glows produced by polarized light, but there were 'happenings' which completely baffled me.

I had also been baffled by a stage magician, by the name of Dante, and I thought there might be a connection between the two forms of presentation. I did not like being bamboozled, and as a result, decided to make a study of the art of magic. I read books on the subject, went to see performances by the leading illusionists, acquired equipment from specialists in London and began to devise and make equipment myself. In due course, I was able to entertain people at charity shows, and later at Home Guard concerts.

One piece of equipment I made, consisted of a large cabinet from which my young sister Mary, could be made to appear or disappear. After I had completed the construction and shown Mary the mechanics of the operation, we thought we would try it out on father. Accordingly, when we later saw him, on returning from work, we placed the cabinet where he would see it and Mary got into the rehearsed postion. When father appeared, I was apparently putting in the last screws and as expected he asked what I was doing. I told him it was a cabinet I had just finished making for my magic show and then commenced to demonstrate what was supposed to happen. I opened up the sides to show it was completely empty and then closed them again. Next I turned the cabinet round, so that he could see it from all directions and then opened it – whereupon, Mary stepped out.

Prior to this occasion, I had never seen father lost for words, but after he had recovered from the shock, he led Mary away and interrogated her, as to how she had so mysteriously appeared from nowhere. I had previously told Mary that magicians never reveal their techniques and as the questioning continued, I realized that I had placed her in a most invidious position. I had no alternative therefore but to explain to father the principle of the routine, after which he merely remarked, "I never realized how easily one could be fooled".

The outcome of my acquaintance with magic was sufficient to convince me that most, if not all, of the 'happenings' I had seen at séances, were capable of being explained on a rational basis.

Another subject I attempted to master by the use of books was ballroom dancing. My tennis partner was an exceptionally good dancer and she inveigled me into attending a school 'Old Boys Dance'. As I was anxious to impress her, I studied the various dance steps most meticulously from a book, which showed the successive postions for the feet by diagrams, rather like a series of footprints. In this way I mastered the waltz, the foxtrot, the tango and many other forms of gyration, to the accompaniment of music played on records. When I arrived at the dance, I was amazed to find that the dancers were not following the footprints as in my book, and what was even more bewildering, was to see my young lady friend executing the 'one step' at such a speed, that made it quite impossible to see where she was putting her feet; yes, that evening was a complete disaster.

Books on the history of pottery indicate that the Podmore family were involved in the manufacture of pottery in Liverpool, round about 1740. In 1755, Robert Podmore moved to Worcester and started a pottery there, but this branch of the family eventually settled in the Potteries and established a pottery in Tunstall. This operated until the outbreak of World War II, when the industry was concentrated, with a view to the production of essential items only. After World War I, father had specialized in the production of materials for the manufacture of pottery, such as prepared clays for earthenware, porcelain and bone china – as well as ground minerals, glazes and a wide range of colours.

When I joined the company, I was first employed in the laboratory, which was mainly responsible for quality control. When there was a complaint from a customer, it was my job to investigate the matter. I well remember one particular problem, concerning a colour for addition to glazes, which we sold as 'Ivory No. 429'. One day, we received an unusually large order for it, from a pottery in Kilmarnock and at about monthly intervals thereafter, we would receive equally large repeat orders – but the strange thing was, that the orders were always made out for 'Pink No. 429'.

Consequently, I thought it would be a good idea to send a representative up to Scotland, to see what they were doing with such large quantities and why they always referred to it as 'Pink'. It transpired that the firm had obtained a contract to supply large quantities of faience tiles to cover the station walls on the Glasgow underground railway, and sure enough, the walls were a beautiful shade of pink. We were happy to receive these orders over a period of several months, until one day, we got a telephone call from a very irate gentleman in Kilmarnock. He said the last consignment of '429' was coming out 'Ivory' and as a result, production on their big order was at a standstill; it was imperative therefore that we should get a replacement batch up to Kilmarnock, as quickly as possible. We explained that, as far as we were concerned, the colour was 'ivory' as described on all the invoices and as obtained by all other users of the product. Furthermore, the last consignment had been taken from the same production batch as the previous delivery, which on their factory apparently produced 'pink'. We also stressed that the material had passed our strict quality control. But in spite of everything, we could not convince them that it was exactly as previously supplied. Consequently, I thought it would be best for me to go to Kilmarnock and take a further supply of colour, together with the relevant fired trial specimens, resulting from the quality control tests.

On arrival at the factory, I asked to see the managing director, who soon gave me a very rough time. He said, "I don't know why you are wasting your time coming up here; you should get back to The Potteries and make us more of the colour you supplied originally". As I could see that I was not going to get anywhere with the man, I asked if he would permit me to see the works manager.

The manager told me they had made no change in the processing but in the course of the conversation, he mentioned that it had recently been necessary to close down the tunnel kiln for repairs. He said the repairs had taken longer than usual, because they were not able to get delivery of the refractory burner blocks from their usual supplier, and as a result, they had been compelled to get them from elsewhere. When I examined the two types of block, a difference in composition was obvious. Investigations showed that the original blocks were based on a chromite refractory, while the substitute blocks contained alumina. To cut a long story short, we eventually found that the high temperature to which the burner blocks were subjected, was sufficient to volatilise traces of chromium compunds, which then reacted with the tin and calcium in the '429' to produce *in situ*, a chrome-tin pink stain. I therefore made trials with traces of chromium oxide added to the '429' to produce the required pink colour. As a result, the greater part of the walls on the Glasgow Underground stations were covered with tiles produced from a modified '429', which was sold as 'Pink 429K'.

As soon as the pottery was back in production, I received a telephone call from the managing director, thanking me for my valued assistance. He apologised for his lack of co-operation during my visit and invited me to dinner, when I was next in the locality. A month or so later, I was able to avail myself of his kind hospitality.

While at university, I had made myself a pair of skis with a view to gaining experience in ski-mountaineering. My first attempts at skiing were on the Derbyshire hills and unlike my introduction to ballroom dancing, I found books on the subject most helpful. Later, I made several visits to the Austrian and Swiss Alps, where I progressed under the watchful eyes of mountain guides – some of which were members of Hitler's SS.

On one of my visits to the Alps, I travelled with a party of university students. After crossing the English Channel, we boarded a train for Basel, in Switzerland, and on arrival, I found that my skis, which were supposed to have been put in the guards-van, were missing. During my previous trip to Basel, the same thing had happened and I was then told the skis would be forwarded to my destination – but I never saw them again. So this time, I decided I would not leave Basel, until I had found my skis, and as it was permissible to have skis in the carriage compartment in Switzerland and Austria, I would not then have any further difficulty. Accordingly, my party continued on its way to Landeck in Austria, while I stayed in Basel. Fortunately, my skis arrived on the very next train from Ostend and I was then able to get a later train to Landeck.

As my train struggled up the Arlberg Pass in the late evening, the guard checked the tickets and when he handed mine back, he told me that the next stop would be Landeck, and as the train was running late, it would not stop long; therefore, when it started to slow down, I must be ready to get out.

About twenty minutes later, the train braked and I got my skis and rucksack close to the door. As soon as the train stopped, the guard appeared and helped me out. I had just put my skis on the ground and the guard was handing me my rucksack, when the train started again. As it disappeared into the distance, I looked around; the night was pitch black and I could not see a light anywhere – and there was certainly no station. Why the train had stopped I shall never know.

In this uncalled for predicament, I decided the only thing to do was to walk along the track in the direction in which the train had just departed. So, shouldering my rucksack and skis, I commenced to walk in the deep snow. Nothing could be seen except the summits of the mountains, silhouetted against the sky and nothing could be heard, except the crunch of snow beneath my feet.

After walking for about an hour, I saw lights ahead, and in due course, came up to a small village, where at the side of the railway track, there was a kind of signalbox in which I could see a man sitting at a desk. I entered and in my best German told him my story, with much emphasis on the fact that I had been put off the train by the guard, in some godforsaken place. He appeared to be very concerned and started tapping out messages on a telegraph key, which resulted in replies being received in morse code. After some considerable time, he conveyed his apologies on behalf of the railway company and said arrangements had been made for me to stay the night at the village inn and that the Vienna express would stop to pick me up at 7.25 a.m. on the morrow. The people at the inn had obviously been well briefed, but appeared uncertain as to whether they should feel sorry for me, or to regard me as some kind of idiot, who should have decided to get off a train into the blackness of the night, between stations, at some remote spot up in the mountains. However, they provided me with a very nice meal and a room for the night. The following morning, they gave me an early call and an excellent breakfast. When I asked for the bill, they told me it was to be paid by the railway company.

I then made my way back to the signalbox, where in the dim light of morning, I could see there was a small siding and provision for local trains to pick up passengers. After waiting a short time, the express came to a stop and two uniformed officials descended. The senior man instructed the other to put my skis and rucksack into a first class compartment, after which they both joined me on the short journey to Landeck. Profuse apologies were voiced regarding the stupid action of the guard and on arrival at my intended destination, they gave me every assistance, and even helped me with my luggage onto the post-bus, which was to take me up to the small village of Weinberg, in the Samnawn Alps.

Here my party, after hiring skis and boots, were just about to depart by horse-drawn sleigh for Compatsch. I was therefore able to rejoin my friends earlier than I had expected. At Compatsch we donned skis and climbed up to the mountain hut on Alp Trida, where we were to commence two weeks of wonderful ski-mountaineering in the Swiss Engadin.

Later I became interested in rock climbing and found much enjoyment and no little excitement, on many of the mountains in Britain. It is not difficult to make friends among the climbing fraternity and as a result, I soon found myself attached to a rope and being led up such climbs as the Inaccessible Pinnacle, in the Lake District and Great Gully on Carnedd Llewelyn, in N. Wales. In due course, I began to lead various climbs in England and Wales, also some in Scotland, such as those in the wilds of Glencoe and the Cairngorms, on the north face of Ben Nevis, and the magnificent Coolins of Skye.

One one occasion, while climbing with a friend in the Coolins, I had just reached the summit of Sgurr Alasdair when to my utter amazement, I saw a forty foot high shadow image of myself approaching from the other side of the mountain. But the most disturbing aspect, was to see a brightly shining halo around my shadowy head; something I considered highly improbable – even in a later life! As I took in the rope, and my friend appeared over a rocky ledge, I was able to get a close-up view of his shocked expression, when he too caught sight of the apparition. We were then, each able to see two figures, but could only see the halo around our own head.

The phenomenon is known as the Broken Spectre, as it was first observed in the Broken mountains of Germany – but rarely recorded since. It is produced when the sun casts a shadow on a well defined cloud bank that is close to, and below the level of the subject; the halo is really a miniature rainbow. When we look at a rainbow the sun is always behind our back and our eyes are on the axis of the arc. In the case of the Broken Spectre, because the reflecting cloud is quite close and below the level of the person, the rainbow is seen as a circle, about two feet in diameter, and centred about the head of the figure. Where the bow coincides with the dark shadow it is indistinct, but where it is reflected from the white cloud it is very bright and has the appearance of a halo.

Among my climbing friends was Maurice Horner, with whom I shared many unforgettable days in the mountains. He also introduced me to cave exploration and classical music. I was happy to introduce him to my elder sister, whom in due course he married.

Life in 1939 suddenly changed with the outbreak of war. I became a member of the LDV (Local Defence Volunteers) which was soon to become the Home Guard. As a Platoon Commander, I had to periodically inspect, at night, several observation posts sited on the neighbouring hills. Travelling in the dark and often in fog, with no lights on the car except for masked headlights with narrow slits, was to say the least, a frustrating and tedious business.

However, life with the Home Guard certainly had its lighter moments. I well remember visiting an observation post on the outskirts of a remote village and being shown a large wooden box, by a very elderly man, who told me that here was his answer to any invasion. He insisted on showing me the contents, and after fumbling with a key for several minutes, managed to open the box to reveal a very ancient shotgun, stripped down into its component parts. With great care he laid out the many bits and pieces and after about half an hour he had managed to put them all together. I was tempted to ask him what he thought the invaders would be doing, while he was assembling his trusty weapon, but as I knew the platoon was to get an issue of American .303 rifles during the following week, I thought it better not to despise his well meaning contribution to the war effort.

My work with the Home Guard brought me into contact with several army units and this eventually led to my deciding to enlist in The Royal Armoured Corps. Before actually joining up, however, I arranged a last visit to the mountains of North Wales with Maurice Horner. We pitched our tent on the lower slopes of Glyder Fach, above Idwal and early the following day, set off over the Glyders and down to Pen-y-pass. Then over the Bristly Ridge of Crib Goch to Crib-y-Ddisgl and up to the summit of Snowdon. Finally, we made our way back to the tent via the summits of Lliwedd and the Glyders – truly a day to remember.

5

LIFE IN THE ROYAL ARMOURED CORPS

I joined the RAC at Warminster Barracks, as a trooper. The first six weeks of training were devoted mainly to squad drill, rifle practice, physical training and driving wheeled vehicles. No matter how much driving one had done previously, it was imperative to learn the army methods. In my squad was a man named Nick Mavrogadato, who had gained a considerable reputation as a racing and rally driver. One day, we managed to get a sight of the driving instructor's report book and against Nick's name was entered, "Will make a reasonable driver after he has gained some experience". After the first six weeks, we progressed to driving tanks over the Salisbury Plain and the time came when I found myself in a 70 ton Churchill tank, with Nick Mavrogadato as the driver. For him, it was full throttle all the way, up hill and down, as well as over ditches – and he was not the kind of man who believed in letting a few trees stand in his way.

We received instruction on the Sten gun, a low cost tommy gun which often jammed. One day, a trooper under instruction was unable to clear a stoppage by carrying out the approved drill. The officer in charge, therefore took the gun and placed the butt on the ground, with the barrel pointing upwards. He then stamped his foot on the 'cocking lever' which cleared the stoppage, but as his foot slipped off the lever, the spring recocked the action and the gun fired – the bullet hitting the officer in the chest. For some minutes, he reproached himself for being so careless; in fact, doing what he had always instructed troopers not to do. Before the ambulance arrived he lost consciousness and died.

While at Warminster, I was interviewed with regard to the possibility of my receiving a commission. The outcome must have been favourable because soon after being posted to the barracks at Bovington, I was sent to St John's Wood, London, to appear before a War Office Selection Board. This involved a stay of four days, during which candidates were comprehensively examined.

One of the tests involved answering, against the clock, a large number of 'mensa' type questions. The candidates were next sent over a hair-raising obstacle course, which included jumping off high buildings, and then immediately given more of the same type of questions to answer. It would seem that some people find it difficult – or even impossible – to think clearly, when subjected to physical stress and obviously, such people would be unsuited to battle conditions. At the end of the four days, I learned that I had been successful and a week or so later, I was instructed to attend an interview in the Chemical Warfare Branch at the War Office, where I was informed that subject to a satisfactory performance at OCTU (Officer Cadet Training Unit) I would be considered for a course of training, which would lead to an appointment on the General Staff, as a Technical Officer (Chemical Warfare). This would mainly involve technical work in connection with poison gas, tactical smoke and flame warfare – it all sounded very exciting.

Life at Bovington now radically changed for me, as I found myself assisting with duties normally carried out by officers, including a spell of about two weeks in the pay office. I was also called upon to give a talk to members of the Toc H Branch. I chose as my subject, *The Discipline of Rock Climbing* and concluded with an anecdote based loosely on fact but suitably embellished to impress the several officers present, who I suspected would be reporting on my performance. Here is my recollection of the story: "Just before the outbreak of war, a party of German climbers from the famous Munich Mountaineering Club, visited North Wales and asked to be shown a rock face that had never been climbed, as they wished to make a new ascent in the name of The Fuhrer. Accordingly, they were taken to a steep crag which had previously attracted little attention – not so much due to the climbing difficulty but because the featureless surface presented little climbing interest. The visitors carefully examined the face and planned a route, which they declared would be climbed on the following day. As might be imagined, a number of local climbers congregated to see the attempt on this new climb. At first good progress was made but as the leader on the rope approached the featureless section, his advance slowed and soon he was in real difficulty. Ultimately, he called down to the second man on the rope, to admit that he could not get any higher. Whereupon, the second man implored the leader to continue in the name of The Fuhrer".

At this point in the story, I stressed the fact that British climbers would never give instructions to the leader and hoped the officers present would take due note. Then I continued: "As the leader was obviously defeated, he hammered a metal *piton* into a small crack in the rock and secured his rope to it. Protected in this way, he was then able to reach up and fix another *piton* and eventually two more, until at last, he was able to bring up the second man and continue the climb to the top. The achievement was followed by hearty rejoicing among the visitors and loudly proclaimed toasts to The Fuhrer. The following day the Munich papers featured a dramatic account of the climb, in which their daring climbers had faced great danger, in order to honour the name of The Fuhrer".

To bring the story to a suitable conclusion, I made the point that British climbers feel that it is just not done to use steeple-jack methods, on climbs which are intended to exercise the technique of rock climbing. So as soon as the Germans had departed, some of the local climbers decided to make the ascent in order to remove the desecrating *pitons*. They not only succeeded in doing this, but managed to complete the climb without them.

There were many interesting characters at Bovington but few more so, than Leslie Welch, who after the war became well known on radio and television as "The Memory Man". He would get people in the studio audience to ask him questions on sporting events, which he would then unfailingly answer from memory, and in a most entertaining manner. While at Bovington, he would spend most of his off-duty time studying record books, such as the football and cricket annuals. As he had apparently been doing this for many years, and was able to retain the information, he had assimilated a vast store of sporting general knowledge. On one occasion, I asked Les what was the most amusing incident he had witnessed on the football field. His reply was roughly as follows:

"A few years ago, I had gone to see Tottenham Hotspur, whom I always supported, and on the particular occasion, three of their players, while travelling to the ground by taxi, were involved in a serious accident. Two players were available as reserves and were therefore included in the team, but this meant they were still one man short. The only other player at the ground was a man who had been playing for a colliery team in South Wales and had just joined Tottenham. In the circumstances, they were compelled to include this new man, whom they put to play on the right wing.

You can imagine that the former amateur, who had not even trained with the Tottenham players, would see this as his great opportunity to make a name for himself. Consequently, right from the kick-off, he ran, he jumped, and he fell this way and that, but by half-time, he had not really had a kick at the ball. The second half continued in very much the same pattern and the poor man was becoming more and more frustrated. No goals had been scored and the game was coming to a close when a Tottenham player on the left wing broke away, and as he swept down onto the opponents goal, he sent over a crashing centre, just as our eager tyro surged into the goalmouth; with a thud, that could be heard all round the ground, the ball hit him on the chest and rebounded into the back of the net. Tottenham had won and as the final whistle sounded, the idol of the hour was carried, shoulder high, off the field".

I recall asking Les what he had been doing before joining the army and he said that he had backed horses. I expressed the view that it is only the bookie who makes money out of betting but Les insisted that it was possible to make really big money as a punter – providing it be done professionally. I was naturally curious to know his technique but at first, found him rather reluctant to say very much. He then said, "Everyone knows that racehorse owners only derive a small amount of their income from prize money. Among other sources must be the winnings resulting from betting on their horses, when they are at the peak of their form and virtually sure to win. All I had to do therefore, was to put a fairly large sum on a horse when I knew that the stable money was on it". I could not wait to learn how he knew when the stable money went onto a horse and therefore put the direct question. Whereupon, he said, "That's the problem, because it is not in the owner's interest for the betting fraternity to know the stables's betting policy and that is why they go to such great trouble to preserve strict secrecy – but you know, not every employee is loyal and therefore it paid me to choose my friends very carefully".

In due course, Les was included on a draft bound for North Africa and as he bid me farewell, he pushed into my hand a piece of paper on which there were three words. "This is to remember me by", he said, "Put your money on this, if it runs in the Derby". Some time later, I happened to hear the result of the Derby and on looking out the note that Les had given me, I found he had certainly got the winner.

6

SOME EXPERIENCES OF AN OFFICER CADET

I was informed that I would be doing my officer cadet training at Dunbar, on the east coast of Scotland, which suited me fine as my fiancée was living in Scotland. Firstly, however, I would have to attend a Pre-OCTU at Wrotham, in Kent. This camp was situated at the top of a limestone escarpment, although most of the training took place at the foot. A steep path led up the cliff and I must have gone up and down it hundreds of times – often when carrying heavy equipment. The instructors had a favourite trick of getting the squad to the bottom of the escarpment for a training session and then at eleven o'clock, they would say, "OK, now you can get off to the Naafi – be back here in twenty minutes". Of course, the Naafi was at the top of the escarpment and even if you ran, it would take ten minutes to get there.

Tuesdays were called 'Doubling Day' and on that day, no matter where you were going or what you were carrying, you had to run at the double. Among the objectives at Wrotham, it seemed, was to eliminate those who could not endure frustration.

Part of the course involved instruction in riding a motor cycle and this could only be avoided by proving that you were a competent rider. I had only done a little riding but did not fancy motor cycling around Kent in winter. Consequently, I claimed to be competent and submitted myself to the relevant test.

For this, I was taken to a nearby disused sand quarry, where there was a suitably attired sergeant instructor and several Norton motor cycles. The sergeant said, "You can ride?" I answered, "Yes sir" – "Then get on one of those bikes and follow me". With that he was off like a shot, with me gingerly following, after I had got the wretched thing to start. For a few minutes we went along a sandy track at breakneck speed and then over a lot of very rough ground, before eventually returning to the quarry. Here, the instructor told me to wait and watch. Thereupon, he drove at full throttle towards the foot of the quarry face, then up an incredibly steep slope, which near the top appeared to be almost vertical. On reaching the summit of the precipice, he shot high up into the air and disappeared from view. A minute or so later, he returned and skidded to a stop.

With a smile, I congratulated him on his death defying stunt – a smile which quickly faded when he said, "Now you do it" – and then he added a warning, "See that you go fast enough to get up that last bit, otherwise you and the bike will fall all the way back to the bottom". That was, of course, obvious to me – what I didn't know was how I was going to land, after the airborne caper at the top.

There are occasions when one can only trust in providence and for me, this was one of them. Suffice it to say, that I got to the top in fine style, shot up into the air and landed some yards from the bike, with the comforting thought that I could not be seen from below. So I quickly gathered myself together, dusted down my uniform, remounted and got back to the instructor as quickly as possible. He merely murmured, "I've seen worse", which for me, was praise indeed.

The following morning, I was told that I had completed my spell at Wrotham and was given a train ticket for Dunbar.

The OCTU at Dunbar was based in the Bellevue Hotel, on the seafront and there we received instruction in leadership, army organization and tactics, etc. But as at Wrotham, everything was done to encourage cadets to request a return to their units and in a number of cases, cadets were obliged to return, without having made such a request.

One form of torment was a sixteen mile cross-country run over the neighbouring hills, terminating in a swim, from one side of the harbour entrance to the other. On the far side, ropes had been hung down the harbour wall and one was expected to climb up them for about thirty feet, before staggering to the finishing line. Those who lacked the strength to get up the wet ropes, were asked what the difficulty was!

There were also the forty-eight hour exercises on the Lammermuir hills, which were designed to test mental stamina when feeling mighty cold (there being plenty of snow), tired through lack of sleep and hungry as a result of having little to eat. The night exercises on the Gullane sands were intended to simulate battle conditions. In these, each cadet was required to organize and lead a mock attack on specified positions, over which live ammunition was fired. The tracer bullets, which of course, show up clearly at night, appeared to be only about four feet above the ground. It was obviously advisable therefore to move in the prone position – and the more prone the better!

For me however, the Passing-out Parade proved to be the most perturbing part of all. I have previously indicated my inability to get on terms with ballroom dancing and in spite of getting a fair amount of practice, I was not much better with drill on the barracks square. Instruction for the final parade was given by the Regimental Sergeant Major of the Scots Guards, who were stationed at the Dunbar Barracks. Much of the drill was done with fixed bayonets in the 'present-arms' position which, on a cold day, rendered the arms completely useless in no time at all.

When, on the rare occasions we were standing 'at ease', the RSM would pass along the ranks and ask each cadet in turn a question. Mine

was, "What's the name o' th' Adjutant?" There was no way in which I
could have got to know anyone at the Guard's Depot, so I gave the only
possible reply, "Don't know, sir". "Then b....y weel fin oot" he roared, as
he waved me towards the main building. With this, I broke ranks and
made for the entrance. Inside I saw two guardsmen who told me the
Adjutant was Captain Cameron. Having obtained the vital information, I
went back to my squad, where I was met with, "Ye there – get fell in an'
tell this lot, the name o' th' Adjutant". Confidently, I called out, "The
adjutant is Captain Cameron". There was a brief silence, during which
the big man appeared to grow even bigger and then he exploded with,
"Git awa wi ye an' I dinna wan tae see yer face agin, till ye kin gi me th'
name o' th' Adjutant". I was now in a real fix and had visions of being
back at Bovington on the morrow.

However, in the main building, I met two other cadets who were on
similar, apparently impossible missions and consequently we decided
to co-operate with a view to finding some possible answers. One of the
boys told me there was a notice-board at the end of a certain corridor
and he believed the name of the Adjutant was on it. I was off like a shot
and sure enough, there it was: "Captain Cameron MC". I had
committed the unforgivable sin, by omitting to mention the
decoration.

Life was not always quite so dramatic; there were in fact, some
pleasant interludes, as for example, when we were free to go into
Edinburgh to buy uniform and all the necessary accoutrements. For me
there was then, the added pleasure of being able to spend an hour or
so with my fiancée.

Relentlessly however, the time approached for the dreaded
Passing-out Parade and on that memorable day, senior members of the
services arrived and were joined by an appreciable audience of
townspeople and others. The pipe band of the Scots Guards took up its
allotted position and we commenced our well rehearsed drill routine –
quite a nerve wracking experience and particularly so, for those of us
who had not previously marched to a pipe band. One of the final
movements in the parade was, "The Ceremonial Advance". In this, after
the appropriate command had been given, the squad – without any
further orders – had to march thirteen steps forward, halt and then
present arms. With an English military band the music stops abruptly
on the thirteenth step, which greatly helps the squad to come to a
crashing halt. But with the pipe band it was all very different, because
while the pipers stopped playing on the thirteenth step, the well known
wailing sound from the drones continued. Consequently, we were
uncertain as to how many steps we had taken and were fooled into
taking an additional step. When it was all over the RSM no longer

regarded us as cadets – he even congratulated us on our performance, but he could not resist having a final dig, by saying that, "Only a bunch o' b....y Sassenachs wud tak therteen an' a haf steps on they Ceremonial Advance". We were, however, now out of his clutches – although I was later to meet up with him in Arnhem – and we were commissioned to serve in the "Service of the Crown" – with all that was to entail.

On leaving Dunbar, everyone was allowed seven days leave, after which, in my case, I was to report to the Chemical Warfare Branch, at the Headquarters of 21 Army Group, which was then based at St Paul's School, in London.

7

CHEMICAL WARFARE TRAINING

On reporting to 21 Army Group Headquarters, I was directed to the Chemical Warfare Branch, where I was introduced to the staff, the most senior being a brigadier, while the most junior was Major Bell, who was to be my superior officer. After he had allocated me a desk, he said, "We can't have you walking around this Headquarters as a second-lieutenant because you would be mistaken for a major – you had better put another 'pip' on your shoulder". So it was, that I found myself promoted to lieutenant, within a few minutes of reporting for duty.

After signing a document headed Official Secrets Acts 1911 and 1920, I spent several days perusing the contents of files, marked "Top Secret" and then I was told that I was to attend a course of instruction at the Army School of Chemical Warfare. This sounded most interesting, but when I learned that the School was accommodated in a large hotel at Glenridding, on the shores of Ullswater in the Lake District, I could hardly believe my luck at the prospect of being back among my beloved mountains once again. On the course, we were worked pretty hard, but we had some free time at the week-ends, during which I would be off up Striding Edge to the summit of Helvellyn or rock climbing on various neighbouring crags.

It was intended that my eventual appointment would be as a Technical Officer (Chemical Warfare) on the General Staff, and hence it was necessary for me to receive training, not only in chemical warfare, but also in the administrative procedures associated with work on the General Staff. In order to gain the necessary experience in this respect, I was posted to Headquarters Second Army, to work under Major Peter Maitland and later to various Command Headquarters; the first of which was Southern Command, then accomodated in the magnificent Wilton House, near to Salisbury.

This large mansion is, of course, one of the great show places of England, having a wonderful collection of furniture, furnishings and works of art. During the war, most of these items were held in store but many of the oil paintings were still in position on the walls. I well remember the night when, as duty officer, I found myself at a desk and alone in the splendid ante-room, with the portraits of famous soldiers from previous wars, looking down on me.

I was sent next to South Western Command Headquarters at Taunton. The buildings were not so grand as Wilton House and I can't remember very much about the work, but I shall never forget being billeted on a most delightful family, who treated me like a long lost son.

My next venue was completely different, being the Chemical Defence Experimental Station at Porton, where the work carried out is highly secret. In the army, the Chemical Warfare branch was mainly concerned with the properties of war gases and their management in battle, both offensively and defensively; also the development and use of particulate clouds as smoke screens and the use of flame as a weapon. I found the research being carried out in these various activities of immense interest. The properties of poison gases can only be evaluated by experiments involving animals. I fully appreciate that some people are strongly opposed to animals being used in live experiments but when, for example, gas mask filters are being developed to provide life saving protection for people – and indeed for some animals – there is really no alternative to performance testing. The animals used were mainly rats, mice, guineapigs, goats and monkeys. All were reared under exemplary conditions, and in the experiments every possible care was taken to avoid any kind of suffering.

Each week, a batch of volunteers from the Services would arrive to participate in experiments. Most of the men suffered no lasting ill effects, but those who did sustain injury received the very best medical attention. I never heard any volunteer complain and indeed some said they would like to return, as they had found the experience so interesting.

In World War I, poison gas was released from cylinders forward of the trenches, when the wind was blowing towards the enemy, but with the rise of air power it became more expedient to put the gas into bombs, which could be dropped from the air onto precise targets.

For the efficient employment of both poison gas and smoke screens, a sound practical knowledge of meteorology is essential and consequently, much of my time at Porton was spent in studying this fascinating branch of science.

Everyone hoped that poison gas would not be used, and it was of course, banned by the Geneva Convention. Nevertheless, it was imperative to take all necessary precautions, in case the enemy should decide to use this dreadful weapon. Many new potential war gases had been developed since World War I and it was obviously possible, that the enemy might employ gases with which we had little or no experience. It was imperative therefore, that Technical Officers should be able to analyse gases of all types and have available the necessary equipment to facilitate evaluation on the battlefield, in order that the appropriate counter measures could be taken with the minimum of delay.

The word "flamethrower" is really a misnomer, because these weapons do not throw flame; they throw an inflammable liquid which

34

produces flame on the target. The liquid is propelled by compressed air and for this to be effective, the liquid must have a high viscosity, otherwise the air would burst through and give a short fierce flame like that produced by a blow-torch. When for example, the viscosity of petrol is increased to that of treacle, by the addition of a suitable compound, the resultant liquid can be propelled through the air like a rod, burning only on the surface. But when the liquid hits the target, it will break up into small droplets and burn explosively. It is a fearsome weapon; men in a slit-trench can gain protection from gunfire, but the liquid from a flamethrower will fall into a trench and produce an inferno. Similarly, flamethrowers are very effective in attacks against pillboxes.

I was sorry to leave Porton, but my next move was not without interest – and certainly not without excitement – as I was to be based at Dover Castle, to enable my participation in exercises at sea, off the coast of France. One of the aims of these manoeuvres may well have been to encourage the enemy to concentrate on the build-up of shore defences in the Pas de Calais area.

I had previously been informed that after my spell of duty at Dover, I would be due for a week of leave. As I did not know whether or not I would get any further leave before going overseas, I thought it would be a good opportunity to get married. As my fiancée fortunately agreed, a ceremony to be conducted by the Revd George Hamlet was arranged in Scotland, with the honeymoon in the Lake District.

Before the outbreak of war, I often visited Oxford to play golf on the University Golf Course, where an uncle – Fred Taylor – was the resident professional. Consequently, when I was posted to the Cowley Barracks to gain more administrative experience, I was able – when off duty – to simply walk across the road and onto the golf course for a round of golf, before enjoying true hospitality at the home of the Taylors.

After completing my period of training, I was posted, towards the end of 1943, to the Headquarters of 1st Corps, as Technical Officer, with the rank of Staff Captain. At that time, the Headquarters was based in a former stately home in Painshill Park, Cobham, Surrey. The beautiful old house standing in delightful grounds was, in every respect, a very pleasant place in which to work.

But now, there was a real job to be done, as it soon became apparent that 1st Corps was going to act as the spearhead in the imminent invasion of France. The 1st Corps sign is, in fact, a white spearhead, against a blood-red background. One of my first tasks, was to organize a series of exercises to develop and evaluate the action to be taken on discovering the first use of gas by the enemy.

It was suggested that the golf course at Gullane, east of Edinburgh, would serve as a suitable location and I readily agreed – particularly as I had not seen my wife for some time. Consequently, over a period of about a month, I made several visits to Scotland in order to stage miniature battles in gas warfare.

About this time, I was fortunate in having the opportunity to attend a series of talks in the War Office, given by General Montgomery – the subject being *The Psychology of War*. He advanced the view that just as each person has an individual character, so does every fighting unit. Hence, it was imperative for all leaders to understand the collective characteristics of their particular unit, in order to make the best use of it, in a given situation. He considered it essential that every soldier should appreciate that he was fighting for a just cause. In this connection, he detailed the events leading up to the outbreak of war and concluded by saying that, as all other means had failed to stop the aggression, honourable men had no real alternative but to go to war. He also stressed the point that it was useless going to war, unless you were certain of victory, and then went on to explain why he was so damn sure we could, and would win.

At Corps Headquarters, attention was now directed towards the many problems involved in landing on an enemy shore from assault craft. The first essential was to be able to swim while carrying full kit – and those who failed the relevant test, did not need to be told to get some urgent practice. One day, we were taken to Southampton and then marched to the docks for embarkation. The streets were lined with cheering well-wishers, who believed the big day had come, but we merely sailed a few miles to a neighbouring coast, where we transferred to landing craft for the run ashore. Succeeding landing exercises became more and more arduous as we were put into rough water, well away from the shore.

In mid-May 1944, I was given a special pass and instructed to report at a secret rendezvous, where I would be briefed in connection with an overseas operation. At the site was a well guarded camp, where I met Major Peter Maitland from Headquarters Second Army; just the two of us sat in a small tent and I shall never forget what followed. After Peter had impressed upon me the importance of absolute secrecy regarding the information I was about to be given, he unlocked a strong-box and took out various documents and maps. He then described in considerable detail, the plans for the landing in Normandy, insofar as they concerned me.

He explained that all units landing during the first three days, would carry full anti-gas equipment, but as it was important to avoid transporting unnecessary stores across the beaches, it had been decided that only personal anti-gas equipment would be taken thereafter, if there was good evidence to show the enemy would not initiate gas warfare, during the first thirty days after the landing.

This critically important decision could only be made by someone in the invasion bridgehead, and consequently, arrangements had been made for me to be put ashore very early on D-Day and it would be my sole responsibility to investigate the situation and report to the Tactical HQ on board the SS *Hilary*, by the evening of D+1. The report would be required to state quite categorically, whether or not the enemy would use poison gas within thirty days of the landing, together with the detailed evidence upon which the decision was based. We then spent a couple of hours discussing how the vital information might be obtained and the specialized equipment that I would require.

During the next few days, I attended a number of planning meetings in London, and it was then, that I came to appreciate the enormous size and complexity of the operation. I was obviously interested in any information regarding the beach on which I was to land, and not particularly pleased to learn that the enemy had recently built underwater steel defences, to the top of which mines had been fixed. In addition, they had just completed a number of large concrete gun emplacements and anti-tank traps – our reception was not going to be exactly hospitable!

One of the meetings, early in June, was addressed by General Eisenhower. Assisted by large maps and various visual aids, he graphically described the strategy for the landing operation and stressed the importance of getting men ashore quickly, before the enemy had time to regroup. It would then be necessary to maintain the forward momentum, with a view to capturing ports, which would be essential to land the vast quantity of stores and equipment, that would be required before the major battles could take place.

On 3 June, I was instructed to check all my equipment, prior to embarkation and to place everything, except that required for the assault, into my steel box which would be sent on to me, in due course. An hour later, I was on my way to Southampton, where I was encamped under canvas, in the marshalling area. Converging on Southampton were vast numbers of every type of military vehicle, including special purpose tanks, such as those adapted for bridging, for flailing mines, and of course, those equipped as flamethrowers. Military police were skilfully controlling traffic and everyone appeared to know exactly where they had to go and what they had to do.

My particular camp was situated in a wooded valley on the outskirts of the town and the personnel were all assualt troops.

Many were marine commandos but there were also a large number of Canadians, including members of the Chaudière Regiment from Quebec, who appeared to be most anxious to get to grips with the enemy. Their commanding officer told me that his job was going to be relatively easy, because ".... all I will have to do, is get this wild lot onto the shore, point them in the right direction – and then turn them loose".

In the camp, everyone was busy; vehicles had to be serviced and waterproofed, while personal kit and weapons had to be checked and made waterproof. I paid particular attention to my box of chemicals and special equipment; ensuring that it was not only waterproof, but also, that it would float!

During the morning of 4 June, I was included in a party of eighteen, who were taken from the camp to the docks, for embarkation on a vessel which had previously seen service as a ferry, on the Holyhead to Dun Laoghaire route. As soon as loading was complete, she sailed down Southampton Water and anchored in Cowes Roads, where many more vessels were assembling. I was allotted a very nice single cabin, while the facilities on board – including an excellent restaurant – proved most acceptable after the spartan conditions in the marshalling area. We were assembled in small groups for briefing and given various items including French money, large-scale maps and two twenty-four hour ration packs. We also received a personal message from General Montgomery, part of which read:

"On the eve of this great adventure I send my best wishes to every soldier in the Allied team. To us is given the honour of striking a blow for freedom which will live in history; and in the better days that lie ahead men will speak with pride of our doings. We have a great and a righteous cause. Let us pray that 'The Lord Mighty in Battle' will go forth with our armies and that His special providence will aid us in the struggle.

"I want every soldier to know that I have complete confidence in the successful outcome of the operations that we are now about to begin. With stout hearts and with enthusiasm for the contest, let us go forward to victory."

We were informed that we should be sailing soon after sunset, but later that evening, it was announced that the entire operation was to be delayed by twenty four hours, due to an unfavourable weather forecast. In the circumstances, we were advised to get a good nights sleep, and then await further instructions.

By the afternoon of 5 June, it was still quite windy but warm and sunny – consequently, we were not surprised to learn that the big show was at last on.

8

MORE THAN A MERE INCIDENT

At dusk on 5 June, our ship and many more, slipped out of the Solent and headed south. As I had made all my preparations, I went to my cabin to get a few hours sleep. At about 5 a.m. next morning, I went up on deck to find the sea full of ships of all kinds, but all sailing in the same direction. Overhead, the sky was full of aircraft, again all flying in the same direction, while the southern horizon shone with a lurid glow, indicating that the enemy defences were already receiving a tremendous pounding.

Many of the men on board were having breakfast and I decided to join them. In the restaurant, one could easily have imagined being on the ferry in peacetime, as the waiters, in their usual uniform with white jackets, were serving a traditional full English breakfast. It was only the passengers who appeared different – and they were very different.

When I next went up on deck, it was just possible to see the French shore, which was still being heavily bombed from the air, but also being shelled by several large battleships. Soon, rocket ships approached the shore and commenced to fire their deadly loads. One could be tempted to believe that nobody on shore could survive this continuous battering, but we feared it would prove otherwise.

When we were about three miles from shore, our ship anchored, and soon several landing craft came alongside to take on board the assault troops. In the landing exercises, men had transferred from the mother ships to the landing craft by sliding down the inside of canvas tubes, and this method had proved eminently successful. Now, however, two things were different; firstly, the sizeable waves caused the assault craft to rise and fall through a height of about twenty feet, against the side of our ship and secondly, the commandos were carrying open knives which cut slits in the canvas, through which some of the men fell into the sea. In the circumstances, it was decided to get the men to jump into the landing craft, when it had just risen to the high point – if the jump was made too late, there was the distinct risk of falling into the landing craft from a considerable height.

After about half an hour the landing craft returned to take in the second wave and consequently, it was now my turn to time the jump to perfection – but firstly, we had to take from the boat, the bodies of two men who had apparently been killed before they could leave the craft.

During the run towards the shore, the high sides of the landing craft provided some protection from gunfire, but also prevented those

39

on board from seeing what was happening around the craft; it was only possible to see the sky, a lot of smoke and some very vivid flashes. Suddenly, there was a terrific explosion under the craft; it lurched violently and water started to pour in. We had obviously hit one of the mines attached to the underwater defences. Within seconds, the vessel was aground, the big ramp at the front was lowered and it was now up to each one of us to make for the shore the best way we could. It seemed that the entire coast was ablaze, as there were flames and smoke everywhere, while the noise was deafening.

On jumping out of the landing craft, I was surprised to find that the water only came up to my chest but after taking a few steps, I apparently dropped into a bomb crater, as I was soon swimming and pushing before me, my box of scientific equipment – I could not help thinking that if it received a direct hit, I might well be the first gas casualty of the war. For my part, however, being almost fully immersed provided a sense of security from the various bits of metal flying around and consequently, I kept as low as possible in the water, until I reached the beach.

Here there were many poor souls for whom the struggle was already over. Among them I fleetingly recognised the face of a young commando officer, who, as he sat at the next table during breakfast, had leaned towards me to say, "It won't be long now". We knew that the most dangerous part of the operation would be in crossing the open ground between the water's edge and the concrete defence wall – so this was covered in one frantic dash. Fortunately, the sappers had just blown a large hole in the wall, and as a result, it was not difficult to scramble over the resulting debris and then across a road to gain cover from a ruined building, where I happened to meet up with some of my colleagues.

We had been put ashore, exactly as planned, about two hundred yards to the west of the railway station, at the small seaside town of Bernières-sur-Mer. The first thing we now had to do, was to remove the waterproofing from our equipment and check our weapons. When I looked around and saw the deadly weapons carried by my colleagues, I could not help but feel rather ill-equipped to face the might of the German army, with just a small revolver and a box of chemicals.

By early afternoon, I had to get to the village of Courseulles – about two miles away – where we were to establish the headquarters for 1st Corps. A reconnaissance revealed that the road to Courseulles was still covered by enemy gunfire and furthermore, a big gun battery by the harbour had not yet been silenced. Very quickly, however, the situation locally stabilized, and vehicles began to pour along the Courseulles road.

My small party started to walk, but we soon found that the verges at the side of the road were mined. We therefore hitched a lift in a truck.

At the bottom of the main street in Courseulles there was a group of French people – the first we had seen – and from the group two women approached us, shouting and wildly gesticulating. We learned that their hostility was due to their German boy friends having been killed in the preliminary bombardment, but the other people immediately dragged the protesters away, and showed most clearly that they were overjoyed to see us. Indeed, after the inhabitants had recovered from the shock of the terrific assault, they could not have welcomed us more warmly, even though many had suffered grievous loss.

Headquarters 1st Corps was located in a small orchard, at the top of the main street and conveniently close to the village pump. By radio, I learned that already, many German prisoners had been taken and some were being held in a compound which was not far away. Bearing in mind that I had to report by the following evening, as to the possibility of the enemy instigating gas warfare, I was anxious to interrogate as many prisoners as possible, in order to find out what gas training they had received and the type of anti-gas equipment they were carrying.

On reaching the compound, however, I was very surprised to find that none of the prisoners spoke German. They were from the *Ostbatalliones*, consisting of men who had been captured by the Germans in the Russian campaign and who had subsequently 'volunteered' to man the Atlantic Wall. They were Mongolian in appearance, unkempt and completely indifferent to their present situation; as for their anti-gas equipment, it hardly existed. Obviously, I was not going to make any progress there – so had to find prisoners elsewhere. I then learned that the Marine Commandos were holding some prisoners near to La Vallette, but when I arrived there, the men turned out to be members of an SS unit and although I was able to examine their interesting anti-gas equipment, there was no way that I could make them talk. I felt quite sure that even if one had threatened to shoot them, they still would not have co-operated in any way. I now realised that I had only twenty-four hours in which to compile and submit my important report, and as yet, I had absolutely nothing of interest to communicate.

The first night on shore was spent in a slit trench. There was some aerial activity, during which a few bombs were dropped, also some enemy gunfire that sounded much too close for comfort, but despite this, I managed to get a few hours sleep.

The next day, I was up at daybreak and after a quick wash at the village pump and a less than hearty breakfast consisting of pemmican, a slab of compacted oatmeal and two Horlicks tablets, I was ready to begin my urgent search for information. Enquiries revealed that no gas ammunition had been found – so that was a good start. In addition, an army store had been captured which was said to contain some anti-gas equipment. This proved to be quite interesting, because I found there, an ingenious instrument designed to automatically analyse gases and some large gas masks for horses, of which the German army had a large number. The most interesting find, however, was a file of documents relating to poison gas and a top-secret reference to a new type of mask filter, which appeared to indicate that some recent development regarding war gases may have taken place.

Later in the day, I was able to locate some German speaking prisoners who were prepared to talk, and who gave me valuable information regarding the training they had received in gas warfare – none however, appeared to believe that the use of gas was imminent. I was now in a position to start drafting my report, but one very important factor still had to be considered.

Poison gas is most effectively employed by loading it into bombs, which can be dropped from the air onto specific targets and the large concentration of troops in the bridgehead would undoubtedly have presented an excellent target. It would, however, be imperative for the enemy to have air superiority over the bridgehead, otherwise the Allies could retaliate with much heavier gas attacks. At the time, we appeared to have complete air superiority and providing this happy state of affairs continued, there would be little risk of the enemy commencing gas warfare.

Consequently, I sought a meeting with the most senior RAF officer I could find and asked for his opinion on the matter. He was quite confident that we had, and could maintain, the necessary air superiority. Accordingly, and subject to this assurance, I was now prepared to state categorically, that the enemy would not initiate gas warfare in the bridgehead, during the first thirty days.

Early in the evening, I went to Beach Control HQ, which was by the Bernières railway station and asked one of the officers if he could get me to the SS *Hilary*. Immediately, a DUKW (An American amphibious vehicle) was made available and off we went with the driver weaving his way between the large number of vessels, until eventually, we found the headquarters ship lying about three miles off shore.

My report was received with interest and duly considered, after which, I was told that it had been decided not to bring further supplies of anti-gas equipment into the bridgehead, so long as the present situation continued. Before leaving the *Hilary*, I was invited to stay for dinner and I must say the delicious roast chicken was a great improvement on the pemmican I had for breakfast.

During the following thirty days, I monitored the situation most carefully, knowing full well that if the enemy commenced the use of gas, without warning, the outcome for the Allies would indeed be disastrous.

On D+2, the headquarters received a number of tents, trestle-tables, chairs, a field-kitchen and a supply of food. At the same time, field-telephones were installed, and as a result, we were now able to function effectively as a corps headquarters. On D+3, Driver Bird arrived with my Austin Utility containing a tent, various items of scientific equipment, a cine camera with a good supply of film and my kit box. I was therefore, now able to set up my 'office', and become fully mobile within the slowly expanding bridgehead. Driver Bird – who was, of course known to everyone as 'Dicky' – turned out to be a most enthusiastic and resourceful character, who believed in making war as acceptable as possible.

The invasion was making good progress inland, but there were some pockets of resistance, one of which was quite near to the headquarters at Douvres la Delivrande. Here there was a radar station, resolutely defended by an SS unit. Several attempts had been made to capture the station but they had all failed. On one side, an extensive minefield had been laid, and consequently the attacks had been made from the opposite side, which was protected by a battery of guns.

As a result, it was now decided to stage a concerted attack and to use the Crocodile flame-throwers. These were, in effect, Churchill tanks equipped with a flame gun; the necessary fuel being contained in 400 gallon tanks mounted on trailers. The entire operation was carefully planned with a view to control by radio.

At the time agreed for the start of the attack, I found a vantage point about 300 yards from the station perimeter, where I could film the operation with my cine camera. Firstly, the target area was covered in smoke, which prevented the defenders from seeing the direction of the attack, then Flail tanks were sent forward to clear a way through the minefield. These specialized tanks were 'Churchills', fitted at the front with a rotating drum, to which chains were attached. When the drive to the drum was put into gear, the chains beat the ground and caused the mines to harmlessly explode. The flame-throwers then went in, following right behind the "Flails", and on reaching the outer defence positions they commenced flaming. At the same time, the artillery put down a barrage on other sections of the perimeter defences.

It is not difficult to imagine what would be going through the minds of the defenders; they would see the smoke and wonder what was going to happen next, they would hear the tanks coming through the minefield, which based on their previous experience was not possible, they would hear shells exploding on other sides of the station – and then suddenly they would see only a few yards away, an advancing wall of flame. It was not surprising therefore, that the defenders abandoned their weapons in panic and surrendered. Casualties among the garrison troops were negligible, while we suffered no casualties at all.

From that day on, I became an enthusiastic campaigner for flame warfare, not just because it produced results but because, contrary to common belief, it saved lives. Very few men were ever killed by a bayonet, but it caused many to surrender. I came to regard flame as a psychological weapon but compared with the bayonet, it had a very much longer blade and a very much sharper point.

One day, I received a message from a commando unit on the eastern side of the river Orne, stating that they had been attacked by mortar bombs, which emitted noxious fumes, and as one of the bombs had failed to explode, they requested that someone should examine it. Consequently, I set off and found the particular unit manning a forward observation post. The officer in charge detailed two NCOs to take me to the unexploded bomb and just as we were about to leave, one of them asked the officer if, on the way back, it would be all right for them to 'sort out' some 'jerries' whom they had previously located. Whereupon, the officer merely suggested that they should not do anything stupid.

With this, the three of us set off in search of the bomb, which we eventually found; it having made a neat hole in the ground, a little larger than a rabbit-hole. To withdraw the bomb, I used a light cane with a piece of bent wire at the end, which could be hooked around the tail flights. After I had defused the bomb, the NCOs told me that they proposed to make a detour on the way back, which would take us to an enemy outpost – this being the one they had decided 'to sort out'.

Although this kind of thing was not in my normal line of business, I had no alternative but to go along with the idea. Consequently, after proceeding for about 450 yards, the NCOs started to cautiously crawl towards a stone wall – with me some distance behind. On reaching the wall, the NCOs looked through a gap and then beckoned me forward to do likewise, whereupon, I was amazed to see, only about 30 yards away, two Germans sitting by a small fire and apparently having a meal. One of the NCOs indicated that I should go back the way we had come and after I had crawled about twenty yards, I saw them tossing hand grenades over the wall. They then came running towards me – so without bidding, I quickly followed their example, while still holding on to my bomb.

When we arrived back at the observation post, the specification of the bomb was discussed, but the incident at the wall was hardly mentioned. On several later occasions, I was to work with the commandos; it seemed that for them, war was like an exciting game of rugby, in which the aim was to score something much more spectacular than a try.

Enemy aircraft were making occasional raids over the beaches and therefore, I was having to organize smoke screens to protect vulnerable areas, such as the prefabricated 'Mulberry' harbour at Arromanches and the very busy quays at Port en Bessin. The only way the efficiency of these screens could be evaluated was to fly over them and take cine photographs. For this purpose, I would obtain the use of an Auster light aircraft of the type used for air reconnaissance. Flying in the smoke and between the almost invisible wires of the balloon barrages, often proved very exciting.

On one occasion, we were asked, while carrying out a smoke mission, to drop a bag containing photographs of enemy positions, at a location occupied by one of our forward units. We were given as a point of reference a prominent landmark, from which we had to fly on a given bearing for a distance of three miles, and then drop the bag where at a stated time, a yellow flare would be ignited. All went according to plan, until we realised we were being shot at from the ground, whereupon, as might be expected, the pilot turned round and flew back on a reciprocal course. After flying for at least two minutes, we saw the yellow smoke and then realised that we had just made a low level flight over enemy territory.

On 7 July, Bomber Command employed 460 aircraft, each carrying a five ton bomb load, to make pin-point attacks on the strongly fortified defences north of Caen. Then on the following day, three Divisions under the command of 1st Corps, fought their way into the city and the suburbs east of the river Orne.

During the course of the following two weeks, further advances were made, which made it possible to move our headquarters from a position north of Caen to a site near Troarn. It was on such occasions that Driver Bird's resourcefulness became evident, as for example, when erecting my tent in the new location. He would first of all, dig a neat slit trench and place the soil to form a barrier on the side facing the enemy. Then he would erect the tent, so that it would come over the trench, with the earth wall just outside. This done, he would next line the trench with a waterproof sheet and after making up my safari bed, it would be lowered down into the hole.

During the move to Troarn, he implied that the rickety table that I used, was not at all suitable; what I needed was a nice desk with drawers. Obviously, I had to agree, but I was most surprised to see, within the hour, a splendid desk with fitted drawers being lifted down from the Austin – I was given to understand that the late Commanding Officer at the Douvres radar station, no longer had a use for it.

During our first night at Troarn, a nearby road junction was very heavily shelled and some of the shells strayed onto the headquarters. From previous experience, on similar occasions, I had come to learn that it was best to stay in my trench, but as soon as the aggravation ceased, 'Dicky' Bird appeared and asked if I had seen outside the tent. When I indicated that I had not, he suggested that I should take a look and on doing so, I was amazed to find that where previously two tents had stood, there were now two deep craters – and both were less than twenty yards from my tent.

Men were quickly on the spot, whose duty it was to deal with problems of this kind and therefore, I decided to go back to bed. Before doing so, however, I thanked Bird for his prompt interest in my safety, and with a dead straight face he said, "That's all right sir, I only came to see if there would be any point in bringing your morning tea". He was a native of Marlow, and as such, normally resided too far from Bow bells to be considered a cockney but nevertheless, he did possess the cockney characteristic of being able to make light of any adversity – something I was to greatly value on many subsequent occasions.

Each day brought a new experience, as on the occasion when I was out with the Corps doctor and we were hailed by a farmer, who asked if we could get his wife to their farm, because she was about to give birth to a baby. Apparently, the woman had been working in one of the fields, and sure enough, on arriving at the farm, the baby was born almost immediately.

The following day, as our work again took us near to the farm, the doctor suggested that we should call to see how our patients were progressing. We found the baby being cared for by a granny, but the mother was back working in the fields. It seemed that giving birth to a baby, was not a valid reason for interrupting the arduous work of a Normandy peasant.

When I returned to my tent, I found a message informing me that American aircraft had bombed our troops at a place near to

Tilly-la-Campagne, east of the Falaise road, and instructing me to investigate and report.

On arrival at the position indicated, I found complete chaos; many men had been killed and many more had been badly injured, while damaged equipment of every kind was scattered over a wide area. My enquiries revealed, that a large number of aircraft had been supporting an advance by armoured vehicles, when one of the planes had been shot down. By a chance in a million, it had fallen onto one of our forward ammunition depots, which contained red coloured smoke ammunition and this had been immediately ignited. It so happened that, in the particular operation, red smoke was being used to mark enemy targets, and consequently, when the following aircraft saw the red smoke rising from the depot, they naturally assumed that it was marking an enemy position and therefore, they released their bombs. It showed that, even with the most meticulous planning, things can, and do sometimes go disastrously wrong in war.

After the capture of Cherbourg, Montgomery's strategy was for the American forces to concentrate in the west of the bridgehead, preparatory to making the breakout, while the British and Canadian forces pushed strongly towards Falaise, in order to join battle with the majority of the German armoured divisions. On 4 August, the American 3rd Army under General Patton, broke through the German defence positions and after reaching Rennes, turned eastwards in the general direction of the lower Seine.

The advance quickly became a rout, as Hodge's 1st American Army and most of the divisions of British 2nd Army pushed southwards to broaden the opening through which Patton's men were now pouring into the very heart of France. This great encircling movement effectively pinned down the German armies, between Falaise and Argentan – and as the Allied advance rapidly continued, the enemy was squeezed into a smaller and smaller area, which became known as the 'Falaise Pocket'. The Germans made desperate attempts to escape towards the Seine, but the RAF Spitfires and Typhoons were able to fly in and make low level strafing attacks on the huge troop concentrations, using cannon shells, rockets and machine-gun fire to destroy everything in sight.

I was given the task of reporting on certain types of equipment abandoned in the 'Pocket', and as the roads were impassable, I used a Jeep, with which I could drive across the fields. The scene I found was one of appalling carnage, from which men had tried to escape across the fields on bicycles, by the use of stolen horses and cars – and even

47

by taking the village fire-engines. The worst destruction was on the roads, where the columns of traffic had been brought to a stop and then wiped out by the RAF.

In a narrow and steep sided defile near to Clinchamps, vehicles of all kinds, together with dead horses and men were piled solid, to a depth of more than twenty feet. It would seem that after one part of the column had been wiped out, another section had endeavoured to pass over the top of it and that too, had then been strafed. The awful sight, the terrible stench and the swarms of flies, all combined to form a never to be forgotten impression. In war, medals are awarded for gallantry in battle, but I could not help feeling that the men, whose job it now was, to clear up this truly dreadful mess and bury the dead, would deserve much more than medals.

Many of the German troops who had managed to escape from the 'Falaise Pocket', were subsequently trapped to the west of the lower reaches of the Seine, as the RAF had destroyed all the bridges. It fell to three divisions of 1st Corps to mop up the disorganized rabble, and here again, the RAF played its part by attacking a large concentration at Quillebouf, where the enemy had been trying to cross the river on anything that would float.

When I reached the banks of the Seine, I was not prepared for what I saw, because the waters were covered by debris of all kinds, together with countless bodies of the enemy and scores of bloated horses. It was now obvious to everyone, that the events of the last few days had been an important turning point in the war.

9

FURTHER WAR EXPERIENCES

At the end of August, 1st Corps crossed the Seine by a pontoon bridge, which had been erected near to Elbouf, and then had the task of clearing the Havre Peninsula, including capture of the very strongly fortified port of Le Havre.

Many of the small towns and villages through which we now passed, had seen no fighting at all, and consequently, had suffered no loss. It was not surprising therefore, that the inhabitants were overjoyed to be liberated and showed their feelings by giving us an unrestrained welcome.

This was particularly so, in the small town of Bolbec. Here, cheering crowds lined the streets for several days, and at times, brought our convoys to a standstill, so enabling the people to shower us with flowers and present gifts of all kinds, including Camembert cheese and bottles of Calvados. The young girls made the most of the occasion to demonstrate typical French *joie de vivre*, by jumping onto the vehicles to hug and kiss everyone they could get their hands on – the thought did occur to some of us, that perhaps life in war torn France was at times, preferable to that in austerity Britain.

At this stage of the war and after four months of hectic activity, we felt entitled to occasional relaxation in the late evenings. Consequently, when we heard that the Lion D'or restaurant, in Bacqueville, was serving fillet steak and pommes frites, we thought it would make a nice change from bully-beef. Four of us therefore, took a Jeep and drove to Bacqueville over a road which lead up a long hill with a series of hair-pin bends – and sure enough, on arrival, we found that we could get magnificent steak and chips. We ordered four large portions, but when we asked about drinks, we were told that apart from mineral water, they only had Benedictine Liqueur, and that was in the small 'tot' bottles.

In the somewhat unfortunate circumstances, we decided to order eight of the small bottles, but by the time the meal was served, we were ready for a further eight bottles. After the wonderful repast, we ordered eight more, and as the 'empties' had not been cleared away, the small table was looking rather cluttered. It was then that the senior member of the party suggested that we should make the most of the convivial evening, by ordering more Benedictine until there was not room on the tiny table for more bottles.

I can only vaguely remember the drive back to the H.Q. but I do recollect that at one point, we became hopelessly lost. On seeing a sign at the side of the road, a member of the party left the Jeep and stumbled up to it. By the aid of a torch, he closely scrutinized the wording and when asked what it said, he haltingly replied, "These verges – have –not been – cleared of – mines". The sight of our colleague attempting to get back to the Jeep, without his feet touching the ground, provided the biggest laugh of the evening. Actually, we got back to the headquarters quite quickly – possibly because the hair-pin bends we had encountered on the way up, had somehow miraculously disappeared.

One day, I was informed that a large enemy ammunition depot had been found at Le Treport, a pleasant little town on the coast, near to Dieppe and it was suggested that among the varied contents, there could well be some gas ammunition. I therefore decided to go and take a look, but as on all previous searches, no gas ammunition could be found.

I had visited Le Treport, once previously, as a young member of a school party led by our French teacher, so I was interested to see if the pension where we had stayed, still existed. To my surprise, there it was, in a small side street, just off the waterfront and looking very much as I had remembered it.

I have to confess, that as I gazed at the once familiar building, I could not refrain from wondering what had become of Marie-Louise, the young maid who used to serve us, early each morning, with *café-complet* in our rooms. She became a heart-throb for all of us, not just because she was so very pretty, but also because she was always prepared to join in the pillow fights and similar tomfoolery – that is, until the French Master appeared, and put an end to our antics, on the grounds that romping with the young lady was most ungentlemanly – particularly when we were still in our pyjamas.

I was expected to investigate anything even remotely connected with chemical processing, so one day, I decided to call at the Benedictine Monastery, near to Fécamp, where the monks produce the famous liqueur. I was very kindly received and shown round the distillery, after which my guide said they would have been very pleased to let the Headquarters have a supply of the end-product, but unfortunately the Germans had left them without any bottles. Whereupon, I asked if they would be able to let us have some of the liqueur, if we were to supply the containers – and immediately I received a favourable response.

On returning to the Headquarters, I told one or two of my colleagues about the monk's kind offer, and as a result, early the following morning, people went over to the monastery with pails, jerry-cans, tin baths and indeed anything that would hold the blessed spirit. For several weeks thereafter, the mess served a generous measure of Benedictine to wash down the bully-beef.

The time had now come to turn our attention to the little matter of capturing the world's most strongly defended port – Le Havre. It was obvious that the operation would have to be comprehensively planned and as by now the effectiveness of flame warfare was held in high esteem, I was instructed to lay on every available Crocodile flamethrower.

In several previous flame battles, it had been found that some of those killed bore no visible injuries, so it was decided that this mystery should be investigated. The medical authorities, in particular, felt that the cause of death in these cases should be established, and as a result, they arranged for a surgeon and a mobile operating theatre to be placed at my disposal.

Very briefly, the plan was for me to lead a number of men who would follow right behind the Crocodiles, and as soon as a dead body was found, without visible injuries, it was to be taken back to the surgeon. This would have to be done very quickly, because some parts of the post-mortem examination would need to be carried out within about twenty minutes of death. Various causes of death had been considered including carbon monoxide poisoning, asphyxia due to carbon dioxide and dehydration from short term exposure to high temperatures.

At 1745 hr on 10 September, 5,000 tons of bombs began to fall on the outer defences of Le Havre, and early the following morning, after the usual smoke screens had been laid, all hell was let loose. The artillery banged away and the Flail tanks cleared tracks through the minefields, along which the flamethrowers advanced, with the intention of scaring the pants off those defenders who had survived the bombing and shelling. My party, equipped with Jeeps, followed close behind the flamethrowers, together with the infantry, who were having a rough time as a result of the unpleasant stuff being thrown at and over the tanks. Each time we found a dead body, without obvious injury, we would put it onto a Jeep and take it, as quickly as possible, to the operating theatre – and then return to the action to continue the grim search. In this way we kept the surgeon quite busy. By dusk on 11 September, and after 37 hours of this exciting business, we entered the city, whereupon the Garrison Commander surrendered, together with 12,000 troops.

After a good long sleep, I made my way over to the surgeon, who incidentally, turned out to be a very interesting young Canadian. Before joining the army, he had been living with the Eskimos in order to carry out research on tuberculosis, and in this connection, had many great yarns to relate. But I was anxious to know, what he had been able to learn from the post-mortems. Surprisingly, none of the anticipated causes of death had proved positive; it appeared, in all cases, that it was just a matter of cardiac arrest. In other words, men who were brave enough to face machine-guns, had died from shock on being confronted by the flame. To me, after merely experiencing the wall of flame at a safe distance, this conclusion came as no great surprise.

There was, however, an unexpected climax to this piece of research, which arose as a result of a war correspondent reporting the matter to the Red Cross, in the belief that the post-mortem examinations contravened the Geneva Convention. There followed a high level investigation, but in due course, we were completely exonerated.

The enemy had found it impossible to hold a defence line on the river Seine and consequently had been forced to fight a rearguard action to the east, across northern France. By the middle of September, they had regrouped on the Antwerp-Turnhout canal and were showing every intention of holding the important town of Antwerp, so as to deny the Allies use of the docks. As a result, 1st Corps was now ordered to move into the area east of Brussels and given the task of clearing Antwerp and thrusting into the Netherlands.

It was therefore, necessary to find a convenient location for the Headquarters, and in view of the onset of winter, it was hoped that a group of suitable buildings could be requisitioned. As a result, it was decided to send into Belgium a reconnaissance party consisiting of five officers – of which, I was one – to investigate the possiblities.

Although the roads were heavily congested with military traffic, and in some places bridges had been destroyed, we managed to make good progress and arrived in the planned locality by early evening. The idea then, was to find a suitable hotel for the night and commence the reconnaissance early on the following day.

The hotel we chose was Le Grand Veneur at Keerbergen, where the proprietor gave us a fantastic welcome. Bottles of champagne appeared, we were given the best rooms in the hotel and the six-course dinner could not have been bettered anywhere. After sleeping rough in Normandy, the wonderful beds, with silk sheets, looked most inviting but we all slept badly; it would seem that even the poorest of beds can, after a few months, become the norm.

The following day, we rose early and over breakfast the proprietor was again dancing attendance upon us. During the course of a wide ranging conversation, we asked him if he knew of a group of buildings in the vicinity, which could suitably accommodate the staff of a large headquarters. He immediately told us about some new barracks, which the Germans had abandoned, just a couple of weeks previously and were only about two hundred yards from the hotel. We decided to view the property and found it to be perfect in every respect. The buildings were in excellent condition and comprised all the necessary facilities, including blocks of offices, mess rooms, kitchens and garages, etc.

We did make further enquiries in the locality, but soon came to the conclusion that we were not likely to find anything better than the barracks. However, as a second choice, we investigated the potential of a moated castle, which was very picturesque, but lacking in many of the preferred facilities. We reported accordingly, and were instructed to requisition the barracks and prepare plans for the allocation of rooms to the various branches.

When we told the hotel proprietor that the 1st Corps Headquarters was going to move into the barracks, he was absolutely delighted and told us that during our stay in Keerbergen, we could use the hotel as an annexe to the officers' quarters, and moreover, the members of the reconnaissance party could retain the hotel bedrooms for just as long as we wished; it all seemed too good to be true. Within three days the entire Headquarters staff had moved into the barracks and everyone was delighted with the excellent facilities.

It was then, that the proprietor of the hotel announced that to celebrate the outstanding success in Normandy of British 1st Corps, he was going to arrange a *Grande Soiree*. This was to consist of dinner, followed by lavish entertainment and dancing. All the officers at the Headquarters were to be invited, as well as, "the most beautiful girls in Belgium". Even if we had wanted to, there was no way in which we could stop the man from going ahead with this mad idea, at such an inopportune time – so Sunday 24 September was fixed for the propitious occasion.

Early in the evening of that day, large limousines (some chauffeur driven) began to arrive at the hotel and out of them stepped the most striking young ladies we had seen for many months. In fact, I feel sure we could not have been blamed if the thought had occurred to us, that if this was war – long may it continue. At the appointed time, drinks were served, introductions were made and in due course, we took our seats in the very fine restaurant. The meal was all that we could desire – so too was the female company. Quite naturally therefore, everyone was looking forward to a highly convivial evening.

During the lively conversation, one of the officers asked his consort where she had come from during the day, and we were very surprised to learn that she had travelled at least sixty miles. He then asked her how she had learned about the *soiree*, whereupon she said she had received an invitation, and on opening her handbag, she withdrew a sheet of paper, which she handed round for us to see; all the other girls had apparently received similar invitations. It proved to be a most amazing document, because in addition to stating that the Headquarters of British 1st Corps was stationed in Keerbergen, the hotel stationery included a map of the locality. One of our security officers immediately realised that the invitation would have gone out on a fairly wide distribution and that it could quite easily have fallen into the hands of a girl, who had a German boy friend.

Accordingly, he felt that it was his duty to show one of the invitations to the Head of the Intelligence Branch.

The outcome was that, within fifteen minutes, the order was given for all officers to immediately leave the hotel and work through the night, with a view to the barracks being evacuated before dawn, and the Headquarters then transferred to the moated castle.

The hotel proprietor was completely dismayed by this sudden turn of events and said he had no idea how he was going to explain matters to the girls. Whereupon, the senior officer present agreed to speak to them on behalf of all the officers, saying that we were very, very sorry the wonderful evening had to come to such an untimely end, but then went on to explain that headquarters were prime targets in war, and consequently, their location had to remain a well guarded secret.

10

ONE OF WAR'S TRAGEDIES

Two liaison officers were attached to the Headquarters; one was Belgian and the other Dutch. The Belgian was Lieutenant Julien Dewolf, who at the beginning of the war, was the editor of a newspaper published by the Belgian Resistance Movement. As might be expected, the enemy persistently tried to discover where the paper was being printed. As a result, strict security was essential and to facilitate this, the presses and the editorial staff were quite often relocated. The Resistance was not merely encouraging passive defence but in addition, was planning and carrying out major offensive operations. It was not surprising therefore, that the Gestapo should employ all available means to track down the members and in particular the leaders, including the editor of the newspaper.

Julien was nearly caught on a number of occasions and when it became obvious that his home was being kept under surveillance he decided to live rough in the open country. Finally, however, it proved impossible for him to continue his work as editor, with the result that he decided to leave Belgium.

After bidding his wife good-bye, he contacted the escape organization that was operating to get Allied airman, who had been shot down over the Continent, back to Britain. They quickly provided him with forged papers and got him into France. He was then passed from one section of the organization to another, all the way through France, over the Pyrenees, across northern Spain and into neutral Portugal, where he was able to join a ship in Oporto, which was bound for England. The Belgian authorities in London, then arranged for Julien to be trained as a liaison officer in the British army, after which he was posted for duty with 1st Corps Headquarters.

When 1st Corps entered Belgium, Julien was able to contact a friend, who told him that soon after he had left Belgium, the Gestapo had arrested his wife, Irène, and that she was now believed to be in the infamous Breendonck Concentration Camp. Apparently, Irène had steadfastly refused to tell the Gestapo anything concerning Julien's whereabouts or the activities of the Resistance Movement, and as a result, she had been taken away.

At this time, the Camp was still in the hands of the enemy, but the troops under 1st Corps were getting ever closer. Consequently, Julien sought out the unit that was expected to liberate the inmates of the dreaded place and as it was believed to have gas chambers, I arranged to co-operate with Julien, so that together, we could get into the Camp at the very first opportunity. The immediate task would then be to find

Irène and take her to relatives who could look after her. Julien had shown me photographs of his wife and therefore, I knew the kind of person I would be looking for.

On the long-awaited day, we followed our troops into the Camp; the warders were quickly overpowered and led away, so that in no time at all, we were free to contact the poor mortals who had managed to survive. We searched and searched in every nook and corner, and we hoped – but just as Julien was beginning to despair, he saw Irène. The photographs had shown a vivacious and strikingly beautiful young woman; the person I now saw, was little more than a skeleton and seemingly devoid of the strength to stand.

She recognised Julien, but appeared drained of all emotion – she just could not believe what she was seeing. We carried the poor woman to a car and took her to a relative, near to Brussels, where she could be nursed back to life.

There was nothing more I could then do at this point, so I left Julien and Irène together and returned to Breendonck. Members of the Army Medical Corps and several Chaplains were administering to the survivors, with a view to transferring most to hospital, from where their relatives could be contacted. Some of the people had first to be released from the manacles that bound them hand and foot. Some had clothes but most had only a collection of rags – it was difficult to contemplate a more depressing sight of squalor and suffering.

It was obvious that the authorities had recently been trying to remove some of the incriminating evidence, but the speed of the Allied advance had forestalled them, and as a result for all to see, were pathetic messages on walls, torture chambers with demonic apparatus beyond even the imagination of normal people, the gallows and the posts to which victims were pinioned before being shot.

I found no evidence to show that significant numbers of prisoners had been killed by poison gas. But facilities did exist whereby various gases could have been introduced into torture chambers, as a means of extracting confessions, because these chambers were fitted with windows and equipped for audio communication.

About a month later, Julien told me that Irène had recovered sufficiently to enable her to meet her friends. They proposed therefore to arrange a celebratory dinner, to which I was invited. In due course, their house was brought back into use and a day fixed for the party. When I approached the house, I saw Julien digging in the garden, which I thought was a rather odd thing for him to be doing, immediately prior to the family reunion – but then, I saw that he was taking a wooden box from a hole in the ground. Apparently, before he had made his escape to England, he had put several bottles of wine into the box and vowed they would not be retrieved until the family could once again welcome their friends and celebrate in a free Belgium.

Irène, wearing a pretty dress, was sitting in a chair and understandably looking very different from when I had last seen her, but she was still very, very weak. When I took her limp hand, she could hardly speak, but a flicker of a smile said all that was necessary. Her mother and several relatives were busy in the kitchen preparing dinner and soon we were to enjoy a truly wonderful meal, comprising many courses, with the main dish consisting of delicious jugged hare. The wine from the garden flowed freely, and everything contributed to a memorable evening – except that, poor Irène could hardly eat anything at all.

Before I left the house, Julien took me over to Irène, and they told me that they would like me to have Julien's Resistance Movement badge, which he had worn behind the lapel of his coat before his escape, well hidden during his escape but proudly worn on his uniform since joining the British Army. It is a small and simple article, but something I will always treasure.

As soon as Belgium had been liberated, Julien left the Headquarters but I continued to keep in touch with him and called to see Irène, from time to time. She never really recovered from the terrible treatment received in Breendonck, but it was remarkable that she did not blame Julien, in any way, for all she had suffered; on the contrary, she was very proud of him and fully appreciated the great risks he had taken to advance the cause of freedom. About two months after the party, I received a note from Julien to tell me that Irène had died. I often feel, that many people in Britain, failed to fully understand what life was actually like in the occupied countries.

11
THE NETHERLANDS AND THE
APPROACH TO GERMANY

Resulting from the interrogation of prisoners, we began to suspect that we should soon find large stocks of poison gas in Germany and therefore, I kept in close touch with the two officers at the Headquarters who were responsible for interrogation. These young men (Captains Spinks and Caldow) had attended universities in Germany before the war, and as a result, were able to speak the language like natives.

It was very interesting to watch these experts at work. Their particular technique would depend upon the type of prisoner, but in general, they endeavoured to commence the interrogation as soon as possible after capture, so that the men would most likely be apprehensive, and therefore, somewhat submissive. The two officers would work a short distance apart, each interrogating one prisoner, while all other prisoners were kept well away.

As they had, by this time, been doing the job for several months, they had accumulated a tremendous amount of information about the various German units, which was to be of direct operational value. In addition, they inevitably collected much lowdown concerning the people in the units, including their foibles and even their vices.

The Geneva Convention requires a prisoner to reveal his name, date of birth, rank and serial number but nothing more. So when this had been noted, the officer would not immediately seek further information, but would begin to talk to the prisoner about the men in his unit, and it would be at this point, that he would draw upon his vast store of scandal. Very soon, the prisoner would conclude that the officer knew as much about his unit, as he did – and possibly more – so what possible harm could there be in talking. In this way, a dialogue would be established, during which the prisoner would be led into conversation on subjects where information was specifically required. The officers would very cleverly toss snippets of the latest gossip, one to the other, in such a way as to make each of the two prisoners believe that the other was talking freely, and when this stage was reached, all questions would generally be answered without hesitation.

The fact that the prisoners saw nothing being taken down in writing, would support their belief that what they were saying was of little importance but later, the officers would make out detailed reports on all new information, which would be circulated to the appropriate Branches of the Headquarters.

The Dutch liaison officer was Captain Harry Stokvis, who before the war, had been a director in the well known firm of Stokvis & Zonen, in Rotterdam. He was a most jovial character and ready at all times to undertake the most dangerous missions. As the Allied forces began to enter the Netherlands, it was feared that the enemy would open the dykes to flood the low-lying ground, which would make further advance difficult, if not impossible. As a result, Harry was questioned with regard to the possibility of contacting the Dutch Resistance Movement, and getting them to guard the vital flood-gates at the appropriate time.

Soon after these discussions had taken place, Harry, without warning of any kind, disappeared. As no explanation could be found, his loss came to be accepted as just one more of war's unsolved mysteries.

Then, about three weeks after his disappearance, I happened to see him strolling into the Headquarters. He was dirty and rather dishevelled, but smiling as ever and apparently quite unconcerned. I went up to him and blurted out, "Where the hell have you been", to which he laconically replied, "I think I should first talk to my boss".

Little by little the mystery unfolded. It would seem that, although at the time, our troops were a considerable distance from the vital dykes, Harry had been under the impression that he was required to personally contact the Dutch Resistance Movement, there and then. As a result, he had penetrated the enemy positions, by swimming at night in the canals, contacted the leaders of the Resistance Movement and made all the necessary arrangements for the guarding of the flood-gates. Having ensured that the people possessed all the necessary resources, he had then made his way back, by again infiltrating the enemy positions. This amazing feat resulted in very little of the low lying land being eventually flooded and greatly contributed to the ultimate rapid advance of the Allies through the southern part of the Netherlands.

In recognition, Harry was appointed MBE. He was heard to say, "Not many people could have been rewarded for disobeying an order – Nelson wasn't so fortunate". After the war, Harry resumed his research work and gained a Doctorate in Economics on the submission of a masterly thesis on the Bretton Woods Agreement.

As the fighting drew closer to Germany, it became possible to detect two opposing types of German prisoner. There was the committed fascist, who believed Hitler's secret weapons were about to be introduced and that they would then quickly bring the war to a victorious conclusion. And there was the other type, who after seeing his unit pushed back, in one humiliating defeat after another, had come to the inevitable conclusion that Germany was already doomed. With this second type very much in mind, the RAF decided to drop leaflets over the enemy to inform the troops of their impossible situation and the advisability of surrender.

As might be expected, the enemy soon joined in this war of propaganda by distributing similar leaflets; the following is a copy of one I picked up near to Breda, which describes the wonderful life in German prison camps awaiting British prisoners:

GERMANY STRICTLY OBSERVING GENEVA CONVENTION

For every soldier, even the bravest, the moment may arrive when fighting on, would mean senseless selfdestruction and no benefit to his country. It is recognised by all nations at war that under such circumstances, the soldiers are justified in surrendering. If you should face a like situation, keep the following points in mind.

First:

You will be taken for a few days to a Dulag (transit camp) right behind the front. The Dulags are not hotels. They are fitted out simply, as the nearness of the front permits, but you will be safe and well-treated. You may send home a message at once via radio "Invasion Calling" telling your wife and family you are alive. If you are wounded or sick you will immediately receive the best of medical care exactly like a German soldier.

Second:

You will be transferred to a Stalag (permanent camp). The Stalags are up-to-date camps with all conveniences. The food is prepared in modern kitchens. It is ample and of the same high quality as the food of the German soldier. Besides, you are allowed to receive a package every week through the International Red Cross. You will be housed in clean airy rooms which you may decorate according to your taste. Lavatories and toilets are of a high sanitary standard. If you wish to work, your qualifications will be taken into consideration. You will be given opportunity to learn a trade, to improve yourself in your own profession and you can even acquire a university degree. All Stalags have athletic fields and modern sporting equipment. If you are artistically inclined, you may carry on your study of the fine arts. You may receive any amount of mail. The forwarding of letters and packages by the International Red Cross is swift and reliable. You yourself are permitted to write 4 postcards and 3 letters per month.

Third:

The fighting will be over for you. Nothing more can happen to you and above all

**YOU WILL RETURN HOME
SAFE AND SOUND AFTER THE WAR**

Our boys used to add between the lines of such leaflets, spicy comments in the colloquial idiom; examples of which would be quite unprintable.

Having regard to recent history, the theme of the following leaflet, is not without interest.

WHY DIE FOR STALIN?

In dying for Stalin your soldiers are not dying for democracy or the preservation of the democratic form of government – they are dying for the establishment of Communism and a form of Stalinist tyranny throughout the world. Furthermore, they are not dying for the preservation of the integrity of small nations (England's old war-cry) but are dying so that Poland shall be a Soviet state; so that the Baltic States shall be incorporated in the Soviet Union and so that Soviet influence shall extend from the Baltic to the Balkans.

Every British soldier who lays down his life in this war is not only a loss to his country; he is a loss to the common cause of European civilisation. Germany's and England's quarrel is a form of traditional rivalry. It is more in the nature of a private quarrel which Germany did not seek. The Soviet Union's quarrel, however, is a quarrel with our common heritage and with all those values – moral, spiritual, cultural and material – which we have, all of us – Englishman and German alike – recognised, cherished and striven to maintain. TO DIE FOR THE DESTRUCTION OF THESE VALUES IS TO DIE IN VAIN. Stalin, with all the diabolical power of Communism behind him, is seeking to profit from Britain's and Germany's preoccupation. The amount of influence which Britain can exercise on Stalin can be measured by the latter's undisputed claims to the sovereign territories of other nations. The only controlling influence left on Stalin is the strength and tenacity of the German Wehrmacht and of the European volunteers who support Germany in her fight for the survival of Europe and its position as the cradle of our common civilisation. Every British soldier who dies for Stalin is another nail in the coffin of

Britain's hopes of maintaining a "Balance of Power" in Europe. Should the "Equilibrium" pass to Stalin then the equilibrium of the world is at an end.

THOSE WHO ARE ABOUT TO DIE - THINK IT OVER!

One day, I had occasion to visit a Canadian unit that was holding the southern bank of the river Maas, and one of the officers told me that during the previous morning, they had been surprised to receive a visit from five Dutch Resistance members, who said they had captured a Divisional Headquarters and wished to know what was to be done with it.

Apparently, the Germans, who were holding the northern bank of the river, had been using a large barge to accommodate their headquarters staff and during the night, some Resistance people had killed the sentry, then jumped onto the barge and fastened down all the hatches. Using a fishing boat, they had towed the barge across the river and handed the lot over to the Canadians. The officer went on to say that they had managed to deal satisfactorily with the very surprised Germans, but now had the problem of getting the Dutch people safely back to the other side of the river. When he asked if I had any ideas as to how this might be done, I suggested he should contact Harry Stokvis at Corps Headquarters, who was the acknowledged expert on that kind of operation.

As the end of the war was now becoming a not too distant possibility, a favourite question for discussion was, "What are you going to do when you get back to 'civvy street'?" The answers were always interesting and often very surprising.

I well remember putting this question to Captain Basil Spence, whose particular responsiblity was camouflage and he told me that he would be designing cathedrals. I felt that cathedrals would be one of the last things post-war Britain would be wanting, and therefore I said, "No, seriously Basil, as a qualified architect, you will surely be required to assist in the rebuilding of the bombed cities and towns?" Whereupon, he replied very firmly, "I could not be more serious; cathedrals have been destroyed and the people will demand that they be rebuilt – not just as they were originally but with new designs, to exemplify the spiritual rebirth of the nation, after this traumatic conflict".

I have to say, that I was not really convinced until much later, when he designed many imposing buildings, including of course, the magnificent Coventry Cathedral.

12

THE ACCIDENT

Early in October, I received a request from the Polish Division for me to visit them and advise on the use of flamethrowers. The Division had been given the task of crossing the Leopold Canal, the northern bank of which was being strongly defended by the enemy. The particular section of the canal passes along the top of a steep sided embankment and the enemy was dug-in on the reverse slope, so making their positions very difficult to neutralize by artillery and small-arms fire. As a result, the Division had been allotted a number of flamethrowers for use immediately prior to the crossing assault. It had received little previous experience, in the handling of flamethrowers and this particular situation was very tricky, due to the height of the embankment and the width of the canal.

Obviously, the objective was to elevate the flame-guns so that the flame fuel would clear the top of the embankment, cross the water and then fall onto the enemy positions. I therefore, considered it advisable to organize a preliminary trial session, in order to determine the optimum gun elevation and the necessary distance from the foot of the embankment, for the flamethrowers to be stationed.

A mile or so back from the canal, we found a hilly ridge, rising to about the same height as the canal embankment and this enabled us to simulate the actual conditions. Here we measured out the width of the canal and put posts in the ground to mark the corresponding positions of the enemy defences. The flamethrowers were placed on the other side of the ridge, so the gunners now had to fire over the ridge and generate the flame at the posts. The particular flamethrowers were mounted on tracked Bren-gun carriers and were therefore fully mobile. Consequently, by moving the carriers forwards or backwards and adjusting the elevation of the gun, it was possible to achieve the required result.

I stressed the importance of preventing the flame liquid from hitting the forward slope of the ridge, because in that case, it would be reflected back to the flamethrower, with disastrous consequences. It will be realized that all my instructions had to be translated into Polish, and therefore, it was difficult for me to ascertain to what extent I was being understood.

However, we successfully carried out several trials and made all the necessary measurements. To conclude the session, it was decided to allow the remaining flame gunners, who had not yet participated in the exercise, to get some experience in hitting the posts.

It was then, that it all went wrong. One of the gunners did what I had particularly warned against, and allowed the flame liquid to hit the forward slope of the ridge, whereupon it rebounded and fell onto the flamethrower, immediately setting both the carrier and the gunner alight. As I happened to be standing right behind the carrier, I jumped onto it and pulled the gunner away. He sustained serious injuries which received prompt attention, after which he was sped away to hospital. The injuries to my hands, chin and chest were comparatively minor.

On leaving the area, Driver Bird headed for the farm track that we had used on arrival and which connected with the highway. We were surprised to see at the commencement of the track, a sign bearing the words, "Danger – Mines" and even more surprised to see a sapper lifting a land-mine from one of the wheeltracks.

Just prior to our arrival at the site, there had been a heavy rain storm and water was lying in the rutted wheel tracks. The car had therefore been driven with two wheels on the centre of the track and two on the side verge. If we had arrived before the downpour, we would have driven with the wheels in the tracks – and in that case, this book would not have been written.

I went back to the Poles, just prior to the assault to see if further assistance was required. Everything appeared to be well under control and soon a dense smoke screen was laid over the canal. Ten minutes later the flamethrowers started firing and this time everything went according to plan – but with me nevertheless, standing well back! The defenders lobbed a few mortar bombs over the embankment but it seemed that they were too much occupied in avoiding the flame, to give a lot of thought to offence. On a given signal, the flaming stopped and immediately the Poles crossed the canal by light assault craft. In a matter of minutes they established two bridgeheads, which after some stiff fighting, were successfully joined. During the following week, the entire area south of the Scheldt was cleared.

About a couple of weeks after the accident, my burns were almost healed but the Headquarters' doctor found that the wounds had become infected. He tried various treatments but as my hands were by then, suppurating quite freely, he arranged for me to enter hospital in Antwerp. There, I spent several days holding my hands in a solution of potassium permanganate, which proved helpful, but as soon as the treatment was stopped, the trouble recommenced.

At this time, the enemy was firing V1 rockets into Antwerp and one night, a rocket hit the hospital, blowing out all the windows and completely destroying one of the buildings. As a result, it was decided

The Accident

to evacuate part of the hospital and fly some of the patients back to England. Accordingly, I was conveyed on a stretcher, by ambulance to a Dakota and together with other patients, flown to an airfield near to Gloucester, where we were put on board a Red Cross train bound for Nottingham.

In the City General Hospital, I was treated like a war hero, which made me feel a complete fraud. I would be asked, "How did you come to get these nasty burns?" Whereupon the ensuing conversation would be something like this, "They were produced by a flamethrower". – "Oh, those beastly Germans". – Actually, it was one of our flamethrowers". – "Where were you fighting?" – "There was no fighting – it was just an exercise". At this point the nurses would generally give up and I fear, come to the conclusion that I was in the wrong type of hospital!

The army services arranged for my wife to be accommodated in a nearby house, and as I was classified 'walking wounded', I was allowed out of hospital quite often – so life was really quite agreeable. But then one day, a doctor told me that I would have to receive specialist treatment, that was not available in Nottingham. I had visions of being sent to London or some other big city but no, I was to be taken to Stoke-on-Trent – my home town – and even more surprising, the consultant was to be Doctor Lindsay-Boyd, whom I knew well. As a result, I found myself living at home and attending the North Staffs Royal Infirmary as an out-patient, under the expert care of Dr. Lindsay-Boyd, who prescribed various treatments, including superficial X-Ray therapy. After about a month, I was pronounced fit to return to my unit.

Subsequent to crossing the Rhine, the Divisions under the command of 1st Corps advanced towards the Rhur and soon we began to find large stocks of poison gas ammunition. The contained gases were of various types but consisted mostly of products developed by the Germans during the war and called nerve gases, because they act upon the central nervous system. These gases, of which Tabun and Sarin are typical examples, cause violent convulsions and rapid death, unless a respirator can be put on within about thirty seconds. Fortunately, the British respirators did provide complete protection against all these deadly compounds.

The end of the war in Europe came quickly on 4 May 1945, with the surrender of the German forces to Field Marshal Bernard Montgomery, who shortly after, issued the following personal message to the British forces:

"1.   On Saturday 25 August, 1945, the 21st Army Group
will cease to exist and the British forces in north-west
Europe will be known as 'The British Army of the Rhine'.
2.   I cannot let this moment pass without a reference to the
past achievements of the 21st Army Group. This Group of
Armies fought on the left or northern flank of the Allied
Forces that invaded Normandy in June, 1944; these forces
liberated France, Belgium, Holland, Luxemburg and
Denmark; they joined hands with our Russian allies: and
thus ended the German war.
The Army Group completed its active operations by
gathering as captives on the northern flank, in the space of
a few days, upwards of two million of the once renowned
German Army. The fame of the Army Group will long shine
in history and other generations, besides our own, will
honour its deeds.
3.   Officers and men of the Army Group are now scattered
throughout the world; many are serving in other theatres;
many have returned to civil life.
To all of you, wherever you may be, I send my best wishes
and my grateful thanks for your loyal help and co-operation.
4.   To those who still serve in Germany I would say that,
though our name has changed, we still have the same task.
As a result of this war much of Europe has been destroyed,
and the whole economic framework of the continent lies in
ruins. We have a job to do which will call for all our energy
and purpose; we have got to help to rebuild a new Europe
out of the ruins of the old.
It is a gigantic task.
But we must face up to it with that same spirit of service
to the common cause of freedom which has so
strengthened us during the stress and strain of war.
Together we have achieved much in war, let us achieve
even more in peace."

13

SOME POST-WAR EVENTS IN GERMANY

My first task after the end of the war, was to organize the safe disposal of 120,000 tons of German poison gas ammunition. Most of it was stored in concrete bunkers, in two very large ammunition depots at Sennelager and Munsterlager, while much of the remainder was held underground, in a disused salt-mine at Hänigsen. The ammunition was of various types and contained several different chemicals, but by far the greatest part was in the form of aircraft bombs, containing the deadly nerve gases.

It was decided to employ German labour, working under the management of the British Forces, to load the various items onto trains, for transport to North Sea ports. At the ports, the ammunition was to be transferred to German barges, which were to be towed to the deep waters of the Skagerrak and there scuttled. I had to ensure that, at all stages, strict safety measures were enforced, because the consequences of spillage, from say a punctured bomb, would have been extremely serious.

Scientists from the Porton Chemical Defence Experimental Establishment, carried out assessment trials on the nerve gases at the Gas Experimental Station, at Raubkammer, in N W Germany. Briefly, these compounds in the liquid state, as contained in the bombs, produce severe injuries to the skin, but when volatilised and inhaled, the affects are too dreadful to contemplate. They act by blocking the action of an enzyme in the body called acetylcholinesterase, which plays a vital role in that part of the nervous system responsible for muscle control. This produces convulsions, so violent as to cause bones to fracture; while the eyes bulge, resulting in blindness. It is, however, the muscles controlling the lungs that fail first, so making breathing impossible and mercifully, bringing about death within a few minutes.

I have often wondered what would have happened if the enemy planes had been able to disperse these terrible gases in Normandy. They have very little odour and are difficult to detect; so the essential warning to put on respirators may only have been given by the sight of our colleagues going into convulsions. Without doubt, my task in the bridgehead would have been very, very difficult. Consequently, our thanks must be forever due to the Allied Air Forces, for gaining the vital air superiority before the invasion and maintaining it throughout the war in Europe.

In the disused salt-mine at Hänigsen, there was 20,000 tons of poison gas ammunition, together with a large variety of other items. The workings in the mine were very extensive, consisting of many large chambers connected by tunnels, through which light railways ran to connect with two large lifts, operating between the surface and the various levels. Here again German labour was used, under British supervision, to bring the ammunition to the surface and load it into railway trucks for disposal, together with the ammunition from Munsterlager and Sennelager.

While I was working at the mine, we gained the impression that certain items were being taken away by the German workers, so the security officer decided to stop one of their buses as it left the mine, and search the occupants. Accordingly, the men were taken from the bus and herded into a room, where they were asked if they were in possession of any property from the mine. All were most indignant and declared that they would not think of taking anything away. The officer told them he was not satisfied and was going to have them searched; it would therefore, be best for anyone who had anything, to own up, rather than be found both a thief and a liar.

As they continued to assert their innocence, each man was taken separately into an adjoining room and again asked if he had anything that did not belong to him. The result was the same in almost every case; the man would deny having taken anything, whereupon, he would be told to start undressing. When he had removed everything except his trousers, he would still be protesting his innocence. But on being told to take down his trousers, it would be seen that he had wrapped around his waist many yards of silk cloth, or some other valuable item. The men were immediately charged with theft and duly brought before the local Court.

On the following day, the security officer said he was going to repeat the operation. I told him it would be a waste of time because nobody would take anything, in view of what had happened to their friends. He merely said, "Do you want to bet?" – so I laid a small wager. Suffice it to say that I lost my bet, but gained an unexpected insight into yet another aspect of human nature.

After all the gas ammunition had been dumped into the Skagerrak, I submitted a lengthy report to Army Headquarters, giving detailed information on the tonnages of various types of ammunition, the casualties suffered and the many problems experienced during the operation. As a footnote to my report, I referred to the 10,000 tons of high explosive ammunition still remaining in the Hänigsen mine and which, as a result of the high temperature, was most likely becoming unstable, with consequent risk of explosion.

About two weeks later, I was informed that the Brigadier wished to see me. Immediately on entering his office, he asked how long I had been a soldier. I toyed with a disparaging reply, but there was something about his manner which made me play safe, and give a factual answer. He then asked if that was not long enough for me to know that in the army, you did what you were instructed to do, and nothing more – to which, of course, I had to agree. He then said, "I understand you recently reported on the condition of the high explosive ammunition in the mine at Hänigsen. You must surely know that you have no authority to make reports on ammunition, other than gas ammunition – accordingly, I have been ordered to issue a reprimand and to warn you that any further such occurance will have very serious consequences. That will be all".

Greatly shattered by this unexpected encounter, I was just about to leave the room, when he said, "Just a moment – I feel you should know that, this morning, the mine at Hänigsen blew-up and it is feared there are more than 120 casualties". I was now even more shattered, and pondered deeply on the whole affair – until a few hours later, when I was walking along a corridor in the Headquarters, I felt a tap on my shoulder and turning round saw the Brigadier, who with a broad grin, said, "I hope you haven't been submitting any more of those unauthorized reports". I eventually came to the conclusion that he had been instructed to 'tick me off' and had done just that, but at the same time, he fully realized that I had a very good reason for stepping out of line. This view was reinforced, shortly afterwards, when I was informed that I had been promoted.

About this time, I learned that a gas chamber had been found at the Spandau prison in Berlin; I was therefore asked to go and inspect it. I joined two other officers, who also had work to do in Berlin and together we drove through the Russian Zone and up to the former capital. My two companions were to have a meeting with the Russian authorities in order to discuss the movement of railway rolling stock. Apparently, trucks that entered the Russian Zone, from the British Zone, were not being returned, and consequently, the number of trucks available to the British was becoming progressively less.

In the Spandau Prison most of Germany's top war criminals were being held, consequently when they were taking exercise in an enclosed yard, I had the unique experience of seeing, at close quarters, men who had played a leading part in the attempt to dominate Europe.

Their expressionless faces failed to reveal any reaction to their momentous downfall.

The room, which had been thought to be a gas chamber, was quite large, had no windows and the doors could be completely sealed. A motorized fan provided a supply of air, after it had passed through a comprehensive series of filters. Leading off the room was a store containing sophisticated apparatus for analysing war gases, together with supplies of respirators and gas capes, etc. Another store contained a refrigerator and facilities for storing food. There were also two cubicles containing chemical lavatories. In the room was a stack of folding chairs, a table with telephone and a library of books.

It was immediately obvious that this was not a gas chamber designed for the purpose of killing people, but on the contrary, had been intended to protect people during a gas attack. Indeed, it would have given the warders complete protection for a very long time – what would have happened to the prisoners was, of course, another matter.

On the journey back from Berlin, I asked my travelling companions how their negotiations had fared. It appeared that they had been received with cordial hospitality, so much so, that during dinner, the vodka flowed in such quantity as to make reasoned discussion quite impossible. The following morning, however, they did manage to get an undertaking from the Russians that they would return the missing trucks without further delay.

There was much concern when a report was received from Sweden, complaining in the strongest terms, about gas ammunition being washed ashore on the southern coast. Naturally the finger of suspicion was immediately pointed at me; the argument being, "You were supposed to dump the stuff into the Skagerrak – if it is now on the shores of Sweden, you had better go there and deal with the problem".

It was very pleasant to be in a country that had not been at war; with the bright lights, the wonderful food and the happy go lucky people – except for those who had been detailed to escort me to the poison gas. I had visions of finding battered aircraft bombs containing nerve gas, and in my worst moments, of actually finding punctured bombs and the inevitable casualties.

Fortunately, it was nothing like that; what I found were a few artillery shells but not of the type we had been dumping, and moreover, they were old smoke shells, which were comparatively harmless. Consequently, I was able to get them quickly gathered up and destroyed to everybody's satisfaction. When I returned to the

Headquarters, I did not tell anyone how wonderful life had been in Sweden, and as a result, they could not understand why it had taken so long to carry out such a simple task.

Shortly after the end of the war, the Board of Trade, as it was then, began to organize visits to Germany by parties of British business men, who were interested in investigating specific industries, with particular regard to reporting on research and development that had been carried out during the war period. As a result, a department had been established at the Headquarters of British Army of the Rhine, in Bad Oeynhausen, to brief these people regarding research for the various industries and to provide them with any relevant research papers.

This activity had been rapidly growing to meet an increasing demand, and as a result, I was asked to manage the department and to improve the service, by co-opting on to the staff, several well qualified people with war-time experience in German industry. This proved to be a very interesting appointment, as it brought me into contact with many of Britain's leading research workers and enabled me to learn much about German developments; some of which (as for example, audio tape-recording) were quite unknown outside Germany.

I was also asked to assist in the organizing of sporting activities for the troops, and in particular, sailing. The Mohne Dam had been breached in a famous RAF raid, but having since been repaired, it provided excellent facilities for dinghy racing.

The large sheet of water known as the Steinhuder Meer, to the west of Hanover, offered sailing for larger craft, and it was there, that I was able to further my own interest in sailing. Ever since reading Dr Manfred Curry's book entitled, *Yacht Racing – The Aerodynamics of Sails and Racing Tactics*, I had become fascinated by the science of sailing and therefore, this was a good opportunity to put Curry's theories into practice.

We had found thousands of skis, which had been provided for the German ski troops, so we commandeered suitable hotels in the Harz mountains, south of Goslar, where our service men and women could spend a short leave and receive tuition in skiing.

I was fortunate in being included in a party of skiers sent to Chamonix to investigate the possibility of using this famous resort for advanced instruction. We travelled by train, with interesting overnight stops in Brussels and Paris. On our first evening in Chamonix, we had just sat down to dinner, in our hotel, when there was an earthquake tremor which left a long crack in one of the walls of the dining room. Immediately, people rushed out of the building, shouting, "*Tremblement de terre*" and in no time at all, we had the hotel to ourselves;

surprisingly, it remained so, for fully half an hour. It seemed a very minor disturbance, compared to some we had recently experienced. When at last the waiters began to trickle back and they saw us still at our table, they felt obliged to apologise for the lack of service.

The skiing at Chamonix, was of course, excellent in every respect, but when I saw the locals descending from the summit of the Brevent, at a death defying speed in thick mist, I could not understand why these same people should worry about a small earthquake.

On one of my skiing trips to the Harz Mountains, I joined a party of four, on a hunting jaunt with army rifles. In a large forest we stalked a wild boar for several miles and eventually, having made a kill, we decided to take the beast back to the mess. The farther we dragged the wretched thing, the heavier it became, and then on emerging from the forest, we saw right ahead, a Russian frontier post.

We could only conjecture as to our fate if we were caught in the Russian Zone with army rifles; we had therefore, no alternative but to drag our spoil back whence we had just come, and then try to find the place where we had inadvertently strayed into the Russian Zone. We must have lugged that animal many, many miles before eventually getting it back to our car.

When we handed it over to the cooks in the mess, it was hardly surprising that we should be asked why boars don't have hair on the side of the body. One of the cooks looked at me and said, "At least it will make a change from venison". This remark was due to the fact that during the previous week, I had hit a deer that did not quite make it across the autobahn and after delivering the unfortunate animal to the mess, we had lived off venison for far too long. In fact, the Mess Officer threatened to impose a stiff fine on anybody who, in future, ran over anything bigger than a hare.

Before the Allies entered Germany, many people believed that in the concentration camps, large numbers of people had been put to death in gas chambers – indeed much information was published to this effect. We were therefore, very anxious to examine these chambers at the very first opportunity, and ascertain how they had been operated.

When survivors from the camps were questioned, many were able to give graphic accounts of inmates being led away to gas chambers and their bodies subsequently cremated in large ovens. To facilitate our investigations into this grim subject, it was necessary to enter the camps as soon as possible after they were liberated, because in many cases, as at Belsen, it was the policy to destroy all that remained, once the survivors had been evacuated.

I did not have an opportunity to visit the camps at Huy and Charleroi but understood the facilities there, were similar to those I have already described at Breendonck. It was not possible for me to inspect personally, the camps in the Russian Zone. A camp near to Lublin, in Poland was said to have gas chambers but as far as I am aware, no technical report was ever published. The infamous camp at Auswitz was also widely reported to have gas chambers, but when the Russians liberated it, towards the end of 1944, the buildings that were supposed to have housed the gas chambers and the crematoria had already been destroyed.

There was no difficulty, however, in liaising with American technical officers and visiting the concentration camps in their Zone, including perhaps the most notorious of all, the camp at Dachau, near to Munich. Here large numbers of people were put to death and the regime is known to have been particularly cruel; moreover, there were, at the time of its liberation, reports of gas chambers and rows of furnaces in which the bodies of victims had been cremated.

I certainly saw the furnaces, which were of the same type as those I had seen at other camps, such as Belsen and Buchenwald. All of these had been used to dispose of the bodies of prisoners who had died from illness, starvation or other forms of horrific ill treatment. The building which had been described as a gas chamber, had been constructed to serve as a shower room, and as such, was equipped with fans to take away the steam.

People could have been led into the room, ostensibly for the purpose of showering; the doors could then have been bolted and a gas such as hydrogen cyanide introduced. The operation thus far would not have been difficult, but it would then have been necessary to remove all traces of the gas, before men could go in and pull out the tangled bodies. It has been suggested that the gas may have been dispersed from the top of the crematorium chimneys but I was unable to find any provision by which this might have been effected. Moreover, such a procedure would have exposed the people in the surrounding locality to grave risk of injury. It has also been suggested that the installed fans could have extracted the gas and passed it through filters, but here again, none of the necessary equipment could be found.

People have postulated that when the nerve gases were researched, it would have been logical to try them out on people and where better to do this, than in the concentration camps. I believe there was strong evidence to show that the trials were carried out at the Raubkammer Experimental Station, where highly specialized facilities certainly existed for the complete evaluation of war gases.

It therefore, remains something of a mystery why so little evidence was found to substantiate this widespread belief, that gas chambers in the concentration camps were employed to kill large numbers of people. Was it just another wartime atrocity rumour – or if it did actually happen, was all the incriminating evidence skilfully removed, before the camps were liberated?

What was proved beyond any doubt, was that prisoners in the camps were forced to dig mass graves and then large numbers of them would be lined-up at the sides, where they would be shot and their bodies pushed into the graves. This was a far simpler, cheaper and more expedient method of disposing of people, than the use of gas chambers could ever have been.

On one of my trips to the American Zone, I visited Berchtesgaden, where Adolf Hitler and Hermann Goerring had possessed magnificent villas. Adjoining Hitler's residence, was a large underground bunker, which had obviously been constructed to serve as an impregnable redoubt. Access could be gained by a lift or a staircase, both of which descended from a blockhouse, capable of being resolutely defended. At the bottom, was a large hall, from which radiated a comprehensive network of tunnels, leading to the well equipped quarters for the SS troops, the armoury, kitchens and the accommodation for the various services such as engineering and communications.

I was particularly interested in the elaborate equipment for anti-gas protection. In principle, the system resembled that which I had inspected in the Spandau prison but here, it was the very last word in sophisticated anti-gas defence. Facilities were provided to draw surface air from several well disguised intakes and then pass it through an elaborate series of filters to remove all known war gases. The filtered air could then be distributed through ducting to the various parts of the bunker.

One system of tunnels was of particular interest, because it communicated with Hitler's private apartment. Starting from the entrance hall, one had to proceed along a corridor, at the end of which was a machine-gun post. This enabled the gunner to fire through a narrow slit, along the length of the corridor. At the machine-gun position, the corridor turned through an angle of 90 degrees into another corridor, at the end of which was a further machine-gun post. In all, there were about half-a-dozen of these angled corridors, each being covered by a machine-gun post. All the gun positions were connected through a separate tunnel arrangement to the SS quarters. Hence, any attacking force would have had to sacrifice the lives of many men, in order to penetrate this ingenious defence system.

Having passed through the angled corridors, one entered an administration area with a map and conference room, various offices and accommodation for the staff. Proceeding farther, the visitor next came to the apartment of Eva Braun, who for several years had been Hitler's mistress; that is until their marriage in the Berlin underground bunker, shortly before they both committed suicide.

Any attacking force, after infiltrating this labyrinth and taking many prisoners, would finally have arrived at Hitler's well furnished suite of rooms, which except for the lack of windows, resembled a luxury flat. In the event of such an attack, and had Hitler been in residence, it is clear that he would have been the last person in the bunker to be taken.

Overlooking Berchtesgaden is a mountain, on the summit of which was Hitler's retreat, known as the 'Eagle's Nest'. To reach it, one first had to drive up a steep, private road to a wide terrace, from which a tunnel had been driven into the very heart of the mountain. At the entrance to the tunnel were large security doors and at the inner end there was a hall, from which a lift ascended directly to the Eagle's Nest. So Hitler, and his very special guests, could be driven up the road, and through the tunnel to the lift. In the ornately decorated lift was one crimson, plush-upholstered seat, provided specifically for Hitler's exclusive use. When I tried it out, I saw that the mirrors on the walls had been set at angles which enabled the occupant of the seat to see his reflection many times.

The principal room in the Eagle's Nest was a beautifully furnished lounge, with a large picture window, looking out on to wonderful alpine scenery, with range after range of snow capped mountains in the distance. It was awesome to think that some of Hitler's most devilish plans were probably conceived in this heavenly abode. It was possible to step out of the lounge and onto a long balcony, from which steps led down to a grassy terrace. I was told that huntsmen would drive deer up to the terrace, so that Hitler could shoot them from the balcony.

Hermann Goerring's residence in Berchtesgaden was not to be compared to Hitler's magnificent villa, but it did contain a unique facility – something which, I certainly, had never seen before. At the end of the the sitting room was a very fine bar, with a door leading to a toilet room containing all the usual sanitary fittings – but in addition, two very special items of equipment. These consisted of extra large wash-basins with robust handles at each side. Apparently, Goerring and his friends were ardent beer drinkers, so when they had consumed their fill, they would go to one of the basins and place a feather into the appropriately positioned holder. Then, while grasping the handles, they would bend over the basin, open mouthed, in such a way as to cause the feather to tickle the back of the throat. The room was referred to as a *vomitorium* and apparently the idea was, that after making use of its specialized service, one could return to the bar with a renewed capacity for more beer. How many times this procedure would be repeated, during the course of a convivial evening, I really don't know.

Early in 1946, the pace of demobilization noticeably quickened and many who had formed close relationships, under the stress of battle, parted – in most cases for ever. I and several of my colleagues were notified that we would be demobilized at the beginning of May and consequently at the end of April, a Farewell Party was organized in the Officers Club. After the party, we found to our surprise, that we only had a few hours in which to pull ourselves together, before we were off to Hamburg and then, via the ferry, to Hull.

On the boat, I had time to meditate, and consider the great change that was about to take place in my lifestyle; in many ways far greater than the change that had taken place when I joined the army. As we began to recover from the bitter struggle, everyone fervently hoped there would never be a World War III, with more terrible waste of human and material resources. At the beginning of the war, it had been necessary to weigh the cost of war, against the cost of losing all our democratic rights and being subjugated under a cruel dictatorship.

Anyone who doubts what would have happened if Britain had been invaded, should consider what happened in Austria – the country in which Adolf Hitler was born and where many people actually welcomed the Anschluss. Of the Austrians who endeavoured to resist, 2,700 were executed, while 33,600 non-Jewish and 65,000 Jewish Austrians died in concentration camps, between 1938 and 1945. The country's cultural heritage was shattered and most of its treasured art works confiscated. I believe the decision to oppose tyranny, taken by Britain and the Allies, was completely justified and trust that in the years to come, people will still think likewise.

War is a strange affair, because in spite of all that is bad, some associated features are highly commendable and worthy of cultivation in peacetime. Comradeship during wartime was almost taken for granted, so that assistance was immediately to hand when required and indeed many of the bravest acts were carried out to help comrades who were in difficulty. To further the common cause, people in general, willingly worked hard and conscientiously. There was very little theft and certainly no vandalism. And strange though it may seem, although in battle many lives were taken, there was – in Europe at least – very little treachery. Apparently, there are rules in war that are not recognised by terrorists.

When the Allies entered Germany, it was feared that the civilians might resort to terrorism, but this was certainly not the case; on the contrary, the great majority co-operated to a surprising degree. When 1st Corps Headquarters was stationed in Iserlohn, at the end of the war, I was for a time billeted on a German family, and they could not have been more kind or helpful.

I feel it should also be said that the German army fought honourably and very bravely. It certainly would not have been vanquished so easily, if Hitler had not been in command to order impossible operations, such as the counter-offensive before the battle of the Falaise Gap, and at a later stage, the Ardennes offensive which was intended to recapture the port of Antwerp.

On arrival at Hull, we were conveyed to Catterick Garrison, where the necessary demobilization documentation was speedily completed. The following morning it only remained for us to collect our free issue of civilian clothing, including a suit from a choice of three designs, and in my case, a rail pass to Stoke-on-Trent.

A few days later, I received a letter from the War Office, in which I was thanked for my services in general and certain ones in particular. I was interested to note official recognition of my being the first technical officer to land in Normandy and that as a result of a War Office recommendation, I had been elected to the Fellowship of the Royal Institute of Chemistry – subsequently, the Royal Society of Chemistry.

For some years after the end of the war, the chemical warfare scientists maintained close liaison, lest our services should again be required. We were kept up-to-date regarding research and development on the various aspects of chemical warfare by attending periodic meetings at Porton, and by the circulation of relevant literature.

14

BACK TO BUSINESS

My brother qualified in engineering at the beginning of the war, and then joined Frank Whittle's research staff, which was engaged in developing the jet engine. By the middle of the war, progress was such as to justify an aero-engine design being put into production.

A principal component of the jet engine is a turbine rotor, incorporating a large number of blades, accurately shaped and finished to a very high degree of precision. Machining these blades from heat resisting nimonic steel, called for a high degree of skill and during the war, people qualified to carry out this type of work were not readily available. Consequently, and in order to keep costs to a minimum, it was decided to cast the blades, using the lost-wax process.

Briefly, this involves making a wax model of the required article – in this case a turbine blade – which is then suspended in a refractory slurry, contained in a metal box. The slurry generally consists of a graded refractory and a cold-setting agent mixed in water. The box, together with its contents, is vibrated to induce the refractory to pack around the model; then after standing for a short time, the refractory sets solid, so enabling it to be withdrawn from the container.

The next stage in the process, is to place the refractory block in a furnace to melt out the wax, so leaving a cavity having the precise shape of the required blade. The heating of the refractory block is then continued, until the temperature approximates to the melting point of the particular metal; at which point the molten metal is poured into the mould. On being allowed to cool, the refractory breaks away, to leave a blade so perfect in shape and finish, as to require no further processing.

I was told that the process was giving good results for the production of small blades, but when attempts were made to manufacture larger blades, the moulds generally cracked during the heating process. Apparently, when the slurry was vibrated, the coarser particles of refractory tended to sink to the bottom, while the finer particles rose to the top; the resulting lack of homogeneity developing stresses during heating, which caused the moulds to crack. As in the mixing of concrete, for which both sand and pebbles are used to ensure strength and a smooth finish, so it is in the mixing of the refractory, where the inclusion of both coarse and fine particles is essential.

When I returned to the family business after demobilization, I was invited to the factory where the blades were being cast and asked if I could suggest a solution to this intriguing problem. As a result I offered to conduct some preliminary trials, with a view to submitting a refractory mixture for evaluation.

It seemed to me, that the obvious thing to do, was to use a refractory mixture, consisting of materials having differing specific gravities. It would then be possible to grade the constituents so that, the smaller particles were prepared from the heavier material and the larger particles from the lighter material. It was therefore, necessary to select a few suitable refractory materials and grade them in order that they would all settle at the same rate. Fortunately, a formula existed which related the rate of sedimentation for particles having differing size and specific gravity, so after selecting the refractories and making a few calculations, it only remained to grade the materials accordingly.

We first of all prepared about 100 pounds of such a mixture and submitted it to the factory for trial purposes. When I arrived at my office on the following morning, there was a lorry, with the driver waiting to hand me a note, which simply read, "Please load a ton or more of your refractory mixture onto our lorry as quickly as possible".

Within a matter of weeks, foundries using the Podmore Investment Mixtures, were producing the large blades and soon they were casting complete rotors. Other foundries started to employ the lost-wax process, in order to manufacture a wide range of articles ranging from the components of bicycles to bacon-slicer gear wheels.

I considered the idea on which the development was based to be so obvious, as to make it not worth patenting, and I was therefore very surprised, when one of the firms using our Investment Mixtures applied for a patent, which was subsequently granted. I could, of course, have rendered the patent null and void by proving prior use, but as they were large users of our products, such an action may well have been counter-productive. In any case, we had by then introduced further developments in the compounding of investment mixtures, which fully protected our position in the market.

Glazes containing lead compounds, as used in the pottery industry, had in the past presented a serious health hazard. Whenever the glaze dried out, as for example on the clothing of an operative, there was alway the risk of the resultant dust being inhaled; so that it would then be dissolved in the gastric juices, and thereby enter the system. Lead poisoning is cumulative and consequently, over a period of time, the amount of lead in the body could build up to an unacceptable level.

Women and children are most susceptible and it was mainly women and young people who were employed in the glazing operation. At one time, the abortion rate in the Potteries was considerably higher than for any other part of Britain – abortion being one of the symptoms of lead poisoning.

It was not surprising therefore, that attempts would be made to combat this problem by the introduction of legislation restricting the use of lead in glazes and in 1947, a new Factory Act prohibited such use, unless the glaze was of the 'low solubility' type.

By melting a mixture of lead oxide and silica in a kiln, a glass is formed, which when ground, can serve as a glaze constituent and moreover, it has a much lower solubility in the gastric juices than the unprocessed lead oxide. In the pottery industry, glasses of this type are called 'frits'. The Act described a method for determining the lead solubility of a glaze and specified the maximum permissible limit.

In the Podmore laboratory, we found that the solubility of a ground frit was proportional to its specific surface (a measure of its fineness expressed as the amount of surface exposed on unit weight of the substance). This made it possible to determine the fundamental solubility of a frit – a value that became known as the 'Podmore Factor'. By testing frits of differing composition, products were developed which had much lower Podmore Factors than hitherto.

This line of research showed that by immersing a ground frit in certain liquids, such as a dilute solution of a silicon ester, and then drying out the frit, a very thin impermeable membrane could be applied to the particles, which could reduce the solubility by as much as a factor of ten. This development not only facilitated the production of safer glazes, but in addition, made it possible to use higher lead content glazes, which still met the requirements of the new Act. This was important because many glazes, and in particular tile glazes, were dependent upon a certain minimum lead content, to give various desirable effects when fired at a comparatively low temperature. Coated lead frits came to be very widely used in the pottery industry – and this time the invention was patented.

At the time when the above research was being conducted, frits were manufactured by loading the various constituents into a refractory tank, incorporated in a kiln which was capable of heating the charge to its melting point. The molten frit was then run out of the tank into water, so giving a granular product suitable for grinding. The tank would then be recharged and the process repeated.

This technique had many disadvantages, chief of which was the high cost of renewing the refractory lining of the tank, after a short period of use. When the cold frit mixture was introduced into the red hot tank, the thermal shock produced cracks in the lining and then, when the frit became molten, it would penetrate the cracks, so causing rapid erosion. The eroded refractory would, of course, enter the frit and result in a contaminated product of variable composition.

It occured to me that if the frit mixture could be melted by a continuous operation, then these various difficulties could be eliminated. As a result, we built a kiln with a long sloping hearth and devised a method of continuously feeding the frit mixture onto the high end of the slope. The molten frit ran down the slope, in a continuous stream and was discharged at the lower end into a trough, along which a rapid flow of water was passing. The granulated frit and water then entered an inclined tube containing an *Archimedean screw,* which separated the frit, and allowed the water to be recirculated to the trough.

There were many initial difficulties, but in due course, the continuous fritting technique proved to be an outstanding success. It was patented in many parts of the world and the sale of licences to operate the process often resulted in contracts for us to build the kilns and train the operatives.

The outstanding advantage of the process, was that it facilitated a complete reaction between the lead compounds and the other frit constituents, which ensured a product having an exceptionally low solubility; so much so, that the coating of frits gradually fell into disuse.

Before the war, we often received enquiries for very finely ground materials and as a result, we endeavoured to purchase suitable grinding equipment, but although we searched in many parts of the world, we could not find a machine that would give the required fineness and an uncontaminated product.

When a given weight of material is subjected to a grinding process, the total amount of surface on the increasing number of particles, progressively increases – and it is found that the properties of powders depend, to a considerable degree, on the amount of surface per unit weight (the specific surface). Consider for example, a red pigment, we are only interested in the 'red' that is on the surface of the particles, because we cannot see the 'red' that is inside the particles. So, if we wish to mix a red pigment into a white paint, a certain amount of pigment will be required to produce a particular depth of colour. If we were to use the same pigment substance, but with double the specific surface, we should find that only half the amount of pigment was required to give the same depth of colour. It is obvious therefore, that the finer pigment would be more valuable; quite apart from the fact that it would result in a superior paint, due to it containing less adulterant.

Many other properties of fine powders are related to the specific surface, such as the rate at which they go into solution and the speed of chemical reactions. It will be appreciated therefore, that for many applications, the finer the powder the more valuable it will be.

It might be thought that to produce a finer product, it would only be necessary to prolong the grinding process. Indeed, when a coarse substance is ground, the increase in specific surface is initially related to time, but after a while, the rate of increase begins to fall off and sooner or later, a stage is reached when no further increase in specific surface occurs. At this stage, the mechanical energy put into the grinding process becomes dissipated as heat, while the grinding medium is worn away and enters the product as a contaminant.

This much I understood before joining the army, and after the war, I would often take a pencil and paper and make calculations relating to the little understood realm of ultra-fine grinding.

I was interested in particles having a maximum diameter of one micron (one millionth of a metre) – by comparison, face powder would be considered very coarse indeed. My calculations showed that in a minute quantity of the required ultra-fine powder – just sufficient to cover a full stop in newsprint – there would be more particles, than there are people in the world. It will be realized therefore, that to break each of the particles in this tiny quantity of powder, would require an enormous number of impacts. In other words, an ultra-fine grinding system must be capable of delivering impacts at very high frequency.

Information relating to the impact force necessary to break standard sized cubes of various substances was available, and it was known that the force necessary to break a particle, is proportional to the volume of the particle. Therefore, it is not difficult to calculate the force necessary to break a particle of a given substance and having a diameter of one micron. When this is done, it is found that the necessary force is infinitesimal. In fact, if it was possible to hit the hardest micron sized particle, with a tiny feather, the force would be far greater than that required to break it efficiently.

So, to facilitate ultra-fine grinding it is necessary to apply very, very small impact forces at very, very high frequency. There is, however, one further essential requirement. When a boxer sees a blow coming towards his jaw, he quickly backs away, in order to avoid or reduce the force of impact. It follows therefore, that when an impact force is applied to a particle, it must be firmly held in position and not given space in which to back away. I realized that it would be very difficult to meet all these requirements, and consequently, much experimental research would be necessary.

When we commenced our experiments, we had a small company manufacturing separators and conveyors which were powered by electro-magnetic vibrators, and therefore, it was convenient to carry out the initial trials with vibrators of this type. We used very small porcelain spheres as the grinding medium and loaded this into a rubber-lined steel cylinder, together with the material to be ground, in the form of a water suspension. We found the vibrated material very quickly packed and prevented free movement of the medium, so that the grinding action soon ceased.

It was obvious that a very different type of vibration was required; we therefore conducted trials using three dimensional vibration, with a provision for phase control. This enabled us to carry out a wide range of experiments with different types of vibration, and in due course, we began to find the necessary conditions to facilitate free movement of the medium.

To prevent the fine particles backing away from the impacts, we experimented with a medium in the form of small cylinders and found that a certain type of vibration would make them line-up co-axially, to give line contact at the sides and face contact at the ends. This arrangement resulted in the charge material being presented in very thin films to the impacts, and greatly minimised the detrimental backing away effect.

At the end of each trial, the specific surface of the product was being determined on a sophisticated optical instrument. One day, when I asked to see the latest results, I was told that the equipment had apparently developed a fault, because it was giving ridiculous readings. Arrangements were made to get it serviced; whereupon, it was found to be in perfect working order – we were, in fact, producing products having an exceptionally high specific surface.

The task then, was to repeat this performance on a commercial scale. Consequently, we had to find a really powerful vibrator, which would enable us to reproduce the conditions obtained in the laboratory. After making worldwide enquiries, we found, by a remarkable coincidence, that the precise vibrator was being manufactured in Stoke-on-Trent, by William Boulton Ltd. We therefore bought one of their vibrators and attached it to a specially designed grinding chamber mounted on compression springs. Various modifications were made during the following months, but finally, we had a machine that operated on a commercial scale and produced a finer product than any obtained in the laboratory.

At this stage in the development, we applied for patents in most industrial countries, and in due course, all were granted. We then arranged for Boultons to make for us a Mark 1 model, in accordance with our design specification. This was soon followed by a much larger Mark 2 design. We ordered a number of both types for our own use, but as we were receiving many enquiries from potential users, we arranged for Boultons, who had a world-wide reputation as manufacturers of industrial grinding equipment, to market the machines (as Vibro-Energy Mills) on a royalty basis.

We first employed the mills to grind calcined alumina, an exceptionally hard material, which was required in a very fine state of division and high degree of purity, for the manufacture of the electrical porcelain insulators in sparking plugs.

Professor Maurice Stacey from the University of Birmingham, while on a visit to Australia, had been given a quantity of zircon sand and asked if he could find an industrial use for it. This mineral was, at the time, being obtained as a waste product in a separation process to isolate rutile, from deposits of sand found on islands, off the east coast of Australia. The rutile was required as raw material in the manufacture of titanium dioxide, but there was no demand for the zircon.

On returning to Birmingham, his department investigated the properties of the mineral and in due course, I received a note which read, "The enclosed sample of zircon sand is remarkably inert and very refractory – just the kind of material to interest a ceramist – can you find a use for it?"

The first thing I discovered about the material was its exceptional hardness, which made it very difficult to grind. In fact, the only way we could reduce it to a fine powder was by processing in the Vibro-Energy Mill. Even when very finely ground, it would not react in frits or glazes, at maturing temperatures, and therefore, when incorporated in a transparent glaze it became opaque.

Opaque glazes are mainly applied to red or buff burning clays, in order to give a white or pastel coloured appearance. At the time, tin oxide was usually added to a glaze to render it opaque, but the oxide was very expensive. It occured to me therefore, that the much cheaper zircon might serve the same purpose. Research soon showed that if the finely ground zircon was incorporated in specially formulated glazes, the product was not only cheaper, but in many ways vastly superior.

The Italian potters in the neighbourhood of Sassuolo, were using the local buff clays for the large scale manufacture of wall tiles. As opacifiers, they were using tin oxide and the cheaper but dangerous antimony oxide. We therefore considered this locality to be eminently suitable for our preliminary campaign in the marketing of zircon opacifiers; a venture that proved so successful, that within a year, most of the potteries in the area were using our new opacifier.

As the zircon could only be ground satisfactorily in the Vibro Mills, we had to put more and more of the machines into production. Tin oxide opacified glazes were being used in many other parts of the world; we realized therefore, that the potential was enormous.

Moreover, it was becoming apparent that the Vibro-Energy Mills could find application in other industries. Boultons had already allocated a large department to the manufacture of the mills, but as they could not meet the ever increasing demand, it was agreed that we should co-operate in the sale of licences to manufacture them overseas. We also established a joint technical service, to facilitate the marketing of the Podmore-Boulton Vibro-Energy Mills, throughout the world.

15

THE LANDS TRIBUNAL AND A TERRIBLE TRAGEDY

Father resolutely believed that coal miners would not continue to work for low wages, therefore the future cost of power was certain to rise. For this reason, he had been instrumental in the purchase of water powered mills at Rocester, Stretton and Stone, in addition to the large mill at Consall. The mill at Stretton, near to Burton-on-Trent, was processing materials for supply to the various potteries in the Swadlincote district. As their demand was increasing and not all the available power at the mill had been harnessed, he was very anxious to enlarge its facilities.

The mill was already powered by an efficient turbine, so an additional turbine, of the latest design, was purchased, together with more processing plant and equipment. Work commenced on the erection of new buildings, while father personally supervised the construction of the concrete turbine housing, the sluice-gates and the new flume.

Then one day, and without warning of any kind, we received a compulsory purchase order in respect of the entire property. As might be imagined, father was completely shattered by this amazing turn of events.

It was later disclosed that a neighbouring water authority proposed to extract water from the river Dove, at a point close to the mill weir and in view of the water rights attached to the mill, the only way in which this could be done was by purchasing the mill. We realized there would be no point in appealing against the order, but we nevertheless resolved to do everything possible to ensure payment of reasonable compensation, to cover our imminent loss.

In due course, the property was inspected and valued by the District Valuer, who came up with a figure which was quite obviously ridiculous. It was immediately obvious therefore, that we were going to have a fight on our hands, before the Lands Tribunal.

In our opinion the District Valuer was not placing a proper value on the available water power. We felt that if we were compelled to move the business to a new site, where it would be necessary to use electricity to provide the required power, then the compensation should have regard to the relevant additional cost. We therefore estimated the cost of electricity over future years and then capitalised the resulting sum. From this figure we were able to deduct the known comparable costs for water power, as incurred at Stretton. In this way, we derived a value for the water power alone, which was far greater than the District Valuer's valuation for the entire property.

In the circumstances, we decided to assemble a strong team of solicitors, quantity surveyors, water engineers and valuers, etc. We also took good care to brief leading and junior barristers, who were well experienced in water engineering projects. Father would, of course, be our principal witness, and it was arranged that I would attend, in order to assist where necessary.

The hearing before the Lands Tribunal was eventually fixed to take place at Leicester, commencing on Monday, 2 November 1958. My wife and I had arranged to drive over to North Wales on the previous Friday, in order to join our two daughters, who were at school in Colwyn Bay. The week-end happened to be the college half-term and a play was to be performed on the Friday evening. I therefore decided to call upon my parents on the Thursday evening, in order to discuss with father outstanding matters concerning the hearing. I found them both in evening dress, as they were about to leave for a Rotary Ball in Cheadle. It was agreed that I should call for father at about 2 p.m. on the Sunday, so that we could travel together, to the hotel in Leicester, where rooms had been booked for all the members of our team.

In Colwyn Bay, my wife and I attended the school play, and the following morning, we were just finishing breakfast in our hotel, when a waiter told me that I was wanted on the telephone. It was a call from my brother, who said he was very sorry to have to convey the terrible news – but both mother and father were dead. He went on to say, that he had been alerted by the postman, who, not having received the usual response, on earlier calling at their house, feared something might be wrong. Accordingly, my brother had immediately gone over to the house and on entering, found mother and father sitting in their chairs by the fireside – but it was obvious that they were both dead. A doctor was called and very soon, the tragic situation was confirmed.

There was no way that the hearing in Leicester could be postponed. It was therefore agreed, that I would deputise for father, in so far as it was possible, while my brother and sisters would attend to the funeral arrangements.

When I joined our team in Leicester on the Sunday and dropped the bombshell, it was obvious to all, that the strategy, so carefully worked out, would have to be significantly modified. Accordingly, the two barristers got us around a table and we worked without stop – except for a short break for dinner – until 2 a.m. the following morning.

The first three days of the hearing were very difficult; particularly as some members of the opposing team repeatedly took advantage of father's absence, to claim having made verbal arrangements with him, that were far from being true. One such claim, was that an undertaking had been given not to place boards on the weir in summer, to increase the head of water at the mill. This was the usual practice and the right to do so, was long established and recorded in the water rights relating to the mill. Nevertheless, they insisted on calculating the available power at the mill, in summer, on the assumption that the weir boards would not be used in future.

In view of the mysterious circumstances surrounding the deaths of mother and father, there was naturally a coroner's inquest; the verdict being that in each case, death was due to carbon monoxide poisoning. It transpired that in the chimney from the central heating boiler, there had been a big fall of soot, which had completely blocked the flue.

The anthracite boiler was of the type in which a thermostat controls a fan blowing air into the base of the fire, so producing an action very much like that in a blacksmith's hearth. When the fall of soot occurred, the fan continued to operate and the products of combustion – containing of course, carbon monoxide – had penetrated the floor boards in the room over the cellar, where the boiler was located. And it was in this particular room, that mother and father were relaxing at the end of the day – no doubt, feeling the effects of the previous late night, at the Ball in Cheadle.

Meanwhile, the battle continued in Leicester, where on the Thursday morning the Water Authority's engineer presented his evidence. This man was well qualified and greatly experienced in water engineering, so we were not surprised when he put forward a very well reasoned argument to support the District Valuer.

After lunch, our leading barrister – who was soon to become His Honour Judge Lyall Wilkes – called me to one side and said that the outcome of the hearing, would most likely depend on the performance of the engineer, when under cross-examination during the afternoon session. He went on to say, that if he were to be allowed free rein, he could well win the day and it was imperative therefore, that a valid reason be found to bring the cross-examination to an abrupt end, within five minutes. It was therefore, with even more interest than usual, that I looked forward to the afternoon performance.

On the resumption, the engineer was called, whereupon he presented himself, together with piles of reference books, reports and maps, etc. It took quite some time for him to place in position the many documents, but finally, Mr Wilkes sarcastically asked, if he might be allowed to commence the cross-examination – and it was then that I looked at my watch.

Lyall Wilkes began by holding up a book and asking, "Have you seen this before?" Without waiting for an answer, he continued, "You should have done because you wrote it; this is the report you submitted to the Water Authority, when you were recommending the scheme to extract water from the Dove. I see you have a copy there – would you be good enough to turn to the appendix, where you have detailed figures for the average summer flow in the river, at the mill weir. Now it is very interesting to see, that these figures are considerably higher than those you gave us this morning, and on which, you have calculated the available power at the mill. It is obvious that when you were recommending the scheme, you used one set of figures and then later, when you came to calculate the compensation payable to the mill owners, you worked on significantly lower figures – no doubt in order to produce a result lower than the correct one. In the circumstances, the evidence you gave this morning must be completely discounted and as you stand as an unreliable witness, there is no point in continuing this cross-examination". As Wilkes sat down, I again looked at my watch – it had taken precisely three minutes.

In the hushed silence that followed, the engineer was left to gather together his large library of unused paperwork, after which the proceedings got under way again in less dramatic fashion. At the end of the afternoon, it was announced that as one of the Water Authority's barristers had to be in London on the following day (Friday), the hearing would stand adjourned until the following Monday.

The funeral of mother and father had been arranged to take place on the Friday and it had seemed that I would not be able to attend, but now as a result of the unexpected adjournment, I was able to return home and join our grief-stricken family for the interment at Wetley Rocks.

The hearing continued, on and off, for five more weeks, (it was already the longest Lands Tribunal on record) during which time, a visit was made by all concerned to the Stretton Mill, where we had ample opportunity to demonstrate the excellent facilities, and to show the considerable quantity of new plant and equipment which had been delivered on site.

As part of the evidence submitted by the Water Authority, much emphasis had been placed on the recent sale of a water mill, near to Nottingham, which had changed hands at a ridiculously low price. As a result, Lyall Wilkes claimed the right for us all to view the said property and in due course, a visit was arranged. The first thing I noticed was that the sluice-gates controlling water to the mill were closed, and what little power was being used, was provided by electric motors. I immediately discussed the position with Mr Wilkes, who then requested a meeting with the Managing Director.

The outcome was that very soon we were all trooping into the M.D.'s office. As we stood around, Wilkes explained the purpose of our visit and then asked the M.D. if he would be prepared to disclose how much his company had paid for the water rights. The M.D. smiled and said, that as a result of the arrangements made for the building of the neighbouring electricity power station, water rights were no longer attached to the mill property. He then went on to tell us that they used virtually no power; the site was of value to them due merely to its isolation – because they manufactured fireworks. I do not know how good the company's fireworks were, but I feel sure, they could not have been as impressive, as those displayed by Lyall Wilkes, as we filed out of that office.

In due course, we received notification of the award. We were to get very nearly the total sum claimed, together with a generous allowance to cover our costs and expenses.

Our long struggle had been rewarded. My only regret was that father had not been present, to see that a valid case could still be made out for the true value of one of his principal interests in life – namely water power.

16

THE BEIRUT INCIDENT

At the beginning of the 1960s, industrial activity in the Lebanon was on the increase, so we decided to send a representative there to establish an agency in Beirut. Good business soon developed and as a result, I arranged to pay a short visit to the new agency, during a tour of Middle East countries.

I arrived at Beirut airport around midday, booked in at the Holiday Inn Hotel and then after a quick lunch, visited the office of the agency, which was accommodated in a tall, modern building, overlooking a square in the city centre. During our meeting, much noise with chanting in unison, arose from the street below. One of the men went over to the window to see what was happening – he said it was just another political demonstration.

After about an hour, we had really completed our work, but I was told that it would not be safe to leave the office until the crowd outside had dispersed. When I went to the window, I expected to see a lot of dejected looking people, marching about and carrying banners, but no, the people down in the square were alert young men bearing machine guns, while some were manning heavier weapons, including field and anti-aircraft guns – and even motorized rocket launchers.

Eventually, they all moved away and I asked if the office could get a taxi to take me to my hotel, but the manager insisted on taking me, as there might well be another demonstration in some other part of the city. We went downstairs and found the door to the main entrance locked and strongly bolted, while the doorkeeper was sitting in a chair with a machine gun on his lap.

However, we reached the hotel without incident and I invited the manager to join me for dinner, which he was pleased to do. I found the conversation during the evening very enlightening, as I had not realized that although the Lebanon had many thriving business communities, the numerous religious and political factions fostered intense enmity, which precluded any possibility of intertrading. Moreover, as some of the groups were being heavily financed by neighbouring countries and much of the money was being spent on armament, future conflict appeared inevitable.

At about 5 a.m. the following morning, the telephone at the side of my bed rang and on the phone was my guest of the previous evening. He said, "I appreciate that your plane is not due to leave until mid-afternoon, but I would strongly advise you to go over to the airport immediately, otherwise you will find it impossible, and in that case, you could be stranded in Beirut for several days". He went on to explain that a senior member of the government had been shot and was to be buried, during the afternoon, at the cemetery close to the airport. As a result, the roads would be blocked and there was bound to be a lot of shooting.

I thanked the man for advising me so promptly of the unexpected development, then dressed very quickly, paid my bill and made my way to the hotel entrance, in order to get a taxi. The hall-porter asked where I wished to go and when I told him that I wanted to get to the airport, he said, "You will be lucky – two parties have already tried it and have returned".

At that moment, a taxi drew up to the hotel entrance and the driver asked if I required a taxi. When I said that I wished to get to the airport, he told me the main road was blocked, but by making a detour through a couple of villages, he thought it might be possible. Whereupon, I said that I was prepared to try it, providing he could guarantee to return me to the hotel, if he failed to deliver me to the airport.

With that we set off, and for the first few miles, all was well, but on turning into a narrow street, we saw ahead, a manned roadblock and a pile of burning car tyres. My driver made a skilful U-turn and tried a different route, but very soon, the performance had to be repeated. He then went down a rough track, which eventually brought us out onto a fairly decent road and after a few more minutes, he said that we should soon be there. We quickly caught up with a large taxi, and as together we rounded a sharp bend, we found ourselves confronted by a roadblock and a lot of armed men. This time there was no possiblity of escape.

The men directed the two vehicles off the road and along a track that ran between several hillocks, composed of very red earth. We soon came to an open space, where there were many more men and yet another pile of burning tyres. Here the two taxis were halted, about twenty yards apart. We saw a number of men go over to the other taxi and with much shouting and arm waving, appeared to be ordering the occupants to get out. The passenger complied immediately and dragged out three large suit cases. But as the driver was obviously resisting, one of the men lifted a burning tyre by the aid of a pole, and pushed it under the vehicle; the driver jumped out in panic, and within seconds, the taxi was in flames.

The men then came over to my taxi and ordered us both out; as might be expected, we readily obliged – with me quickly retrieving my light grip. We were told that, "Big man come – he good man".

Whereupon, I speculated upon his use of the word 'good', but hoped for the best. My fellow companion in distress, turned out to be an American business man, and he was not at all happy with the situation. Soon the 'big man' arrived in a delapidated jeep, and I was pleased to find that he could string a few words together in passable English, because trying to converse in Arabic, while looking down the barrel of a gun, had never been one of my accomplishments.

The first thing the man did, was to order my driver to take the other taxi driver back to Beirut, which he promptly did. As the taxi disappeared, I could not help thinking that it was the first time I had not been asked for the fare.

The 'big man' then demanded to see our passports and as he flicked through the pages, he asked if we had been in Israel – to which pointed question, we both gave the appropriate answer. He told us that they were Palestine refugees from the camp at Bourj el Borajneh and that they were controlling the particular road to the airport. He then said, "If you want to get to the airport, show me how much money you have?" My American buddy withdrew a fat wallet, from which the alleged 'good man', appeared to help himself to a considerable sum, before next turning to me. When leaving a country in that part of the world, I always took good care to take out as little of the particular currency as possible, because it generally had little value in any neighbouring country. Therefore, the sum I lost could not have been worth more than about £60.

I was already wondering what the next stage in this bizarre episode would be, when we were told to get into the jeep – so we piled in our luggage and climbed aboard. We were then driven off down a bumpy track and in a few minutes came to signs of habitation; our driver announced with much emphasis, "This is Bourj el Borajneh – I will show you the terrible conditions in which we have to live. If, when you return to your nice houses, you will support the poor people here, I will take you to the road that leads to the airport. I can only go part of the way, because government troops are guarding the airport with tanks".

After we had voiced acceptance of this arrangement – not that we had any alternative choice – he drove around sufficient of the camp to prove his point.The buildings appeared to have been recently bombed or shelled and for the most part were without doors or windows. Many people, however, were living in rough shelters, with only pieces of hessian to provide protection from the weather. Everywhere there were piles of rubble and rubbish. The people, who were dressed in little more than rags, just lazed about and stared at the two strangers.

None too soon, we were being driven away from the squalor of that dreadful place and across some open ground, during the course of which, I caught a glimpse of the distant airport control tower. Eventually, our driver brought the jeep to an abrupt stop, and pointed out the direction in which we then had to walk. Very much 'tongue in cheek', we thanked our escort, picked up our luggage and set off. When travelling by air, I always believe in taking as little luggage as possible, and therefore, my light grip was no problem at all. As, however, my new found friend could just about struggle along with two of his three, large suit-cases, I was obliged to carry the other one for him.

After what seemed an eternity, we reached the dual carriageway that leads down to the airport, but found it completely devoid of traffic – in fact, there was not a soul in sight. We could see the airport buildings – and also the tanks, with their guns pointing towards us. It seemed absurd that all they had to confront were two weary westerners, who could hardly put one foot in front of the other.

On reaching our adversaries, we were told to open our luggage and when we did so, the contents were tipped out onto the ground and kicked around. What they expected to find remained a mystery, but after a short time, the soldiers walked away, and left us to gather up our belongings and repack them the best way we could. This done, we made our way into the building, which to our great disappointment was completely deserted.

During our approach to the airport, we had seen one aircraft land and two take off, so we knew that some part of the airport was in operation – the problem was, how to get to that particular part. We decided to try a corridor, which we thought might lead towards the departure lounge and soon my friend found a trolley, on which to pile his luggage. A little farther on, we came across two women with mops and pails. They were surprised to see us and certainly did not want to know us – that is, until my friend produced money from his hip pocket. It was fast becoming obvious to me that, as a business man, he certainly knew how to get by, in the Middle East. He was also an expert in sign language, because by showing his passport, pointing to his luggage and then giving a realistic audio visual impression of an aircraft taking-off, he managed to persuade the women to lead us through a maze of corridors, which eventually brought us to a place where we could hear voices, and on opening a door – there was the transit lounge.

My friend was quick to notice that the bar was actually in operation and with only cursory thanks to the women, he rushed forward and ordered a double brandy. There was also an information desk, with a girl in attendance, where I was able to enquire about my flight to Tehran. She told me that all flights had been cancelled, except those scheduled to refuel in Beirut before mid-afternoon. My plane, coming from Paris, was expected to land on time and then leave for Tehran.

I then went over to the bar, where my friend was already on his second double brandy – or maybe his third – and suggested he should check on his flight. I felt it would be advisable for him to do so, while there was still a chance of him being understood. He was informed that his flight to Rome would be boarding in about forty minutes and the last I saw of him, was when he was going out to the aircraft supported on each side by willing helpers.

My plane duly arrived, and as I walked outside to go on board, I could hear much rifle and gunfire, that sounded uncomfortably close to the airport. As the plane took off, I could see great columns of smoke rising from many parts of the city.

Ever since that day, the various factions in the Lebanon have been at war; business gradually came to a standstill and our agency unfortunately had to close. I find it very difficult to understand which group, if any, has benefitted.

There was a strange sequel to the Beirut incident, when about two months later, a man who said he was from the Lebanese Embassy, phoned me and requested a meeting. When I asked what he wanted to discuss, he was very guarded and said that he would explain everything when we met.

In due course, he called at my office and after producing various official looking documents to establish his credentials, he said, "I understand you were recently in Beirut and that you visited the camp at Bouj el Borajneh". I agreed it was so, but pointed out that it was not quite true to say, I had visited the camp. He then asked how I had come to be there and after I had briefly related the unfortunate circumstances, he asked if I had seen various things or places, to which he gave Arabic sounding names. I could not, of course, assist him beyond giving a general description of what I had seen, as we were whisked through the place in the jeep. He then questioned me in detail, as to how we had got from the camp to the airport and how much money had been extorted. When I asked why these matters were of interest to him, he said, "Very few Englishmen have got out of Bourj el Borajneh alive, and we are very interested to know how you managed it".

17

THE DOMAIN OF ULTRA-FINE GRINDING

The rapid increase in business, resulting from the invention of the Vibro-Energy Mill, made it necessary to build a new factory, in which a large number of the mills were installed – in fact, within less than three years, it was to become the largest vibration grinding plant in the world.

Improvements in the design of the Vibro-Mill were made from time to time, and for some applications, a semi-toroidal shaped grinding chamber, with the vibration unit located at the centre, was found to give an improved performance.

Generally the feed material is in the form of a water suspension, which facilitates the essential free vibration of the grinding medium. In some cases, as for example where the process material is soluble in water or reacts with water, it may be convenient to use a liquid other than water, but in most cases, it is then preferable to resort to dry grinding.

Initial attempts at dry grinding in the Vibro-Mill were unsuccessful, due to the grinding medium becoming locked by compacting of the process material. We eventually found, however, that it was possible to fluidize the material, by introducing a continuous stream of compressed air into the base of the grinding chamber. The action of the air bubbling through the powder then produces conditions similar to those in wet processing, so facilitating efficient grinding. The stream of air leaving the mill, carries away in suspension the finer particles and this makes continuous grinding feasible, by feeding the mill at a rate equivalent to the rate of product removal. This new technique proved to be very successful and was patented worldwide.

As mentioned in a previous chapter, lead silicate frits are made by melting in a kiln a mixture of red lead and silica, and as one of the principal manufacturers in Europe of lead frits, we required large quantities of red lead. The traditional method of making this material, was to melt lead in a large metal container and to scrape from the surface the accumulated scum, which consisted mainly of litharge. This was then ground and calcined in a rotary furnace to yield red lead. The process was not only inefficient but extremely dangerous. We decided therefore, to investigate the possibility of processing lead in the Vibro-Mill.

Lead ingots were first granulated by melting and pouring into water. The granules were then fed continuously into a Vibro-Mill arranged for dry grinding, with lead spheres as the grinding medium.

Air under pressure was introduced at several points in the base of the grinding chamber, while the air leaving the chamber, with the product in suspension, passed to a cyclone separator. This delivered the fine material to a silo and returned the oversize fraction to the mill for further processing.

The arrangement was found to give very satisfactory results, particularly as the air circulation could be made to operate below ambient pressure. This prevented any possiblity of the dangerous powder escaping into the atmosphere; something that often happened when operating the traditional process. Lead is oxidised by the air passing through the mill, to give a mixture of sub-oxides, which can easily be calcined to yield red lead of a quality eminently suitable for the manufacture of all types of lead frit.

In the past, lead was considered to be unreactive to water and therefore, lead pipes were extensively used for its distribution. The Roman baths, at Bath, are lead lined and although warm water has been flowing over the lead for almost 2,000 years, the lead is still intact. On the other hand, if one merely spits on the ultra-fine lead from the Vibro-Mill, it will immediately burst explosively into flames. This shows very clearly, that the properties of solids depend, to a considerable extent, on their state of division.

In all grinding processes the grinding medium inevitably wears away and enters the product as a contaminant. The rate of wear on the medium in the Vibro-Mill is exceptionally low, but nevertheless, in order to ensure the highest degree of product purity, it is essential to select an appropriate material for the medium. When grinding lead, as described above, the medium consists of lead spheres and this, of course, provides the ideal solution. But in applications where the process material and the grinding medium cannot have the same composition, it is necessary to employ a very hard medium and one that is sufficiently inert, as to have a negligible effect on the required properties of the product.

Most ceramic products are inert and some porcelains are very hard, so we experimented with various types, to discover those most suitable for use as media. We found that alumina and zircon porcelains gave a particularly satisfactory performance. To process these, we therefore installed automatic presses to form the small cylinders and kilns to fire them at the required high temperature.

When the Vibro-Mill was initially developed, it was envisaged that it would be used mainly in the ceramic industry, but it soon found application in many other industries. The processing of pigments and printing inks, might have been anticipated, but many eventual applications were quite unexpected.

Audio tape for the recording of music, etc., consists essentially of pvc tape, coated on one side with a lacquer containing fine particles of gamma iron oxide. The particles are needle shaped and magnetic, so that when a recording is made, they align themselves under the action of the magnetic field induced by the sound, in such a way that when the tape is played back, the magnetic field produced by the tape, reproduces the original sound. Now to produce high quality tape, it is essential to disperse the oxide uniformly in the lacquer, without breaking the needles. It was found that the Vibro-Mills could be adapted to perform this function very effectively, and as a result, many mills are now used around the world, in the manufacture of high quality magnetic tapes.

When people have a headache and take an aspirin tablet, it is unlikely that they will read the contained instructions, but if they did, they would most likely find that, "The aspirin has been microfined for instant action". Aspirin has to be very fine indeed, if it is to be quickly absorbed into the system. The Vibro-Mill effectively processes aspirin, as well as a very wide range of other pharmaceutical products.

Chocolate is not purchased for its food value, as there are many superior foodstuffs; it is bought in order to savour the unique taste. In order to derive the taste, it must dissolve in the gastric juices, while in the mouth, so that the resultant fluid can stimulate the taste buds. In the case of ordinary chocolate, very little goes into solution, and therefore, most of it passes into the stomach, without imparting the pleasant taste for which it was bought. If, however, the chocolate is ultra-finely ground in the Vibro-Mill, the product will give an overwhelming taste sensation, so enabling a considerable quantity of other desirable constituents to be introduced into the particular confectionery, without loss of the desired chocolate taste.

It has previously been mentioned that when lead is dry ground in the Vibro-Mill, a chemical reaction takes place, resulting in the production of sub-oxides. The fact that such chemical changes can take place during grinding, has been exploited to produce new compounds. In some cases, a reacting gas is used to fluidize the charge material, while in other applications, the material is often ground as a suspension in a reacting liquid.

Metal castings and pressings usually have thin flanges and other imperfections, which have to be removed by abrasion – a tedious and often dangerous process for the operatives involved. If, however, the components are loaded into a Vibro-Mill, together with a suitably graded abrasive such as corundum, the burrs can be quickly and safely removed, while the surfaces will be highly polished – an essential requirement, if the articles are to be subsequently electro-plated.

Similarly, Vibro-Mills are now extensively employed in the pottery industry for processing the biscuit ware, before application of the glaze. When articles are cast in multi-part plaster moulds, they always retain small projections where two parts of the mould have come together. These are normally removed by the use of a knife, while the article is in the leather-hard condition – a process known as fettling. After the ware has been biscuit fired, it is advantageous to polish it, in order to smooth any remaining fettling imperfections and also to remove the adhering refractory, used to bed the pieces during the firing process. In the past, the polishing was done manually, and due to the dust entering the atmosphere, the risk of incurring silicosis was considerable.

But now, the various articles can be passed through the process chamber of a Vibro-Energy Mill, containing a suitable polishing medium, which rapidly and efficiently ensures a perfect result. A feature of this operation is the uniformity of the polishing action; the inner surfaces of cups, for example, receive the same amount of processing as the outer surfaces. Some vitreous pottery – particularly red ware – is not glazed at all, instead it is highly polished and for this application, the Vibro-Mill has proved eminently successful. All these polishing processes are, of course, carried out in closed vessels, and as a result, they are dust free and completely safe.

18

OVERSEAS MARKETING

By 1966, in addition to the manufacture of the Vibro-Energy Mills at the Boulton plant in Stoke-on-Trent, they were being produced under licence in Australia, Belgium, Canada, Japan and the USA. We had sales agencies in most countries throughout the world to market the various Podmore products, and the Vibro-Mill; there was also a plant in Italy manufacturing our zircon opacifiers, with plans for the erection of a similar plant in Spain. Product research for all these facilities was carried out at our central laboratories in Stoke-on-Trent.

To co-ordinate the work of these varied activities, involved a considerable amount of travelling, particularly for those who were involved in the technical marketing of the Vibro-Mill, to the many different industries. When visiting an overseas company interested in ultra-fine grinding, it was necessary to obtain samples of the particular raw materials and the ground products, which would then be sent back to Stoke-on-Trent for examination. The raw material would be processed in a laboratory Vibro-Mill and the product forwarded to the interested company for evaluation; after which a further visit would be arranged. Invariably, the Vibro-Mill would be found capable of producing a much finer product than that obtained by the company. The question would therefore arise, as to whether or not, a finer product would prove advantageous; in many processes, the finer material would be found to give vastly superior results.

Most of the travelling was by air and to reduce the amount of to-ing and fro-ing, the staff began to carry some scientific equipment which enabled them to conduct preliminary investigations at the factory of the interested company, and thereby, avoid the delay occasioned by all the work having to be done in Stoke-on-Trent. We found, however, that the equipment suffered considerable damage in transit, and moreover, as it was very often held in customs, considerable inconvenience was caused.

As a result, we began to investigate the possibility of equipping a motor yacht, as a mobile laboratory and with sufficient accommodation for the technical sales staff. The idea being that it would then be possible to travel to the various countries, and carry out on board, much of the necessary experimental work. It was also envisaged that the vessel would provide facilities for the related administration, while a radio-telephone would enable direct communication with the staff in England.

Since my sailing in Germany, I had owned two yachts, the second of which, I used for off-shore racing. The new vessel would have to be very different, and after considering the many specialized requirements, we came to the conclusion that a sturdy steel-hulled motor yacht, about 65 feet long, should be capable of carrying the necessary scientific equipment, as well as accommodating a crew of eight. It so happened, that some of the technical staff were yachting enthusiasts, and hence, we anticipated that when the yacht was at sea, they would stand watch as yachtsmen, but on arrival in harbour, they would perform their normal duties.

A design for a suitable vessel was quickly agreed and the construction put in hand. The hull, engine beds, bulkheads, decks and the fuel and water tanks were fabricated in steel at a yard in Southampton, after which the vessel was fitted-out in Cowes. Two Rolls Royce diesel engines were installed to give a continuous cruising speed in excess of eleven knots, while to provide the necessary power for the laboratory equipment, in addition to the yacht's normal requirements, a heavy duty electricity generator was provided. Other equipment included: a water distillation plant, stabilizers, radio-telephone, radar, echo-sounder, automatic pilot, direction finder and comprehensive navigation instrumentation. We decided to call the yacht *Keramos*, this being the Greek word from which our word 'ceramic' was derived.

After completing performance trials in the Solent, we crossed the Channel to Cherbourg before continuing to Ostende, from where a visit to the Vibro-Mill manufacturing plant in Brussels was made. Then on to our agents in Rotterdam, who had arranged accommodation for *Keramos* in the delightful little harbour at the Royal Maas Yacht Club and where we were berthed alongside the royal barge. After visiting agents in Hamburg, we made the interesting passage through the Kiel Canal and then on to Copenhagen, where we anchored close to the 'Little Mermaid' statue at Langelinie.

The principal of our agents in Copenhagen was a member of the Danish nobility, but he traded under the name of Chris Fahrner. In addition to his office in Copenhagen, he had associate companies in Sweden, Norway, and Finland; to keep in touch with these widely scattered business interests he piloted his own twin-engined aircraft. I often accompanied him, and in view of my interest in navigation, he would generally leave that task to me. At sea, if you are not sure of your position, you can always stop, but in the air it is rather different. Consequently, flying over the high mountains in cloud, was an exciting affair and I have to admit, we did not always land where Chris had intended.

I well remember a flight back to Copenhagen after a busy time in the north of Sweden. It was a very hot day and Chris said, "I am going to land on the island of Anholt, so that we can have a swim". When I told him that I did not have a swim-suit, he said, "That's no problem – not many people on Anholt wear clothes in summer". After a very bumpy landing on an airstrip among the sand dunes, we had a refreshing swim – and he was certainly right about the absence of clothes.

Chris had a wonderful command of languages; speaking all the Scandinavian languages, in addition to English, French, German, Spanish and Italian. On one occasion, he landed his aircraft on the outskirts of a small town, in Finland, and as it was only a short distance to our hotel, we decided to walk. Soon, however, we were completely lost. Chris stopped a man to ask the way in Finnish, but the only response was a vague look. He then tried a string of Scandinavian languages in quick succession, with similar results. While this was going on, I noticed that the man was wearing an Ocean Racing Club tie, so I asked, "What kind of a yacht do you race?" Whereupon, I found myself with two very surprised gentlemen.

Chris Fahrner was one of the best salesmen I ever met. People were always pleased to greet him and he appeared to have the gift of being able to obtain large orders, as if by magic. One day, I asked him for the secret of his success. After some reluctant hesitation, he told me how he had studied marketing and salesmanship in Paris. He had been shown how to enter a buyer's office, how to display his trade samples and of course, how to make his sales spiels in various situations. This type of training had continued for three years, at the end of which he graduated with honours. He then got a job as a salesman and began to put into practice all that he had learned at college, but he soon got the sack, because he did not sell a thing.

However, he decided to try again and one day, he came to the conclusion that instead of him doing all the talking, it would be better to encourage the customer to talk – simply by asking questions. In other words, it was more important to know what the customer wanted, than to tell the customer what he was trying to sell.

It was therefore, quite an education to sit in with Chris, when he was with a buyer. He would ask for the expiry date of contracts relating to goods, that were not being bought from him; he would probe for information on any problem areas and he would enquire with regard to new projects and product development. Then, when he thoroughly understood the pitch on which he was batting, he would start to make his runs – and it would always be a worthwhile score.

After leaving Copenhagen, *Keramos* sailed to Sweden and Norway, before crossing the North Sea and making an interesting passage through the Caledonian Canal. As I had to meet people in Glasgow, we then passed through the Crinnan Canal and berthed in Rothsay.

I also had calls to make in Northern Ireland, after which, *Keramos* sailed south to the Republic and berthed in Arklow harbour. Here we were only a few yards away from the main entrance to the Arklow Pottery, where we very soon met many old friends. This visit proved to be exceptionally strenuous, not so much due to the work but due to the rip-roaring cordiality, which continued almost non-stop, throughout our stay.

We commenced the day on *Keramos* with a working breakfast, at which we would be joined by several of our Irish friends, and this then merged into a continuous series of tea and coffee breaks. Lunch on board would be a buffet affair, with much coming and going. Things would quieten down somewhat during the afternoon, as we prepared for a formal dinner; after which, we would be invited ashore, to live it up until the early hours of the following morning.

While on our way to Cowes, and just as we were approaching St Alban's Head, we saw a distress flare, sent up from a very small sailing yacht. At the time, there was a moderate on-shore wind and poor visibility, but nothing that would normally give rise to an emergency. However, on going alongside the tiny boat, we found two French boys who had just sailed across the Channel. They were completely exhausted, had no idea of their position and were very much afraid of being swept onto the nearby rocks by the breaking swell. We threw them a line and suggested that we should tow them into Poole harbour.

Our offer was graciously accepted, so we set off together at a low speed. Very soon, we ran into thick fog and the land disappeared from view, which made it necessary to rely on radar to reach harbour. Being a member of the Royal Motor Yacht Club at Sandbanks, I was able to speak, on the radio, to the Secretary and arrange for our sailors in distress to be allocated a temporary berth and for the usual hospitality to be extended. After seeing the boys safely into the club house, I explained that I would have to continue to Cowes, as I was now much behind schedule for a business appointment.

It would seem that after the boys had used the Club's facilities to get a warm shower and some refreshment, they had then made enquiries as to the owner of *Keramos* and obtained my home telephone number. The result was that my wife received a call from a boy, speaking French, who was offering profuse and heartfelt thanks because – so he said – Mr Podmore had just saved his and his friend's lives. About two weeks later, my wife received from one of the boys, the largest box of chocolates I have ever seen, together with a kind note which concluded by advising that something was to follow for Mr Podmore.

Months passed and nothing more was heard and then, one day, a large parcel arrived which contained a magnificent water colour of St Alban's Head in mist, with *Keramos* approaching a small sailing yacht. The accompanying letter offered more grateful thanks and mentioned that the painting had been made by the boy's father. It was obvious that he must have been given a very vivid – and I am afraid, rather exaggerated – description of the incident, but nevertheless, I was very pleased to receive such a delightful gift. I later learned that the father was a well known and much esteemed artist in France. The following Christmas, we received a beautiful card bearing a reproduction of a fine water colour by the father.

The laboratory on *Keramos* was proving to be of great assistance and therefore, while back in Cowes, we took advantage of the opportunity to augment some of the facilities. We had recently sold a licence to a company in Portugal, in respect of a continuous frit plant and we had contracted to supervise the construction of the kiln. Consequently, we put on board *Keramos* all the necessary drawings and specialized instruments, etc. and then set off for Lisbon.

The proprietor of the particular company, also owned one of the two daily newspapers published in Lisbon, and consequently, he was able to keep us up to date with news in Britain, by delivering on board various telex messages.

As it happened to be the time of the 1970 general election, we were able to get the results, within a few minutes of them being declared. The Conservatives were doing well and looked like winning, so when the proprietor came on board, he said that as soon as the Conservatives were shown to be in an unassailable position, he would issue a special edition to announce the election of the Heath government. I told him that Mr Wilson would have to capitulate, before Mr Heath could assume office, and therefore, what people would want to know, was when Mr Wilson had capitulated.

With this he went away and about half an hour later, a boy arrived on *Keramos* to deliver a newspaper and a note for me, which read, "I trust this is what you want to know". I opened the paper, and there on the front page was the banner headline, "MR WILSON CAPITULATES".

While an engineer was supervising the building of the frit plant, I arranged to fly back to England. At the Lisbon airport, I was informed that I would not be permitted to board the plane, because the fact that my passport had not been stamped, on entering Portugal, proved I must have entered illegally. When *Keramos* entered the port of Lisbon, she had been boarded, in the usual manner, by customs and immigration officials, but they had not stamped any of our passports; this did not surprise us, because passports are not stamped in all ports. At the airport, however, they insisted that passports had to be stamped on both entry and departure. Meanwhile, over the public address system, an excited voice was exhorting Mr Podmore to join the plane immediately. I had been urging the bureaucratic official to phone the port and verify the position, which he eventually did, so enabling me to board the plane just as they were closing the doors.

After I returned to *Keramos*, we sailed south to the small town of Setubal, in order to visit a nearby pottery. I had taken from England, a replacement fitting for the water injector on the exhaust system of the electricity generator. This was a rather complicated piece of pipework containing various types of unions. The engineer removed the original component and as it was very badly corroded, he threw it into the sea. But very soon, he realized that on the discarded item there was an essential union, that had not been provided on the new fitting. I suggested we might obtain a union of the required type in the town, but the engineer was adamant that it would not be easy to find one in England and "quite impossible in this one-eyed place – particularly as the union has a gas thread, which is quite unknown outside Britain".

As I had previously decided to take a walk into the town, I contended that nothing would be lost, by taking the fitting with me and making a few enquiries. I started by visiting a garage, as I thought it would prove a likely place to find someone who spoke some English and also knew something about pipe fittings. A mechanic there recommended a man whom he thought might be able to assist, and on a scrap of paper, he indicated where I would find him. Following the instructions, I came to a back street in a poor part of the town and finally saw the place recommended – a small ramshackle building, with a stable door.

It was so dark inside, that on entering from the bright sunlight, all I could see was a rough bench and behind it the vague outline of an old man. I put my pipework down on the bench, and merely by pointing, indicated my requirement. Without even touching the piece, the man turned towards the inner darkness and shouted three or four strange words. After a brief silence, I heard slight noises coming from deep within; then I saw a small boy approaching. He could not have been more than about nine years of age, wore only a pair of ragged shorts, was filthy from head to foot, but in his little hand he grasped a gleaming piece of brass, which he put onto the bench. I just could not believe my eyes, for it was the very piece I wanted. I paid a mere pittance for the precious item and within about thirty minutes of leaving *Keramos,* I was back on board. I did not think anyone could be more surprised, than I had just been – but I had not reckoned on the reaction of the engineer.

In Valencia, there was another assignment awaiting the engineer, so I again decided to return to the Potteries for a few days. On the far side of the harbour there was a good boat yard, and I therefore thought it would be a suitable opportunity for the skipper to get *Keramos* onto a slipway, in order to get the barnacles scrubbed off the hull.

As I had a duplicate set of clothing, etc. on *Keramos,* it was not necessary for me to carry personal luggage when returning home. On this occasion, however, I took a suitcase containing a miscellaneous collection of items, that were in need of repair or replacement. There was an oil pump, an automatic switch with several emerging wires, part of a sheet winch and many similar bits and pieces. When I arrived at the customs in Manchester airport, the officer posed the usual stock questions, which resulted in the following dialogue: "Is this all your luggage, sir?" – "Yes." "How long have you been away?" – "One month." "Where have you just come from?" – "Valencia." "What was the purpose of your visit?" – "Travelling on business." "Would you mind opening your case?" For almost a minute, he simply gazed at the contents and then said, "I have been doing this job for eighteen years and in all that time, I have never come across anyone, who would want to travel about for a month, with luggage like that".

Before returning to *Keramos,* I phoned the skipper and arranged for him to meet me at the airport with a car. On arrival, however, I was surprised to be met by the cook, and when I asked where the skipper was, he told me that the policia had taken him away and he was now behind bars. I therefore lost no time in getting over to the comissaria, to find out, just what had been going on.

In due course, I was able to see the skipper, who told me that after *Keramos* had been put back into the water, he had crossed the harbour and berthed alongside one of the town quays. A customs official had promptly appeared and asked for the name of the port of departure, whereupon he had pointed across the harbour and said "I have just come from over there". The man obviously did not understand, because he kept on repeating his routine question, "Port of departure?" The skipper then went on to say that he could see the wretched fellow had got to put the name of a port on his bit of paper, and therefore, he

▲ 1. The author's early introduction to sailing.

▲ 2. Podmore China plaque, circa 1910. The decoration was made by applying black enamel over a white glaze and then scraping away the enamel to produce the white design.

▶ 3. The author in the Normandy bridgehead, conducting experiments at the back of his Austin Utility.

▲ 4. After the liberation of Belgium, the Resistance Movement sought retribution on Nazi sympathisers.

▼ 5. A typical warning for troops entering Germany.

▲ 6. *Keramos I* in Paris.

▶ 7. *Keramos II* under sail, before the wind.

▲ 8. Vibro-Energy mills ultra-fine grinding alumina.

◀ 9. The author takes a sextant sight in mid-Atlantic.

▲ 10. The huge statue of Christ on the summit peak of Corcavado, Rio de Janeiro.

▼ 11. The yacht harbour in Rio de Janeiro, Brazil.

▼ 12. The three spirits of the Amazon. The upper spirit guards the icon's possessor against accident, the middle one preserves the owner's health, while the lower one protects his (or her) loved one.

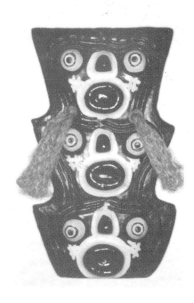

▲ 13. The San Blas Island chief and members of his family aboard *Keramos*.

◀ 14. A San Blas mola.

▼ 15. The onset of a storm. The lack of visibility during a full storm makes photography impossible.

▲16. Murray with playful sea lion pups and fur seals, Galápagos.

▼17. The dragon-like Galápagos marine iguana.

▲ 18. Galápagos cattle being lifted by the horns prior to shipment.

▼ 20. The island of Ua Pou in the Marquesas.

▲ 19. Benedictine was believed to have led to the demise of the last king of Tahiti; hence the large bottle surmounting his tomb.

had given the name that seemed most appropriate and that was – Valencia. Whereupon, the official bawled, "This Valencia, you fool". At this juncture, the skipper admitted that he had made a big mistake by loudly laughing, because the official immediately called the policia, who without a word of explanation, brusquely marched him off. I was of course, soon able to put the record straight and get the sadder but wiser skipper back on board.

We next had to visit Castellon de la Plana, where a new plant was in course of construction to produce zircon opacifiers. *Keramos* was accommodated in the nearby fishing harbour, where we soon found many friends to keep us well supplied with a wonderful variety of fish. The manager of the new factory was an enthusiastic yachtsman and the champion tunny fisherman of Spain, but I have to confess that I enjoyed the tunny fishing better than the tuna, in view of the superior alternatives. A friend of the manager had a large orange plantation and each day, he would have delivered to *Keramos*, a branch off an orange tree, containing about thirty of the most delicious fruit.

A few weeks later *Keramos* was in the port of Mahon, on the island of Menorca, where the potential of the flourishing activity in craft pottery was being investigated. We had decided to carry an additional small anchor and this had been sent from England, and was already in Mahon, when we arrived. As I had made arrangements to visit our plant in Italy and then fly on to London, I asked the skipper to attend to the customs clearance for the anchor and get it on board. While I was away, I phoned the skipper on several occasions and each time, he told me that he had not been able to obtain clearance for the anchor, due to the customs officer being reluctant to discuss the matter.

When I returned to *Keramos* the anchor had still not been cleared. I therefore decided to visit the custom-house myself and investigate the problem. The officer had a beautifully furnished office, with a highly polished marble floor. He sat in a huge armchair, behind a magnificent desk, but as there were no chairs for visitors, I was obliged to stand before him. The poor man was unfortunately suffering from Parkinson's disease and as a result, his entire body was shaking in a most distressing manner. He either could not, or would not speak English. At that time, my Spanish was of the tourist phrase book variety, so I could not do much more than make an appointment for the following day.

In the circumstances, I asked our skipper if he knew of anyone locally, who might be prepared to act as an interpreter. After much thought, he said there was an English girl working in a nearby hotel to improve her Spanish. She was on vacation from university, where she was in her final year, reading Spanish. He said her fluency was impressive and he thought she would be prepared to assist us. Her credentials seemed satisfactory and therefore, I asked the skipper to see the girl, and if possible, make suitable arrangements for the following day.

When I first saw our interpreter, she was standing outside the custom-house and I must say, she was unlike any of the girls I had once known at university. She was wearing an exceptionally shapely T-shirt bearing a bizarre design, together with the briefest of mini-skirts; she wore no shoes and her long blonde hair fell about her pretty face.

After the skipper had introduced us, we entered the officer's sanctum and the three of us stood in line before the big chief. He took one long, hard look at our interpreter – and then began to shake more than ever.

I asked the girl to explain, that I had important business appointments in Italy and that I must leave Mahon, with *Keramos*, within the next couple of days. As she translated into Spanish, she only got as far as the word "appointments", when she was interrupted by a loud outburst, which was translated as, "I am the customs officer – I don't care a damn about your business arrangements". In the diatribe that followed, he made it very clear that *Keramos* would not be permitted to leave Mahon, until all her equipment was on board – and if we left without permission, he would send a gun-boat to bring us back. I then asked when the anchor could be cleared, whereupon he gave a completely non-committal reply.

It was obvious that the man had no intention of being reasonable, so I asked the girl to tell him, that in order to get away from Mahon, I would be prepared to make a gift of the bothersome anchor to the British Embassy and in that case, because the Embassy is recognised as British territory, I would not then be leaving the anchor in Spain. However, as soon as she mentioned the word "Embassy" he went completely beserk, shouting and storming for fully a minute, before snatching the telephone to speak to the British Embassy.

Within ten minutes a man appeared, who introduced himself as the First Secretary at the Embassy and after he had spoken briefly to the officer, he asked us to step outside. He then stressed, that under no circumstances, were we to leave without the anchor or without permission; the officer had previously sent out a gun-boat to bring crews back for incarceration and he would not hesitate to do so again. The Secretary then undertook to do everything possible to solve the dilemma; in the meantime we were to do nothing – and with that he departed.

By this time the poor girl was looking very forlorn. With much feeling, she told me that she had been under the impression she was merely required to assist in collecting a small anchor; not for one moment, had she contemplated the apparently simple task developing into a threatened gun-boat incident. She said, she had spent the morning on the beach and had considered her beach attire to be appropriate; if she had known that she was expected to attend a formal meeting, she would have dressed accordingly. But it was clear that what had upset her most, was the fact that the officer, instead of raving at me, had shouted and shaken his fist at her, as if she had been responsible for the content of what she was trying to say. She was obviously and quite justifiably, very distraught, and in the circumstances, I felt the least I could do to make amends, was to invite her to join us on *Keramos* for dinner.

Later that day a smartly dressed and sophisticated young lady stepped aboard. The long unruly blonde tresses were now neatly coiled on her head and tied in a red ribbon, the skirt was at least eighteen inches longer, while the long nether limbs, which were so much in evidence during the morning, were now discreetly hidden, except for a glimpse of silken hose and a natty pair of high-heeled shoes. It is said that, "manners maketh man"; what is supposed to "maketh" woman is not generally disclosed, but as far as that young woman was concerned, a change of clothes certainly produced a very different woman! I sometimes wonder if, when we met the customs officer, the girl had been more formally dressed, he would have been less hostile towards her.

During the morning of the following day, a lorry approached *Keramos* and the driver was seen to drop our anchor onto the quay, after which he went away without leaving documents of any kind. I phoned our friend at the Embassy, who told me that everything had been settled; the necessary exit permit was being delivered by hand and on receipt, we were free to collect the anchor and go. We lost no time in getting out to sea, but as Menorca disappeared over the horizon, I could not resist an occasional glance astern – thankfully that gun-boat never appeared.

While on a visit to Greece, we engaged a new skipper; a resourceful character named John Kirby, who promptly set about checking *Keramos* over, from stem to stern. Among the matters that he found called for the services of a boat-yard, was a slight leak from the header tank on the air-conditioning system. Our first opportunity to get this repaired, occurred when we arrived in Malta. Accordingly, John got the tank disconnected and took it to a nearby yard.

The manager arranged for John to see the man detailed to do the work, in order that he could explain directly, what was required. The man was shown the place where the tank was leaking and John asked him to patch and braze the affected area. As the tank was fitted with a safety-valve, the man was also instructed to water test the tank after repair, and re-set the valve at 30lb/sq.in.

The following morning, when the man brought the tank back to *Keramos*, John immediately noticed that the outlet on the safety valve had been brazed over, so making it inoperative. Naturally, John was very angry and demanded an explanation. The man said that when he had tested the tank, water had come out of the little opening and therefore he had brazed it over. At this, John threw up his arms in dismay and shouted, "You blithering idiot" – the man scowled and departed without a word. The next thing we knew was that all the workers at the yard had downed tools and were on strike, due to one of their number havng been rudely insulted.

In the circumstances, I thought it best for John and I to see the Managing Director and explain matters. The M.D. listened politely to John's story but then made it quite clear that the men were determined not to resume work, until John had apologised in front of them all. I was amazed to hear John immediately undertake to comply with their demand, because he certainly was not the kind of man who would normally allow himself to be pushed around. However, the workers were assembled in the canteen, and John stood on a table, to face the angry men and their loud incomprehensible catcalls.

What followed was one of the best impromptu speeches I have ever heard. John started by relating, in down to earth terms, precisely what had happened, and then said, "In England, we would not hesitate to call a man who put a safety valve out of action, a blithering idiot. I am sorry I don't know what you would call such a man in Malta, but apparently you would not call him an idiot. I am also sorry I don't know what kind of a man you would describe as an idiot; perhaps you feel that the man who put the safety valve on the tank was an idiot. . . .". After about five minutes of this kind of thing, during which the word "sorry" had been used many times, but not once in the pertinent context, the men gradually became quiet; no doubt because they were totally bemused. Being a gifted raconteur, John rounded off his discourse with a couple of relevant stories, at the expense of management. Soon he had the men falling off their chairs with laughter; so much so, that when he finally got down from the table, they gave him a round of applause. The Managing Director arranged for a different man to set the safety valve correctly, apologised for all the trouble, and waived the charge for the job.

During the time *Keramos* was engaged on work in the Mediterranean, she returned to Britain and adjacent waters several times for short periods. On one such occasion she sailed up the Thames and was berthed in St Katharine's Docks, by Tower Bridge and on another occasion we took her up the Seine to Paris. While we were there, the rainfall was quite exceptional and the level of the river rose to such an extent, that when it was time for us to leave, we found *Keramos* (even with the mast lowered) could not pass under the arch of the Pont de l'Alma.

The water-level of the river is judged by looking at the statue of the *Zouave* (an Algerian soldier), which stands on the bank, at the eastern end of the bridge. During the great flood of 1910, the water rose up to his chin, but the river is considered dangerous when he has his feet in the water. When I consulted the *Zouave*, the water came up to his ankles.

After being delayed for several days, a river official was able to tell me the height of the arch apex above water level. This enabled me to calculate that the radar scanner would just pass under the bridge, with a clearance of about three inches – there would be a greater clearance under all the other bridges downstream. To maintain steerageway, we would have to keep the speed through the water above 2½ knots and as there was about 4 knots of current, this would result in *Keramos* approaching the bridge at a minimum 6½ knots. If therefore, at some point, there was not sufficient clearance, we would not be able to stop, before sweeping away our radar scanner.

So, in order to make the approach at a controlled speed, I decided to let the current push *Keramos* stern first, towards the bridge and to keep her going forward through the water, at a speed just below the speed of the current. In this way she could be directed towards the centre of the arch, at a low speed relative to the bridge, and if at any time we should wish to pull away upstream, it would only be necessary to increase the engine revs.

Accordingly, with one member of the crew stationed on top of the wheelhouse, to observe and report the clearance, we slowly approached the bridge stern first, and carefully manoeuvred *Keramos* so as to pass under the highest part of the arch. Then, just as we were about to go under the bridge, I saw a barge coming upstream towards the same arch, and as the crew on the barge would obviously conclude that we were going upstream, we had to go quickly forward and away from the bridge, in order to give them a free passage. This also happened on two subsequent approaches, but on the fourth attempt, we passed very slowly under the bridge. We were pleased that we had taken prudent action because, in some places, the clearance was only about two inches.

The work being done by *Keramos* in Europe, was proving most valuable, but it soon became apparent, that similar work needed to be carried out in many other parts of the world. The fuel capacity gave her a range of about 1,100 nautical miles and this was obviously insufficient for long ocean passages. We decided therefore, to sell *Keramos* and purchase a larger vessel, specifically designed for world cruising.

Several people showed interest in buying the yacht, but while we were in Malta, a yacht broker advised me that a French client was planning to fly his own aircraft out to Malta, in order to inspect *Keramos*. In due course, the prospective purchaser arrived on board, together with a very attractive young lady, whom he introduced as the stewardess on his aircraft. I provided every facility for a thorough inspection, including a trial run, and when it began to appear that he would pay the asking price, I extended mindful hospitality to the couple, during their stay on board.

Finally, the man said he would sign a contract for the purchase of *Keramos* subject to agreement on four supplementary conditions, which were very briefly as follows:

(a) Nothing apart from personal equipment, to be removed from the vessel.

(b) The vessel to be delivered to Cannes within five days.

(c) On arrival in Cannes, the vessel to be put on a slipway to facilitate a Lloyds Survey, at the purchaser's expense; in the event of the vessel failing the Survey, the purchaser to be under no further obligation whatsoever.

(d) Members of the *Keramos* crew, while in Cannes, to treat in strict confidence, everything relating to the Malta visit.

On the way to Cannes, we encountered strong gales and snow blizzards, but we reached our destination within the stipulated time limit, only to learn that the purchaser could not be found anywhere. Eventually, the brokers managed to locate him in a neighbouring town; he apologized for his absence and excused himself, by saying that he never expected the trip to be completed in such terrible weather.

In due course, *Keramos* passed the Lloyds Survey and as the man was satisfied that the four supplementary conditions had been met, the contract of sale was duly signed. The transfer of ownership was registered, with the name *Keramos* being retained for future use, on the new yacht.

19

KERAMOS II AND SOME EARLY INCIDENTS

The new *Keramos* was designed by E.G.van de Stadt, with interior decor by J. Bannenberg. She was built by Southern Ocean Shipyard Ltd in Poole – a brief description being as follows:

Length overall 75ft. Beam 17.5ft. Draft 9ft.

Displacement 40 tons. Thames tonnage 92 tons.

Construction: Built to Lloyd's specification +100A1 and L.M.C.

Hull built by Tylers Ltd, of heavy moulded GRP, stainless steel reinforced. 10 tons of moulded lead ballast, encapsulated in the keel.

Hydraulic steering with autopilot.

Engine: MAN 5 cylinder, 4 cycle, 135 hp, marine diesel, giving a maximum speed under power of 10.5 knots and a range of 1,800 nautical miles approx. The heat from the cooling system being utilised to operate a distillation plant, producing 400 gallons per day of fresh water from seawater.

Electricity generator: 15kw, 240v, AC, auxiliary diesel generator, in a soundshield.

Air-conditioning throughout. All-electric galley with microwave oven, refrigerators and large freezer unit, etc.

1,200w, radio transmitter, with worldwide coverage.

VHF radio/telephone for local communication.

Comprehensive navigation equipment, including radar, echo-sounder, radio direction-finder, wind speed and direction indicators, speedometer and log, etc.

Accommodation: Berths for 10, in 3 principal cabins and crews quarters – all cabins with *en suite* shower and toilet. Saloon (with navigation section to starboard), galley, engine room, wheelhouse, lazarette and laboratory.

Tender – carried on retractable stern-davits.

Ketch rig, with 3,600 sq.ft working sail area. Spinnaker 3,450 sq.ft. For trade wind sailing, a pair of Yankees each 940 sq.ft sheeted to two poles. Slab-reefing on main and mizzen sails. 19 two-speed winches, manually and electrically operated.

After completing comprehensive sea trials, we took delivery of the new *Keramos* on 15 December, 1978 and sailed to St Malo for the maiden voyage. She was then returned to the builders for final adjustments to be made, after which we sailed to Vilamoura in Portugal. There, we made preparations for the long passage to Rio de Janeiro, where we planned to promote the sale of the Vibro-Mills, for the grinding of coffee and cocoa, and later visit our agency in São Paulo.

From Vilamoura we sailed to Funchal, on the island of Madeira and then to Pasitos Blancos, Gran Canaria. As we approached the Canary Isles, the wind increased appreciably, so we decided to take down the big spinnaker. Somehow, the heavy spinnaker pole became detached from the mast coupling and as it crashed to the deck, it caught the cook (Terry), a glancing blow to the side of the head. Immediately on arrival in port, we took Terry to see a doctor at the British-American Clinic, as by that time, he was in much pain and unable to hold his head erect. The doctor prescribed a suitable treatment, but said that under no circumstances was he to sail across the Atlantic, until he had completely recovered.

On a slipway in the harbour, an American named John Calvert, assisted by a local craftsman, was building a very fine yacht in narrow planked African teak. The interior fittings had been made previously in Malaysia, to John's specification, and were real works of art, embodying much intricate carving in traditional designs.

One day, while I was watching John at work, Terry walked by; John eyed him closely and then asked what had happened to him. I briefly described the accident and the nature of the injury, whereupon John said, "He needs specialist treatment urgently, otherwise he will suffer for some time". I was very surprised to hear this coming from an unshaven man, wearing dirty overalls, and with an old cap set at a rakish angle, so I asked what made him say that. He explained that he had qualified as a chiropractor at an American university and specialized in manipulative treatments. He claimed that he could treat Terry in a matter of seconds and after the treatment, which would be painless , he would be completely fit and able to sail across the Atlantic without delay.

I told Terry about the conversation and his reaction was predictable. He retorted, "I am not going to let a man like that touch me; how am I to know if he is qualified – he might make matters a lot worse". Other members of the crew, however, felt that if John guaranteed the treatment would be painless, and the recovery immediate, then there would be nothing to lose, and possibly much to gain, by giving it a try.

After much discussion, it was agreed that I should invite John on board, so that he could examine Terry and explain matters to him personally; after which, it would be for Terry to decide. Accordingly, John joined us on *Keramos*, still in his dirty overalls, and while he made his exmination, the rest of us sat around in the cockpit and watched with much interest. John described, in detail, the type of injury and what was necessary to rectify matters. In due course, Terry became reasonably convinced that John knew what he was talking about and finally, with some encouragement from the onlookers, he decided to put himself at John's mercy – though still with some trepidation.

John asked Terry to stand and fold his arms tightly. Then positioning himself behind Terry, he put his hands under Terry's elbows and quietly said, "I want you to relax completely – let everything go limp – I am not going to hurt you, so just relax – relax". And then, without a warning of any kind, he suddenly lifted Terry up about two feet and brought him down with an almighty crash, as his feet struck the deck. Terry stood transfixed and muttered, "Oh my God" – while we looked on, in shocked silence. John, in a calm matter of fact voice, told Terry to sit down for five minutes, have a cup of tea – "then, jolly well get cracking in that galley". As Terry sipped his tea, I asked him how he felt. He replied, "Marvellous – there is absolutely no pain and I can now move my head again".

When I asked John how much his fee would be, he laughed and said, "I am only a scruffy boat builder now". I invited him to join us for dinner, and when he later returned, I welcomed on board a different man, for he now looked very smart in his white tropical suit.

He turned out to be a most interesting character, with several skills in addition to boat building and manipulative surgery. We learned that he had made six films in Hollywood and toured the world as a stage magician. Apparently, he had specialized in spectacular illusions, and described one in which he would drape an elephant in a large, brightly coloured sheet; then, on the sound of a trumpet, the sheet would slowly flutter down to the stage. Whereupon, his lady assistant would roll up the sheet and a little Indian boy, in traditional robes, would appear with a dustpan and brush, to remove the droppings – all that remained of the elephant.

After dinner, he entertained us with some amazing feats of magic, using simple items of equipment that we found for him on board. Finally, at some late hour, he said he would really have to go, and asked me for the time. I looked at my watch – but it was not on my wrist. To the amusement of all, John said, "Here you will want this", as he then handed me my watch – but the loud laughter gradually subsided, as many other personal items were restored to their rightful owners.

Terry did not have any further difficulty, so we finalized our arrangements for the 3,800 mile passage to Rio de Janeiro and made our departure from Gran Canaria at 1900 hr on 6 June, 1979 – 35 years to the day after the start of a previous adventure, on D-Day in Normandy.

If one were to draw a straight line on a chart, from Gran Canaria to Rio and then sail on that course, the distance would be less than 3,800 nautical miles, but the time taken would be significantly longer, than that required to sail on a course which made the best use of the prevailing winds and currents. Charts can be obtained which show the direction and strength of the winds and currents for each month of the year; by reference to the June chart, I decided to sail east of the Cape Verde Islands, then follow the coast of West Africa, at an off-shore distance of about 200 miles, for 250 miles – after which, we would gradually change course to SW by the time we reached the equator. Beyond the equator, I planned to hold this same course for 500 miles and then progressively change to SSW by the time we reached the Tropic of Capricorn, when we would steer directly for Rio. (All distances in sea miles, ie 6,080 feet).

On 8 June, we crossed the Tropic of Cancer and soon after, the Sun was directly overhead at noon – a situation which called for a special technique, when determining the latitude from the noon sextant sight. As a member of the Royal Institute of Navigation, I had for many years, taken a keen interest in the various methods of ascertaining position at sea and had obtained Board of Trade Certificates for both coastal and ocean navigation. On the first *Keramos,* I had used a method that I had developed and which was published in the *Journal of the Royal Institute of Navigation*, Vol.28-No.1, 1975. But on the new *Keramos*, I was using a computer specially designed for navigation at sea, and which incorporated in its program, my method for obtaining position line data.

I would have liked to call at one of the Cape Verde Islands, but at that time, the people were not particularly friendly towards Britain, so we passed them by, at a safe distance. A few days later an entry in the ship's log stated:

"Swarms of moths came on board; as we are more than 200 miles from the nearest land, they must have existed over the water for a considerable time. We continue to get land birds alighting on deck, but in spite of our efforts to care for them, none live longer than about three days. Notwithstanding the wonders of bird migration, it is obvious that their navigation can sometimes be faulty, resulting in millions of them being lost at sea. There are many flying fish; those that land on deck go to the galley – good to eat but very bony. A strong easterly wind during the night, deposited a layer of red dust from the Sahara on the decks, and badly discoloured the sails. Day temperature well over 100°F and not much cooler at night".

On 13 June, we were in the Doldrums, where sailing ships have sometimes been becalmed for a month or more. We did experience a few periods without wind, during which we used the engine, but for the most part, the wind was light and very variable. This called for much sail changing – generally during a violent thunderstorm, accompanied by a tropical downpour.

At 0905 hr on 18 June, we crossed the equator and celebrated according to tradition. Two days later, we began to derive significant assistance from the fresh N.E. trade winds, which enabled us to make 10 knots, under the twin headsails and mizzen. The ship's log recorded:

"A huge swell with the wave crests at least a quarter of a mile apart. We saw our first ship since departure (the *Shira Maru*) and although the large vessel passed only half a mile away, she disappeared from view completely, when *Keramos* was in a wave trough".

One member of the crew appeared to have little trust in navigation techniques and after so long at sea, he would look at the chart, on which a succession of crosses recorded our progress, and then ask, "How sure are you really, that we have sailed as far as that?" It so happened that he was on watch with me, on the night of 29 June, and I told him he should be able to see the loom of the beam, from the lighthouse on Cabo Frio, at 0310 hr, if he were to stand on top of the wheelhouse.

He could not wait to see some evidence of land, so at about 0300 hr, he eagerly climbed up onto the wheelhouse – but was disappointed not to see the light. I reminded him that I had said the light would appear at 0310 hr – therefore he must be patient for a few minutes. I kept my fingers crossed, but fortunately, his confidence in celestial navigation was soon to be ameliorated, when the light appeared on time to the minute.

The entrance to the harbour at Rio, is considered by many, to be the most beautiful and spectacular in the entire world. So after lunch, we assembled on deck and gazed ahead in eager anticipation. I had previously read about an incident which became known as the 'Rio syndrome', and concerned a man whose life's ambition was to sail into the harbour at Rio.

After saving his money for many years, he was eventually able to book a passage on a cruise liner, scheduled to call at Rio. On the long awaited day, he went up on deck with his camera, and as the off-shore islands and the spectacular Sugar Loaf mountain came into view, he began to take photographs. He was completely overwhelmed by the compelling beauty of it all, but when the huge statue of Christ on the summit of the Corcavado mountain suddenly appeared, he forgot all about his camera and just stared into the distance with misty eyes. After some considerable time, he came to realize that he was alone on deck – no other person was sharing this unforgettable experience. As the ship docked, he went below – and found that everyone was playing bingo!

20

COASTWISE IN BRAZIL

After rounding the impressive Sugar Loaf mountain, we dropped anchor close to the Rio Yacht Club, where we received a warm welcome and were granted honorary membership for the duration of our stay. The club is one of the finest yacht clubs I have ever visited; being superbly equipped and furnished – and having a first-class restaurant. There is also a magnificent swimming pool with a very popular snackbar, which serves the most wonderful toasted sandwiches. A particular favourite combined a filling of cheese, banana and cinnamon; none of the ingredients could be tasted individually, but the unique blend was quite delicious.

The Sugar Loaf mountain towered above *Keramos* and we could clearly see the cable cars taking people up to the summit. One day, while sitting in the cockpit, I was amazed to see two men standing on the roof of the descending car. When it drew level with the ascending car, both cars stopped and the two men jumped onto the other car and appeared to start attacking its occupants. I could not believe my eyes. I picked up my binoculars and clearly saw that the two men were engaged in a fierce hand to hand fight against a tall man and a fair haired girl. After some minutes of rough-and-tumble on the roof tops of the cars, I saw the tall man hook something onto the cable and while holding on to it with one hand, he grabbed the girl round the waist with the other. The next moment, the pair were making their escape, by together sliding down the steeply inclined cable – it was not possible to see what happened to them on reaching the foot of the mountain.

I subsequently learned that this was a scene being shot for the James Bond film *Moonraker*, featuring Roger Moore and Lois Chiles. When I later saw the film, I managed to catch a glimpse of *Keramos* in the far distance – but it was not possible to see the bewildered man in the cockpit!

I had some business engagements in Rio, but our agents were located in São Paulo. So after a few days, *Keramos* sailed south to the Ilha Grande Bay – an area of outstanding beauty, with more than 370 tree festooned islands and over 2,000 superb beaches. We anchored off the small town of Parati; a place of considerable interest, because it was here in 1660, that the Portuguese settlers came, and from where they shipped the plundered gold. The two narrow streets, laid out in the form of a letter T, were planned to provide defence against pirates. The original Portuguese colonial architecture still remains and is well exemplified by the three fine churches, which were built separately for each of the races: Indian, black and white.

Here, I left the crew to make preparations for the next stage of our voyage to the north, while I went with an engineer to São Paulo. At the time of our visit, it was the fastest growing city in the world. Back in the 1880s, it was a sleepy, shabby little town of 30,000 inhabitants, while today, it has a population of 19 million, increasing at the rate of 150,000 each year.

It is a city of shining skyscrapers and extensive parks; a vibrant metropolis covering an area three times that of Paris and whose industrial districts engulf more and more villages and even townships, as they spread incessantly outwards. To all Brazillians it is the city of promise, offering large rewards for initiative and enterprise. However, some immigrant peasants, who are unable to adapt or meet the demands of modern industry, inevitably drift to the outskirts of the city where they live in slums, unmatched anywhere in the world, for filth and squalor.

Most of the world's major companies are represented and many have factories in, or close to the city. Commerce is the very lifeblood of the place, and every kind of business service is therefore available. Consequently, we spent a very interesting and fruitful week in the great city – and it would also have been most enjoyable, but for the terrible smog, which made our eyes run continuously, and the throat so sore, that all the wonderful and varied food tasted no better than the incessant diesel fumes.

After leaving Parati, *Keramos* returned to Rio, to refuel and take on stores. It would have been unforgiveable to leave the captivating city, without seeing some of the sights. I therefore went to the summit of the Sugar Loaf, and was enthralled by the magnificent views of the coast, with the shining beaches and the many off-shore islands.

I also went by funicular to the top of the 700 metre high Corcavado mountain, which is surmounted by the huge statue of Christ the Redeemer. This impressive figure with outstretched arms, is 40 metres tall and said to weigh 1,200 tons.

I visited the famous Maracanã Stadium (then the largest in the world), to see Flamengo, the local football team, play Capa Grande. The home team won 3-0 and the great Zico, the successor to Pelé, scored a wonderful goal. This was a very fine game of football, but it was also an unforgettable experience, due to the infectious Latin exuberance, stimulated by the continuous beat of the drums and the orchestrated chanting. Whenever the ball approached a goal, the entire crowd jumped up and down, while the roar became quite deafening.

Of all the many fine beaches, perhaps the best known and certainly the most popular, is the 5 kilometre long, Copacabana beach, with its wide stretch of golden sand, lapped by the warm, azure-blue water. It attracts large numbers of people to frolic in the sea, to take part in every kind of beach game, or just to lie and sunbathe on the hot sand.

All kinds of refreshment can be purchased from vendors, who mingle with the people and attract attention by putting on an act, such as dancing or singing; those selling oranges usually show their skill by juggling with their merchandise. The boys carry large pressurized tanks of Coca-Cola on their backs and perform balancing acts with the great stacks of plastic beakers. It pays to say, "No thank you", very quickly and firmly, to these persistent salesmen, otherwise you can find yourself with a beaker of Coca-Cola in each hand, a packet of cigarettes in the breast pocket and a bag of crisps behind each ear. The young girls mostly sell sweets and ice cream; some of them sing, but all attract attention by the abundance of their feminine charm and the almost complete absence of attire.

There are many other beaches extending, in all, for more than 35 kilometres; each has a particular character and attracts a certain type of individual, depending on the principal interest in the locality. Some districts are famous due to their luxury hotels, others for the night life; Arpoador is a popular surfing spot, while Ipanema is renowned – as proclaimed in the well-known song – for its young and very beautiful girls, who disport themselves on the beach, but more particularly in the many sidewalk cafés.

While in Rio, I decided to adjust the ship's compass. This is done by taking bearings on three or more prominent landmarks, the direction of which can be determined from the chart. One of my chosen marks was the statue of Christ – I suppose not many people can claim to have swung the compass with the assistance of Christ.

Before visiting Amazonia, it is necessary to be immunized against yellow fever. I went to a clinic to get the appropriate treatment and asked the receptionist if she spoke English. She replied, "Five words". After a brief interval she said, "Come", so I followed her into the surgery, where she said, "Sit" – I have often wondered what that fifth word was. The clinic was designed to immunize large numbers of people by the use of equipment resembling a petrol pump, but having a needle at the end of a thin plastic hose. Whether or not the needle was changed after each jab, I do not know.

It was extremely hard to bid goodbye to Rio, but we had to continue our voyage. So, as the sun rose on 14 August, *Keramos* slipped out of that most majestic of all harbours, and set sail to the north. I had heard that in the neighbourhood of Búzios, there is a deposit of clay which attracts some eminent craft potters; it was also said to be a good place in which to buy all kinds of fruit and vegetables, at prices much lower than in Rio. I decided therefore, to pay the place a short visit.

On arrival, we anchored close to a salvage vessel and soon the owner came over to *Keramos* for a welcoming chat, which resulted in us being invited to his house, to meet the family. They were engaged in salvaging treasure from HMS *Thetis*, which sank off Cabo Frio in 1830. Some members of the family assisted Phillipe on the salvage work, while his wife, Claudine, supervised a team of workers at the house, who were engaged in cleaning and restoring the many valuable items. They showed us some of the fine pieces recently salvaged and Phillipe gave me a Bolivian coin, which had been recovered from the captain's cabin.

Besides their undoubted skill in the salvage business, the various members of the family were accomplished musicians and dancers. The daughter, Rosina, demonstrated the tricky art of samba, which requires every part of the body to twist and gyrate to the pronounced beat of the music, while keeping the head absolutely still. Her attempts to teach us how to perform the dance, were not particularly successful, as she stood on a chair to hold the tiro's head, while pleading, "Come on – let those hips spin". Seafarers make friends very quickly, but unfortunately, they are so often lost, just as quickly – as was the case on this occasion.

A very pleasant sail, during which we caught two large marlin, took us to Vitória, where I had a business engagement. The entrance to the harbour rates only second to Rio, for the beauty of its setting. Apparently, yachts seldom stay in the city centre, as there is a more salubrious anchorage upriver. But I decided to anchor just a few yards from the principal street in the business quarter, and on the opposite side of which, was a large office block. Possibly because the office girls in the building rarely had an opportunity to welcome yachts, dozens of them leaned out of the windows to greet us by waving frantically. In such a situation, it was only natural for the crew to assemble on deck and acknowledge the reception by waving back. Soon large pieces of cardboard were being hung from the windows bearing inviting messages, including names, redezvous, times – and much more! That evening I found myself alone on Keramos – at any rate that is my story.

When it was time to leave Vitória, we were refused clearance because we had insulted Brazil, by displaying a Brazillian courtesy flag, that was smaller than the British ensign at the stern. Normally, the courtesy flags are about eighteen inches long (as was ours) and to fly them is not obligatory – nevertheless, the port official maintained that we had committed a serious offence.

Accordingly, we were reported to the British Vice Consul, who later that day, came on board with a police officer. When the Vice Consul confirmed the situation, I suggested that to solve the problem, we would fly a very small ensign. This, however, was not acceptable, as the insult had already been committed. To get the required port clearance, it would be necessary to go into the city and buy a Brazillian flag larger than our ensign. The only one we could find was enormous and cost the equivalent of £22. We flew the wretched thing for about ten minutes and when out of sight, from the port, it was taken down. We eventually sold it to a port official in Amazonia, for about £25.

Our next port of call was Salvador – until 1763 the capital of Brazil. The city is of interest because it is on two distinct levels, connected by four large lifts. As it is the centre for the coffee industry, I was anxious to ascertain how the coffee was processed, because I envisaged the possibility of it being ground in the Vibro-Mill. Indeed some time later, 50 of the mills were bought by the Brazillian government, for shipment to Salvador.

During the previous April, the builders of Keramos had sent a consignment of spare parts to Madeira, for collection when we arrived there, but due to some strange blunder, the parcel arrived in the Azores. After much delay, it was returned to England and then forwarded to Salvador. Consequently, one of the first things we did on arrival, was to enquire about our long-lost parcel. Nobody knew, or wanted to know, anything about it, but when we went over to the airport, we were told that we could look for it in the parcel store. We were then shown into a room, where there were quite literally, thousands of packages piled on top of each other, to a height of more than six feet. After three of us had worked for about a couple of hours, during which time we must have handled most of the store's contents, we found our much battered parcel. On taking it to the check-out desk, the official demanded a considerable sum of money; when I asked what it was for, he said, "It is the normal handling charge".

All the items in the parcel had been wrapped individually in newspaper, and I vividly recall the sight of the crew carefully unfolding each scrap of paper, in order to glean news that was more than six months old.

When we came to leave Salvador, we had another brush with officialdom, due to a particular individual wishing to put his personal pursuits before duty. The crew member who spoke Portuguese, would go to the official's office and find him leaning back in a big armchair, with a girl on his knee. When asked for the necessary exit document, he would say, "Can't you see I am busy – come back when I am not busy". On being asked when that would be, he would reply, "I don't know –you had better ask her". Fortunately, the time came when the poor man required a respite from his arduous duties; a junior then deputised, from whom we succeeded in getting the required clearance authorisation, to leave for Recife on 17 September.

Recife has a large commercial harbour, but the entrance to the yacht harbour is along a narrow winding channel and as the tide was at about half-ebb, we only had a few inches of water under the keel. In the harbour, we met up with a couple of yachts seen previously, but we soon found many new friends. On one yacht, we met Emilio Salvi, the Belgian Consul, who had previously held the world championship for the Snipe Class of racing dinghy. He had a 300 acre farm on which he raised beef cattle and also a large orange grove. We were happy to receive gifts of magnificent beef and sacks of superb oranges. He had spent many years developing a new type of orange and kindly brought us some from a recent crop; I can honestly say they were easily the best I have ever tasted – large, easy to peel, juicy, very sweet and with a wonderful distinctive flavour.

On the next yacht to *Keramos*, was a psychologist who was employed on research work for the Brazillian government. He was visiting prisons to interview criminals, whose brothers were outstandingly successful in life. The object was to find out why two men, with the same parents and the same environmental background, should come to find themselves in such widely different situations. At the time, his work was not complete, but he was convinced that psychological factors would be shown to provide much of the answer to the fascinating problem. He told me that in many cases criminals had followed the same route, which very briefly was: envy of the bright brother – desire for equal success – frustration – desperation – criminality.

Previously, he had been researching candomblé, the local Africa-derived religion, which is the counterpart of Rio's macumba. He had found that the people who practised candomblé were generally very gullible and therefore, easily raised to a state of frenzy by a kind of mass hynotism; this being induced by rhythmic drum beats to stupefy the audio senses and rhythmic movement – swaying from side to side or bobbing up and down in unison – to stupefy the visual senses. After the assembly has been appropriately conditioned by such means, the various religious rites are enacted, and when the people have witnessed them a few times, they soon come to be accepted as a normal experience.

The followers of candomblé take very great care to ensure that nobody photographs the rites, but my friend, as part of his research project, had attended many assemblies with a well concealed camera. Consequently, he was able to show me just what goes on – and I can quite understand why they do not want the world at large to know.

One of my reasons for calling at Recife, was to visit Ceramica Santa Antonio, a large tile works where I found much interest and was able to introduce the President to the use of zircon opacifiers. I also visited their associate company, which produces industrial alcohol from sugar cane.

In Recife, our crew was augmented by the arrival from England of Alan Kirby, who had kindly agreed to assist us on the voyage into Amazonia, and subsequently to Grenada. Alan, in addition to being one of Britain's top nuclear scientists, is an experienced and enthusiastic yachtsman and an accomplished photographer, specializing in the production of audio-visual programmes. He had periodically sailed on the first *Keramos*, including her last voyage under my command, when she made the passage from Malta to Cannes in very bad weather. When he arrived in Recife, he was heavily laden with letters, parcels, and by no means least – a comprehensive collection of English newspapers.

It took a long time to bid farewell to all our good friends, before making our departure from the lovely city of Recife – known as the Venice of Brazil, due to its many waterways, canals and picturesque bridges.

A great deal of survey work was being carried out in Amazonia, with a view to the future exploitation of its various mineral resources. Some of the minerals were of interest to the ceramic industry and as these were being handled by companies in Belém, I planned to go there, in order to locate a suitable shipping agent. To reach Belém, it was necessary to enter the Amazon delta and then sail up the mighty river. As the distance to Belém from Recife is about 1,300 sea miles, I decided to break the voyage about half-way, by calling at Fortaleza, where we could take on stores and obtain first-hand information regarding navigation on one of the world's most dangerous rivers.

We were away from Recife at 0910 hr, on 4 October and soon *Keramos* was crashing through majestic dark-blue waves, under full working sails. As the N.E. corner of Brazil is littered with coral reefs and wrecks, we kept about 25 miles off shore. The ship's log records many tropical sea birds and some exceptionally playful dolphins, one of which could make two complete rolls while airborne. These and the quite fantastic sun sets, kept Alan very busy with his camera.

It is a scientific fact that when the sun sets, there is a green flash at the precise moment when the red orb sinks below the horizon; it is only observed under certain conditions and is best seen at sea in the tropics. Accordingly, during every sunset, Alan would be found wedged into a strategic position on deck, with his camera aimed to the west and waiting for that decisive moment, when he could record on film the elusive green flash – it was to be a considerable time before his patience was ultimately rewarded.

We made good time to Fortaleza, where we dropped anchor in the open roadstead during the early hours of 7 October. The town has an excellent market where we were able to purchase long term provisions, in addition to a wide range of wonderful fresh fruit and vegetables. As a fishing port, it is famous for the *jangadas* – the quite remarkable local fishing craft. These consist of a raft, made by lashing together a number of bamboo poles, and a free standing mast carrying a lug-sail, consisting of old sugar sacks stitched together.

They are manned by a crew of two; one man steering with an oar and trimming the sail, while the other attends to the fishing. They stand on the bamboo poles, which are continually awash, as the frail craft skim at high speed over the waves. The skill with which these simple craft are handled in the big seas is quite remarkable; indeed it has to be, to enable them to venture far out to sea. They return with their day's catch around mid-afternoon, during the strong on-shore breeze, and to see the dozens and dozens of craft racing home and running up onto the shore, is an unforgettable sight.

We left Fortaleza at 1730 hr, on 15 October and soon found the favourable trade winds to speed us on our way to São Luis. Here navigation became very difficult, due to the mudflats which extend more than ten miles out to sea. Farther out still, there is a maze of coral reefs, on one of which the *Marie Celeste* foundered. It was necessary therefore, to steer a careful course through the narrow channel between the mudflats and the reefs, without the aid of radar, as the land hereabouts is very low lying. Our task was made even more difficult by a violent electrical storm and tropical downpour. But at the very moment when all our difficulties lay behind us, the clouds rolled away and we then had a clear blue sky and a blazing hot sun.

21

THE AMAZON ADVENTURE

While we were still 350 miles from the Amazon delta, the colour of the sea began to change, and soon it was chocolate brown, due to the huge amount of mud brought down by the great river. It is said that at times, the waters of the Amazon can discolour the Atlantic for more than 300 miles out to sea; as the delta is about 185 miles wide, a vast area of muddy water is then produced. The river also brings down great quantities of debris of all kinds, including huge trees. Sometimes, large pieces of forested embankment, covering several acres, break away and float down river and out to sea – taking with them the indigenous animal and bird life.

The Amazon is 4030 miles long, but if one adds to this distance, the length of the shipping route through the delta, it becomes the longest river in the world – then being 50 miles longer than the Nile. However, where the river exceeds all other rivers by far, is in respect of the volume of flow; in one day the quantity of water would be sufficient to supply London for more than 20 years. Of the twenty longest rivers in the world, ten are tributaries of the Amazon, and some of these are considerably greater than many famous rivers such as the Danube, Euphrates, Rhine and Tagus.

The river is tidal for 500 miles and therefore, I planned to enter the delta on the flood tide, to get some assistance against the strong adverse current, and to reach the most difficult part of the channel by about half-flood on 21 October. By the afternoon of 20 October, we had reached Salinópolis, where we anchored in the open roadstead. I considered this would be a suitable starting point from which we could precisely time our approach to the delta.

Although the water was very discoloured, it was teeming with fish and in no time at all, we had caught sufficient to top-up the freezer. There were a few very small fishing craft – similar to the *jangadas,* but having brightly coloured triangular sails, with the apex pointing downwards. These appeared to be making big hauls without much effort, while the thousands of brightly coloured sea birds were swooping over the water and diving to get their share of the spoils. We were surprised to find *Keramos* surrounded by a large number of turtles. No doubt they too, were finding a plentiful supply of food, but why they should wish to congregate around a yacht, remained a mystery.

Soon after midnight we weighed anchor, and proceeded along the coast. After passing a low powered lighthouse on Pta. do Algodoal, there were no further navigation aids of any kind, to assist us in finding the entrance to the narrow, winding Espadarte Channel. All that could be seen was a maze of mudbanks, many of which dry-out completely at low tide. The Channel is well out of sight of land and all identifiable features are out of radar range, so one is compelled to rely upon careful dead reckoning, with an accurate assessment of the speed and direction of the strong and variable current. The Espadarte Channel is only used by small local vessels going as far as Belém; larger vessels going up to Manaus, or beyond, use one of the Macapa Channels, which are 175 miles or so, to the north.

The prime necessity was, of course, to monitor the depth of water on the recording echo-sounder and this task was allotted to Alan. I was laying-off courses on the chart and whenever Alan reported a reduction in depth, I would order the helmsman to make a course change; if the depth then decreased more rapidly we would alter course to the other side of the channel – in this way we endeavoured to keep in the deepest water.

After groping along in this manner for some time, we located by radar, a reflector on the vast Espadarte Shoal, the position of which is shown on the chart. This enabled us to accurately determine our position and set a new course. All on board had an important duty to perform, including the lookout man at the bow, who was relied upon to guide us round the floating debris – large clusters of mangrove being the most prevalent.

Eventually, we sighted the island of Mosqueiro and altered course to leave it close to port. From this point onwards, navigation became somewhat less hazardous and as the adverse current eased, we began to make good progress towards Belém. When we estimated the city was about twenty-five miles away, we were amazed to see on the skyline immediately ahead, many tall buildings, towers, shining domes and indeed all the signs of a large conurbation. It was all very mysterious, as we knew there was no other urban development in the locality and our navigation could not have been as bad as that! Then after about five minutes, the apparition slowly faded, and we realised it had been a mirage. A couple of hours or so later, the same skyline reappeared – but this time it was for real.

In due course we anchored off the fishing boat quay. By this time it was quite dark, except for the vivid and almost continuous lightning flashes. To say it was also raining would be to give entirely the wrong impression, because it was more like standing under a waterfall. So, with all the hatches closed and the air-conditioning working flat-out, we all went below to enjoy a well earned meal. The log-book records a repast consisting of some of the recently caught fish, breadfruit chips, wonderful bread made while we were at anchor off Salinopólis and tropical fruit pie, with ice-cream.

The anchorage was exposed to a strong current, which would have made getting ashore in the tender quite difficult, and therefore, early the following morning, we took *Keramos* farther upriver and anchored close to the Pará Yacht Club.

On going ashore, we were given handbills printed in Portuguese, French and English, which were advertising in glowing terms, what was claimed to be the world's largest house of ill repute, with a cosmopolitan staff of over 3,000. I was later told by a shipping agent that the clients are mainly *garimpeiros* – men from the essentially all-male communities in the interior of the country, who are prospecting for gold. Periodically, they visit Belém, either by boat or light aircraft, to sell their gold, to make essential purchases, but also to have a wild night out on the town. The girls are said to be paid in gold dust, the basic rate being five grams per session, and such is the volume of business, that twenty tons, or more, of gold are believed to reach the bullion market indirectly, by this surprising route, during the course of a single year.

Belém provides a strange mixture of modern shops and old established markets, such as the *Ver-o-Peso*, where every stall has a large set of brass beam-scales, to enable customers to 'see the weight'. Originally, it was a fish market, so seeing the weight made sense, but now, the market sells a wide range of goods, which all go on the scales and are sold by weight – even items such as shoes.

Another old market is in the business of selling superstition and witchcraft, in the form of sparrow-hawk skeletons to ward off the influences of the evil eye, alligator and shark's teeth, dolphin-eye amulets to prevent the loss of a loved one, essence of *uirapuru* (a legendry Brazillian songbird) to attract lovers, music shell rosaries, jaguar tails, boa-constrictor skulls, sea horses and many pottery figures designed to combat every kind of evil.

Belém is just south of the equator. It is not surprising therefore, that the temperature is generally well over 100°F and the humidity close to 100%. It is said to rain on every day in the year. During our stay it rained very heavily on three or four occasions each day, but there was always a very heavy downpour during the late afternoon. On *Keramos* we operated the air-conditioning continuously, and thereby enjoyed a comparatively cool 80°F. All the air-intakes were covered by mosquito screens, because the Amazonian flies can cause pain, distress and in some cases quite serious illness. We were able to obtain gadgets, which when plugged into the electricity sockets, produced an aromatic vapour which instantly killed any fly or insect that found its way below deck. In that part of the world, malaria is particularly rampant and therefore, we had been using an appropriate prophylactic treatment since our arrival in Recife.

Alan was anxious to get away from the city and see something of the real Amazonia. Consequently, after I had completed my business, he invited me to join him on a most interesting expedition. We started by flying in a DC3 over the waters of the Amazon to the island of Marajó, which is the largest fluvial island in the world. We landed at Soure and then transferred to a small launch, which for 2½ hours chugged along a succession of waterways and through spectacular rain forest, until we reached Fazendas Bonjardlm. Here we met Castro Ribeiro and his charming family, who in addition to being our esteemed hosts were to act as guides and wildlife mentors during our stay.

Immediately on arrival, we were taken by Land Rover to see water buffaloes, crocodiles, monkeys, a great variety of colourful birds, including the rare scarlet ibis and swarms of psychedelic moths, the size of dinner plates.

One evening after dining on crocodile steaks, we went out with torches to look for the live reptiles. When the light from a torch falls on the eyes of a crocodile, two characteristic pinkish lights are reflected. In this way, we were able to locate about twenty of these treacherous creatures, which would not normally have been seen in daylight.

Another day, Alan and I took out a heavy punt onto a swamp, to enable Alan to silently approach and photograph birds in the overhanging trees. We were told that in addition to crocodiles, the water was teeming with *piranha*, whose teeth are as sharp as razors. Indeed we could distinctly see the *piranha* in the clear water, and occasionally they would leap two or three feet into the air. Then, just as Alan had succeeded in stalking a particularly colourful toucan, one of the leaping *piranha* landed right in the boat and flapped around in a threatening manner. Fortunately, while we were trying to decide who was going to tackle the intruder – it jumped back into the water.

The population of Amazonia is very low, but the importance of the area to the world's ecology becomes apparent, when it is realized that its vast rainforests supply half of the world's oxygen and a fifth of the supply of fresh water. The fauna of Amazonia includes 250 types of mammals, 1,500 species of fish (the Congo basin, its closest rival, has less than a thousand) and 1,800 identified species of birds.

All too soon, it was time to leave this wonderland of nature and return through the majestic forests to Soure, where we hired a small four seater plane to take us back to Belém. Only from the air can one really appreciate the complexity of the vast delta system.

To make the best use of the tides for our return through the Espadarte Channel and back to the Atlantic, I decided to anchor overnight, off a small island (Ilha Jutuba) which lies about 50 miles from the start of the difficult section. On the island, we found a village community living in houses built on twenty feet high stilts, in order to provide protection from the river when in flood. Access to the houses was by crude ladders, up which many scared children scampered, when they saw strange white men approaching from a boat, the like of which they had most likely never seen before.

We weighed anchor at 0700 hr, on 31 October and made good progress for the first few hours, but just as we reached the tricky channel, we had one of the worst tropical storms we had yet experienced. It was therefore, with much relief, that we eventually located the radar reflector on the Espadarte shoal; surprisingly it showed that we were right on course.

After safely reaching open water, we sailed well out to sea before turning north, so as to avoid the many wrecks which litter the mouth of the river. Consequently, we did not cross the equator until 2147 hr. During the following twenty hours, as we sailed past the world's greatest delta, the colour of the sea remained a drab muddy brown.

Many of the creatures that live in these waters, where visibility is virtually non-existent, have evolved senses other than sight, to facilitate mobility and the search for food. Some have developed the sense of touch, such as the cat-fish with its long tentacles and the river dolphin with its long sensitive nose, while the electric eels react to magnetic influences.

Quite suddenly, during the following morning, we found that we were once again sailing over the familiar dark blue waves, flecked with white – and we realised that we had at last left behind, the waters of the prodigious Amazon.

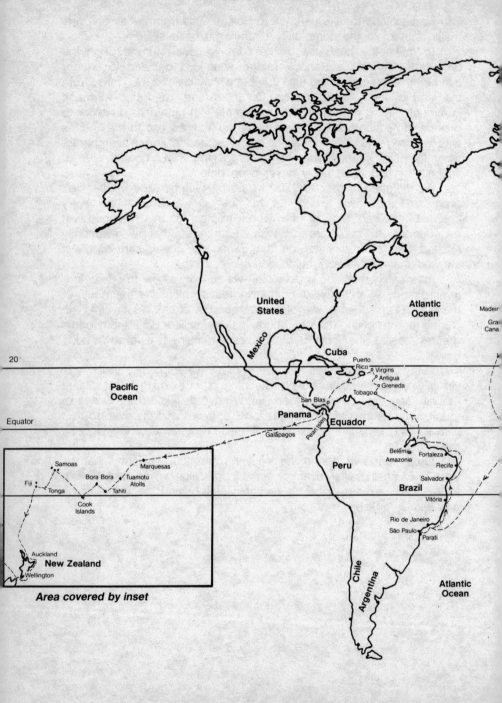

United States

Atlantic
Ocean

Madeir

Gra
Cana

20

Mexico

Cuba

Puerto
Rico

Virgins

Antigua

Greneda

Tobago

San Blas

Pacific
Ocean

Panama

Equador

Galápagos

Pearl Isles

Belém

Fortaleza

Equator

Amazonia

Recife

Peru

Salvador

Brazil

Vitória

Samoas

Marquesas

Fiji

Bora Bora

Tuamotu
Atolls

Tonga

Tahiti

Rio de Janeiro

Cook
Islands

São Paulo

Parati

Auckland

New Zealand

Wellington

Chile

Argentina

Atlantic
Ocean

Area covered by inset

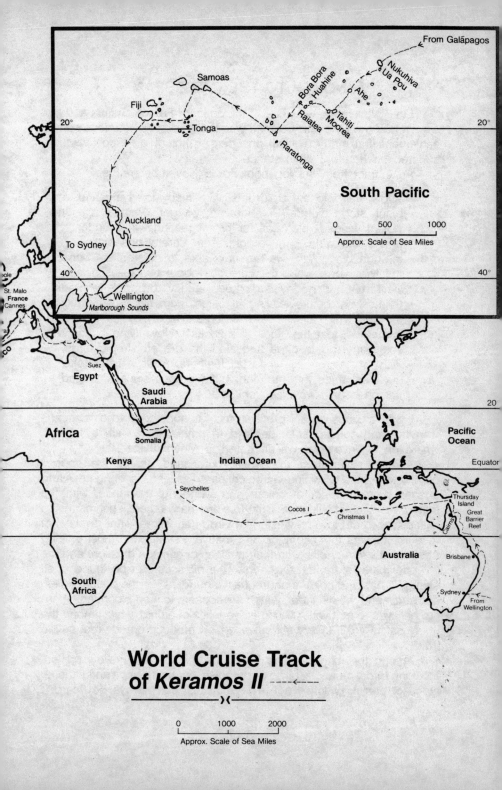

From Galápagos

Nukuhiva
Ua Pou

Samoas

Bora Bora
Huahine
Ahe

Fiji

20°   20°

Tonga   Raiatea   Tahiti
                                                        Moorea

Raratonga

South Pacific

0   500   1000

Approx. Scale of Sea Miles

Auckland

To Sydney

ole

St. Malo
France
Cannes

40°   40°

Wellington
Marlborough Sounds

Suez

Egypt

**Saudi
Arabia**

20

Somalia

Africa   **Pacific
Ocean**

Kenya   **Indian Ocean**   Equator

Seychelles
                                                    Thursday
                                                    Island
                              Cocos I   Great
                                        Christmas I   Barrier
                                                                 Reef

Australia   Brisbane

**South
Africa**
                                        Sydney
                                              From
                                              Wellington

World Cruise Track
of *Keramos II* ---◄----
—✕—

0   1000   2000

Approx. Scale of Sea Miles

22

NORTH TO THE CARIBBEAN

On 3 November, we were off the coast of French Guiana and had Devil's Island on the port beam. It was in the island's notorious convict settlement that many political prisoners – including Alfred Dreyfus – suffered an horrendous existance.

An extract from the log book for 5 November reads:

"Now well into the Doldrums, with many low-lying and very black storm clouds. Under some, we get torrential rain and violent winds, which call for promt reefing, while under others, the wind is quite light. After careful observation through binoculars, we are now able to differentiate between the two types, while they are still about two miles away. White capped noddy birds keep landing on deck to preen themselves, before leaving to catch more flying-fish, which they do while the fish are airborne. The flying-fish are so numerous, that they look like flocks of low flying birds. We see many frigate birds and also the graceful tropic birds, with their yard-long white tail feathers. A large fish broke our steel trace this morning, but we have since managed to get on board two nice *bonitos*".

I was anxious not to proceed too far north, due to a hurricane warning, and consequently decided to pay a short visit to Tobago, where on 7 November, we anchored in Mount Irvine Bay.

After a swim from the white, coral-sand beach, Alan and I penetrated inland to explore a tropical paradise. The flowering trees and bushes provide a riot of colour and wonderful fragrance, with the *frangipani* much in evidence. But there are many others, such as the so called Queen of Flowers, which is a large tree with brilliant displays of rose-like flowers in white, pink and mauve. Perhaps the most striking trees are the *immortelle*, with their masses of crimson blossom and the lavender blue *jacaranda*. Of course, the *hibiscus* can be found in all shapes, sizes and colours and equally abundant are the *bougainvillea, poinsettia* and the *oleander,* which never seem to stop blooming. There are believed to be over 700 named varieties of orchid, while among the many palms are the very tall *pewa*, which produce orange-red, edible fruit.

Among the many striking birds, are the toucans, yellow orioles, mocking birds, motmots, birds-of-paradise, humming birds and various types of parrot, which if not always visible, can always be heard.

Our anchorage was quite close to the famous Bucco coral reef, where the wonders and beauty of the underwater world can easily be seen without diving, providing a visit is made at low water. The depth on the reef is then only about four feet, so providing suitable shoes are worn, it is possible to walk on the sea bed. The various types of coral can be found in isolated clusters, and due to the crystal clear water and the light reflected from the white sand, everything can be clearly seen as if illuminated from below by arc-light.

The countless millions of tiny, soft-bodied creatures known as coral polyps build themselves protective shelters in limestone and when they die, the skeletons remain to add new layers of limestone to the reef. In this way, the reefs grow, year by year, to create fantastic and beautiful shapes and forms. The different types are often named after natural objects, which their shapes resemble; typical examples being star coral, stag's horn coral and brain coral. Most coral is white, but it can be found in any colour and is then exceedingly beautiful when illuminated by the bright light.

Feeding on the coral are thousands and thousands of small fish, on which the larger fish feed. These are to be seen in all the glittering colours of the rainbow, while the variety of species is quite incredible – over 300 have been identified on this particular reef.

Some of the most spectacular are the kingfish and the *wahoo*, which can be as much as 6 feet in length and 80 pounds in weight. Also the moonfish, so called because of its vivid silver colouring and large bright eyes; the striking bluestriped grunt, with its alternating blue and yellow stripes on head and body, together with a bright red mouth; the very colourful queen angelfish, being almost luminous with its yellow-orange and bright blue stripes; the foureye butterfly fish, which owes its name to the large eye-like black dots near the tail, which together with the black band through the true eyes, is thought to provide protection by confusing predators; the long and thin bodied trumpet fish, which hang vertically in the water and the many varieties of striped parrotfish, which are to be found in a vast range of colours and patterns.

We learned that hurricane David had caused tremendous damage in the Windward and Leeward Islands, but as it had then moved away to the north, I concluded that it would be prudent to continue the voyage to St George's in Grenada, where, after a fast passage, we arrived early on 9 November. The customs officer told me that I reminded him of a friend of his, who came fom Surinam. He said, "For one moment, I thought him was you". Then after a pregnant pause, he added, "No, I mean you was him". I am still trying to fathom his logic!

Unfortunately, it was now time for Alan to return to England but he was able to take back a large number of exposed films, with which to prepare an audio-visual programme that was to provide a lasting record of our adventures in Amazonia.

The only facility in the West Indies for getting *Keramos* out of the water, was in St George's. I had therefore, previously arranged for this to be done, to enable the under-water hull to be scrubbed clear of barnacles and then sprayed with anti-fouling paint. The necessary paint had been despatched, a month previously, by air from England to Grenada via Barbados, but on making enquiries, I was informed that the paint was still in Barbados. In spite of all our efforts, we failed to get it delivered to St George's and consequently, the boatyard had to use an American paint that they happened to have in stock.

St George's is an attractive, but quaint town, with much of its charm being derived from the blend of French and English cultures. The people are exceedingly friendly. Possibly because of my age, everyone insisted on calling me, "Dad" – I did not mind when this came from the adults, but it could be rather embarrassing when groups of young children loudly hailed me by yelling, "Dad".

In all our ports of call, the crew were always eager to integrate with the local people – this certainly applied to Murray Aitkin. After graduating in Chemistry, Murray worked for several years in South Africa. He then sailed In a race from Capetown to Montevideo and joined *Keramos* in Rio. During our stay in Grenada, he visited a village disco and later gave us an amusing account of the experience, in which he said, " . . . the lights were so dim and the girls so black, that all I could see when dancing, were a pair of shining eyes and two rows of flashing white teeth. In fact the only way you could differentiate betwen the girls and the fellas was by the pitch of the voice – and even that was sometimes deceptive. When I was dancing with one girl, a boy tried to 'cut-in', but the girl pushed him away saying, 'I'm checkin out this one first".

Murray could always be relied upon to spin a good yarn. I well remember him telling us that, when he was very young, his mother opened two bottles of stout, preparatory to making Christmas puddings, but while his mother's back was turned, Murray drank the contents of both bottles. On discovering what had happened, his mother rushed him off in great panic, to a doctor, who after carefully examining Murray, said, "I don't think he will come to any harm, but I must say that right now, he is the happiest wee boy I have ever seen".

After I had changed the position of the anchor a couple of times in Vitória, because I was not content with the security of the holding, it was

Murray who was heard to say, "When H.L.P. gets to Paradise, if the anchorage is not to his satisfaction, I don't think he will be staying long".

Much interest and often humour, is to be found by noting contrasting attitudes, in various countries, towards everyday situations. For example, when I went into a music shop in St George's, the records were not classified as 'Pop', 'Classical' and 'Easy Listening', as we might find in Britain, but as 'Hot', 'Sweet' and 'Jumpy'. Outside the shop men were mending the road, and apparently for the benefit of nearby residents, a large sign had been erected which read, "NO TOOTIN".

After leaving Grenada on 27 November, we called at several of the delightful small islands to the north, known as the Grenadines, before visiting Barbados, where we anchored in Carlisle Bay and close to the Holiday Inn.

Barbados is a beautiful island, which is still known as 'Little England', due to its long association with Britain. It retains the English legal system and of course, everyone speaks 'some' English. I had previously arranged for money to be transferred from England, to a Bank in Bridgetown and when I went to collect it, the teller said the manager would have to deal with the matter. When the manager appeared, he asked for my address, I replied, "Yacht *Keramos*" and before I could continue, he asked me to spell it. Whereupon, I spelled "K-E-R-A-M-O-S" – he then said, "Please spell 'yacht'".

On the approach of Christmas, arrangements were made for members of the crew to fly back to England, for a couple of weeks vacation, and for my wife and daughter Diane to join me, and assist in sailing *Keramos* to several of the interesting islands in the West Indies, including Antigua, where we arrived on 23 December.

We had been told by various yachtsmen, who had visited English Harbour, that we should anchor in Freeman's Bay and await a visit from the harbour master, who was a notoriously difficult character. I therefore acted upon this advice, and when the harbour master eventually came on board, I saw that he had two decidedly black eyes. I learned later, that on the previous day, the crew of a French yacht had not been prepared to take his insults, and after blacking his eyes, they had thrown him overboard and departed. It was not surprising therefore, that we should find him quite amenable, but it was not to be all plain sailing because he made it very clear that we would not be permitted to take *Keramos* into the harbour, until we had completed an 'Entry Form'. When I requested a copy of the said Form, he told me they could be obtained from a particular stationers shop in St John's and to get there would take at least half-an-hour in a taxi – then with an impertinent smile, he added, "It'll be no use going now, because the shop will be closed this afternoon".

After all the hassle, we eventually managed to get *Keramos* moored stern-to, on the quay of the delightful harbour, where Horatio Nelson had established a fine dockyard and based his squadron. His well preserved house overlooks the harbour, as does Clarence House, built by the Duke of Clarence, who was later to become William IV of England (the Sailor King). English Harbour has, by tradition, become a rendezvous for British yachtsmen at Christmas. Consequently, we were able to celebrate the festive season with all the usual convivial merrymaking, and as the next yacht had a Scottish crew, we enjoyed a wild Hogmanay (complete with bagpipes) as a bonus.

While *Keramos* was in Antigua, we made two crew changes. The first to join us was Kenneth Isted, an ex-naval officer and an enthusiastic yachtsman, who for several years, owned and sailed a fine old ketch from his home town, Lymington. Also joining us was Nicholas Allen, an engineer with considerable experience in marine design and construction. He had recently crossed the Atlantic from England in a small yacht.

The anti-fouling paint that should have arrived in Grenada, for use when *Keramos* was out of the water, was at that time still in Barbados. Consequently, I had arranged for it to be retained there, for later collection. However, when we subsequently arrived in Barbados, I found that it had been sent to Grenada. I therefore gave instructions for it to be forwarded to Antigua. On our arrival in Antigua, I learned that the itinerant paint had been returned to London. Accordingly, as Murray was on vacation in England, I asked him to bring it back as personal luggage, together with various other items for *Keramos*.

When Murray returned to Antigua, it was discovered that he had all the parcels except the paint. Enquiries revealed that it had not been taken off the plane in Antigua, so was once again back in Barbados. In desperation, I contacted a shipping agent in St John's who arranged for the wretched paint to be delivered to Antigua by boat, with the result that it finally reached *Keramos* the day before she made her departure, *en route* for the Panama Canal, on 16 February, 1980.

After visiting several of the Virgin Islands, we sailed to Ponce, the second largest town in Puerto Rico. The short stay there, is memorable due to Ken's kind invitation for us all to join him for dinner at the Yacht Club. Apparently some time earlier in the day, the staff at the club had attended the birthday party of one of their number; as a result, all the waiters were blind drunk – the waiter at our table being the worst of the lot.

When we attempted to place our orders, he regarded the matter as one huge joke and fell about in uncontrolled laughter. It came as no surprise therefore, to find that what we were eventually served, bore no relation whatsoever, to what we had endeavoured to order. As he was quite incapable of carrying any of the dishes, everything had to be brought to the table on a trolley, but as we could not persuade him to take any dishes away, those remaining from previous courses just piled-up on the table.

The highlight of the hilarious evening occurred, however, when Ken gave his camera to our jovial waiter and asked him to take a photograph of us, at the table. The man held the camera to his eye and while swaying all around the place, kept backing away in order to get us all in. At the next table there was a young couple, closely *tête-à-tête*, and obviously wanting to be very much left alone. Soon our waiter cum photographer was leaning backwards over their table, at such an angle, that the young man was no longer able to gaze wistfully into the eyes of his beloved – whereupon he unceremoniously pushed the waiter away. What the waiter then said, we shall never know, but he appeared to be trying to explain, that he had been asked to take a photograph, and that was what he was jolly well going to do.

During the wrestling bout that followed, flashes from the camera could occasionally be seen, and it was not surprising therefore, that when Ken eventually got the film developed, there was only a miscellaneous collection of photographs of the ceiling and close-ups of the angry young man and his scared inamorata. There were however, one or two impressionist images, showing a group of people and a table – apparently hurtling through the air at great speed.

As we left the club, I thanked Ken for the much appreciated hospitality. He said he was sorry the service had been so diabolical. I had to agree it could have been better, but stressed that what it lacked, was more than made up for, by the excellence of the floor-show.

23

THE UNIQUE SAN BLAS ISLANDS

We made our departure from Ponce, at 1700 hr on 29 February, to sail the 800 miles across the Caribbean Sea to the San Blas Islands, prior to our passage through the Panama Canal. The islands lie off the coast of Panama and are about 125 miles from the entrance to the Canal. The direct course would have taken us close to the coast of Columbia but we had been warned to keep well clear, due to the risk of piracy. Apparently, many yachts were being stolen at sea, for subsequent use in the smuggling of drugs. Consequently, we kept a very careful look-out, with our various weapons close at hand.

The immediate objective was the small island of Porvenir, to the north and east of which, lie extensive reefs. In order to make the approach, it was therefore, necessary to determine our position very accurately, and then steer a course to clear the shoal water. Soon we could just make out the palm fringed island and the big seas breaking on the reefs.

The only local aids to navigation are the many visible wrecks, and as the position of some were marked on our rough chart, we were able to find a way round the western end of the island and then via a twisting pass, to the anchorage on the leeward side. After some very anxious moments it was a relief to finally drop anchor and dive into the warm, crystal clear water for a refreshing swim.

We were now about 300 yards away from Porvenir but we could see three other islands, none being more than about 250 yards in diameter. On each, there were many closely packed palm-leaf huts, under the shade of tall and graceful coconut palms. Three of us went ashore on Porvenir and discovered a world, such as we had never seen before.

The San Blas Islands are the legal and exclusive territory of the dwarf Cuna Indians, who are believed to be the last of the true-blooded Carib strain, that inhabited the Caribbean before the Spanish conquest. These people, who have occupied the islands since the dawn of history, have never been conquered, and are today considered unique in having preserved their tribal customs, by freely resisting the so-called benefits of Western culture.

Work is divided equally between men and women, but women play a dominant role in household affairs and the social life. Brides not only choose their husbands, but the young couple will live with the bride's parents, in one *bohio*. This female dominance is reflected in the mode of dress, for while the men dress simply in subdued colours, the women are spectacularly attired in brightly coloured wrap-around skirts, and blouses which are adorned, front and back, with the dazzling molas. These are panels of cloth on which have been worked intricate coloured designs.

The designing and making of molas, by a technique known as reverse appliqué, is quite definitely an art. The method of construction involves the selection of several pieces of cloth, each of a different colour, which are placed one on top of the other and then stitched together at the edges. Holes of the desired shape are then cut in the upper layers to expose cloth of the required colour, after which the layers of cloth are tacked together at the boundary of the shape. This procedure is repeated as required, until an intricate, multi-coloured design has been built up.

The designs incorporate a motif, such as a bird, specific to each island and a further motif, specific to each family. But, in the main, the designs are highly imaginative and fanciful, so that quite often the symbolism is completely incomprehensible to all, except the particular family. Among the components of designs can be found stylized birds, fish and beasts, together with angels and christian crosses – as well as devils and pagan images.

The girls learn the art and craft of mola making at an early age and most, later in life, become highly skilled. Every woman has a collection of molas for daily use, but she will have spent many long hours making one, or more, specially for use on ceremonial occasions. The molas can be bought, but as might be expected, the really good ones are very expensive.

The women make themselves even more colourful, by applying pink rouge high on the cheeks and by drawing a black line vertically down the nose. Their elaborate gold and silver jewellery is worn throughout the day and includes necklaces, earrings, armlets and nose rings; they also wear leg and arm wraps of colourful beads. The various items of jewellery, and in particular the gold nose rings, have been handed down through many generations, since long before the time when South American gold acquired a commercial value.

The huts in which the people live are, more or less, open structures, consisting of a thatched roof of palm leaves, supported on bamboo poles. Inside, there is virtually no furniture, as the people sit on mats placed on the white coral-sand and sleep in hammocks, which are folded during the day. The huts are built close together, while the sand between them is carefully raked to provide a smooth clean surface. There is no ground vegetation, which no doubt, accounts for the absence of animals, snakes and insects.

I was anxious to visit some of the more inaccessible islands in the group, which visitors do not normally reach, in order to see the people living as they have done, almost without change, down through the centuries. So, early one morning, we sailed out through the pass and then in a roughly S.W. direction to the Golfo de San Blas, where we soon found ourselves amidst a maze of reefs and small uninhabited islands, most of which were not shown on our crude chart. A warning note on the chart did, however, state that the information had been taken from an ancient Spanish chart and ". . . . should not be relied upon". The problems of navigation were further compounded, by the edges of the reefs being almost vertical; as a result, the echo sounder failed to give advance warning of danger. In the circumstances, it was necessary to estimate the depth of water by observing its colour from an elevated position – where the sea bed consists of white sand or coral, the stronger the blue colour, the deeper the water.

From information obtained on Porvenir, I knew roughly where to find our small cluster of inhabited islets and eventually, after diligently following a meandering course, we saw rising smoke on the horizon. Soon, we found ourselves surrounded by young boys in dug-out canoes, who until our arrival, had been engaged in fishing. With this excited escort, we made our way towards the smoke and before long, we could see two small islands on which there were many huts.

I had been warned never to approach an island when red flags were being flown, as this indicated the carrying out of a devil exorcising ritual, which might last for a week or more; any stranger who interrupted these proceedings would certainly be taken to the meeting house, where the *Saila* (village chief) would pronounce the appropriate punishment. It was with some relief therefore, that no red flags could be seen. Consequently, we anchored close to the larger of the two islands.

We gathered from one of the fishermen, who spoke some Spanish, that this was Isla Tupo and if we wished to go into the village, we should first obtain permission from the *Saila*, whose hut he pointed out to us. We already knew that visitors were not allowed in the villages after dark and as by now, there was only about one more hour of daylight, we decided to defer our meeting with the *Saila*, until the following morning.

As darkness fell, not a glimmer of light could be seen from the island, nor a sound to be heard – it was difficult to believe that several hundred people were living within 400 yards of *Keramos*.

We had been told tradition demanded that we should make a presentation of a suitable gift to the *Saila*, when being granted an audience and that the most acceptable gift was tinned meat. So early the next day, and well armed with a large tin of bully-beef, four of us went ashore to call upon the *Saila*. We were received, with broad smiles, by the women of the household, who, after inviting us to enter one of the huts, gave us to understand that the *Saila* would soon see us; meantime we were introduced to several babies and felt much abashed, when they were thrust into our arms to hold. When I think back to the sight of my worldly fellow crew members, each holding a naked black baby, I cannot refrain from laughing – as I was obliged to do on that occasion.

Fortunately, the *Saila* soon appeared and we were relieved of our nursery duties. After being ushered into his inner sanctum, I handed over the gift, which by that time was regrettably somewhat moist – and not by sea water. However, it was graciously received and in a mixture of Indian, Spanish and a little English jargon, he asked what we required. I explained that we had sailed from Britain and were on our way to the Pacific, but would like to meet his people and see something of their activities.

He proved to be most co-operative, and insisted on personally showing us round the village to see the building of huts, the construction of dug-out canoes, weaving, and of course, the making of molas. Some of the women kindly dressed for us in their ceremonial costumes, and wore' large quantities of exquisite jewellery.

We were shown the fermentation of coconut milk to produce a potent liquor, which was to be consumed during the forthcoming fertility rites. From what we could make out, the young girls on reaching the age of puberty, take part in a day-long ceremony, in which their hair is cut short. Then while water is made to slowly drip onto their heads, the age-old rites are enacted. After the ceremony, there is much feasting, drinking, dancing and general merrymaking.

We were invited to attend the ceremony, but while it would undoubtedly have proved most interesting, we believed that our presence would have been an unreasonable intrusion into their private lives. Regretfully therefore, we felt obliged to decline. We did, however, agree to stay a further day with these kind people, during which we were granted the freedom of the two islands, over which our friendly *Saila* presided.

We endeavoured to return the hospitality, by entertaining many of the people on *Keramos* and joined the boys in their dug-out canoes, to try our hands at paddling and sailing these very unstable craft. There were many capsizes, and although communication was difficult, fortunately the language of laughter recognises no barriers.

Before leaving the islands, we entertained on board the *Saila*, two of his daughters and a granddaughter. The girls were dressed in their special occasion clothes and as they stepped on deck, they each presented me with a small mola. We handed round a large tin of assorted biscuits, into which they dipped both hands, cupped together and with the hands still held together, they very quickly disposed of the lot – they had no need for the plates which we offered. Tumblers containing orangeade were also held in both hands, just as they would hold a drinking coconut – while fizzy lemonade was regarded with deep suspicion. Sweets wrapped in paper were closely inspected but not eaten.

When we took the girls below deck, the first problem was to get them away from the large mirror in the saloon; by the way they kept performing and laughing, it was obvious they had not seen anything like it before. The galley with its array of cooking equipment made no impression on them at all. They seemed to accept that we slept on the bunks in the cabins but were obviously puzzled by the wash-basins. By miming, I tried to convey that we used them to wash our hands and faces, but when I turned on one of the taps and they saw the water gush out, they fled in terror back to the cockpit.

After one or two drinks, other than orangeade, the *Saila* became quite talkative. He told us that he had a wife and family on each of the two islands, but the family on one island is never permitted to visit the other island – only the *Saila* is allowed more than one wife. There is no water supply on the islands, other than by the collection of rainwater, therefore, the reaction of the girls to the sight and sound of tap-water was understandable.

He explained the significance of the jewellery worn by the girls, as each bangle, anklet and ring, conveys some personal message, from the previous wearer to the present wearer. He was particularly proud to tell us that the magnificent breast-piece worn by the granddaughter was of solid gold and of great value, not simply because of its considerable weight, but due to the very rare, pagan design. The San Blas Indians, it would seem, are God-fearing people, but their supreme God is a Cuna Indian presiding over Paradise, which is a white coral island in the sky. Suddenly, the *Saila* said he would have to leave, because in addition to his administrative duties, he was also the islands' doctor and it was necessary for him to visit a very sick boy, who was expected to die at sunset.

As the girls gleefully jumped into the tender, I feared that one of the precious gold items might disappear below the water, but all were eventually delivered safely on shore without undue incident – and we were left with treasured memories of these simple but fascinating and most kindly people.

Early next day, about thirty canoes assembled around *Keramos* and most came alongside, to enable the excited youngsters to jump aboard and bid us farewell. They left with us many gifts, including nuts, a wide selection of delicious fruit and some of their powerful alcoholic liquor. As we slowly sailed away, many of the canoes followed, until one by one, they left us and returned to allow their occupants to resume their unique way of life, which had been so rudely interrupted by our visit.

As the unforgettable isles faded in the distance, we fell into a deeply contemplative mood. During our short stay among the simple people of Tupo, we had learned much. While they had no understanding of modern transport, communication systems, the paraphernalia of war or even domestic items such as refrigerators and washing machines – which many of us consider indispensable – we had nevertheless, come to realize that there was nothing the 'developed world' could teach the islanders about the fundamentals of life, such as comradeship, compassion, sociability or even diligence. Indeed, if the yardstick for worthwhile existence was the sheer joy of living, then the primaeval culture of these kind people would, without doubt, reign supreme.

We retraced the tortuous path to Porvenir and then continued to historic Porto Bello, on the mainland, where we decided to stop overnight. It was here, in this peaceful spot that the adventurous Admiral Drake died and was buried at sea, out in the bay. Columbus used the natural harbour in 1502, and for more than two centuries, it was a Spanish garrison town. Still remaining, is the treasure house where gold from Peru was stored, prior to shipment by the galleons to Spain.

The following morning, we sailed over to Cristobal, preparatory to making a transit of the Panama Canal. This was to prove another most interesting experience.

24

THE HISTORIC PANAMA CANAL

Many books have been written on the building of the Panama Canal, but one of the best, must be David McCullough's, *The Path Between the Seas*, which is highly recommended to anyone wishing to fully appreciate the eventful history of this stupendous undertaking. The feat of connecting the two oceans by a canal, was not only a very great engineering accomplishment, but a continuing battle against overwhelming odds.

Around 1879, various routes for a canal were being considered, but Ferdinand de Lesseps, who had already succeeded in completing the Suez Canal, favoured a route closely following the line of the Colon to Panama City railway. He believed it would be possible to excavate a sea-level canal, without the need of locks, and for a venture of this kind, he succeeded in attracting sufficient investment to form a French company – but unfortunately, he badly underestimated the difficulties, and therefore the eventual costs.

His visit to Panama had been made during the dry season and consequently, he did not envisage the effect of the torrential rains in the wet season. The annual rainfall is about 120 inches, but it is because a great quantity of rain can fall in a short period of time, that was to prove so disastrous in bringing down the sides of the excavations. This was a particularly big problem in the Culebra Cut, where the planned depth of excavation was over 100 feet, with the anticipated width at the top about 670 feet. Here, steam bucket-excavators moved along railway tracks laid on a series of terraces, which were repeatedly washed away, taking with them the tracks and the excavators. As successive rain storms washed down more and more of the soft earth, the quantity of material that had to be removed continually increased, until finally the width of the Cut at the top was over 1,800 feet.

Equally disastrous was the great loss of life due to mortal diseases, chief of which were malaria and yellow fever. The typical malarial attack commenced with a feeling of intense cold, which brought on shivering, chattering of the teeth, and shaking so violent as to cause the patient's bed to move on the floor. This stage would be followed by high fever, burning thirst and drenching sweat. Those who survived (about 30%), would be left feeling completely debilitated mentally and physically. Acute depression would set in, to produce the melancholia that became so prevalent; encouraged no doubt, by the knowledge that a further distressing attack could occur, even if the person moved to a country considered free from the risk of malaria.

The onset of yellow fever was similar to that of malaria, with intense shivering, high fever and insatiable thirst, but additionally, it produced terrible headaches and pains in the back and legs. The patient would become extremely restless and begin to turn yellow, particularly in the face and eyes. During the final stages, he would spit mouthfuls of dark blood – the infamous and terrifying *vomito negro*, and within eight hours or so, he would be dead.

The man appointed to direct this immense project, the most ambitious engineering effort the world had, as yet seen, was Jules Isidore Dingler. He set about the gigantic task with great energy and declared that all the problems could, and would be overcome. He maintained that, "only drunkards and the dissipated take the yellow fever and die". To prove his point, he took out to Panama his wife, son, daughter and the daughter's fiancé. They were all enthusiastic equestrians and being reluctant to leave their magnificient mounts behind, arrangements were made for them to be taken over from France. Within three months, the eighteen year old daughter contracted yellow fever, and in a few days was dead. A month later, the son showed signs of the dreaded disease and he too, soon died – as did the daughter's fiancé.

By this time, forty-eight officers of the canal company had died and labourers were dying at the rate of more than two hundred a month. The precise number of deaths could only be estimated, as the bodies of many of the black workers were quickly disposed of among the excavated spoil taken to the filling grounds.

On New Years Eve 1884, just over a year after arriving in Panama, Madam Dingler died of yellow fever. After the funeral, Jules Dingler took all the family's horses, including his own, up into the mountains and shot them. Within eight months, he was a broken man, on the verge of physical and mental collapse; he returned to France and was never to see Panama again.

After this, things began to fall apart. Panama had experienced an earthquake, a costly armed uprising, vast quantities of equipment had been destroyed in the many landslides, and three funeral trains were running to Colon each day. No wonder everyone soon became disillusioned, as the undertaking fell deeper and deeper into debt. The official end came on 4 February 1889, when the Tribunal Civil appointed a liquidator; the Compagnie Universelle du Canal Interoceanique was no more.

From all accounts, one Frenchman remained undaunted and full of vigour; that was Ferdinand de Lesseps, who, at the advanced age of 65 married for the second time, his bride being a stunning twenty year old

French girl, who bore him twelve children. There were those who believed his prowess as a canal builder was even surpassed by that as a father.

During the ensuing years, people in the United States came to realize, that an inter-ocean canal was vital to the future economy of the country, and the then president – Theodore Roosevelt – began to actively campaign for the building of a canal by an American company, with the favoured route being through Nicaragua.

Ironically, just after the failure of the French company, an English physician – Ronald Ross – discovered the cause for the spread of malaria. He showed that a certain type of mosquito carried the disease from an infected person, to other people. Consequently, if appropriate action was taken against the mosquito, the disease could be eradicated. Later it was also shown that similar considerations applied to yellow fever.

About this time, tentative approaches were being made to the government in Columbia, by certain Americans, with regard to the possibility of continuing the work in Panama, but the terms demanded by the Columbians proved completely unacceptable. The economy in Columbia was in a parlous condition; consequently, there was much unrest – particularly in the State of Panama. The situation gradually deteriorated and the discontent culminated in open revolution. With some encouragement and assistance from other quarters, the State of Panama was eventually able to secede from Columbia and become the Republic of Panama.

The interested Americans immediately approached the new government, which proved co-operative and after purchasing the rights and assets of the old French company in Panama, they set about the task of completing the canal project. There were, however, to be several alterations to the route, particularly in Limon Bay. But the greatest eventual change resulted from the decision to build a huge dam at Gatun, so as to form a long navigable lake and to construct a series of locks at each end.

Many of the French buildings, railways, dredgers and excavators, etc. were repaired and brought back into use; while much new equipment was shipped from the United States, including large 95 ton Bucyrus bucket-excavators – so that by the end of 1905, steady progress was being made. An army doctor – Colonel William C. Gorgas – was made responsible for directing the fight against disease, in accordance with the techniques devised by Ronald Ross.

During the succeeding years, work continued at an ever increasing pace, until by 1909, no less than 68 of the Bucyrus excavators were being employed in the Culebra Cut alone; with 160 trains, each day, taking away the spoil. In fact, there was more tonnage moving per mile, than on any other railway in the world. Superlatives became commonplace, as one realized that in the entire world, the Gatun dam was the largest, the locks were the highest, the artificial lake the longest and of course the Culebra Cut was by far the deepest. When the volume of earth excavated is considered, no other excavation up to that time, was even remotely comparable – and all this was accomplished in the face of unspeakable trials and tribulations.

When at last the canal was complete and the first ship could make the historic passage, it might have been expected that there would be great celebrations; no doubt there would have been, had it not been for the fact that the ship *Cristobal* made the first ocean-to-ocean transit, on that fateful day in 1914, when war broke out in Europe.

On entering the canal zone, we were instructed over the radio, to proceed to Yacht Anchorage 'F', which was in part of the original French canal. We were soon cleared by the customs and immigration officials, after which the 'Admeasurer' came aboard to make the necessary measurements, on which the toll would be charged.

At that time, the canal administration was in the hands of the Americans and this we found to be very efficient indeed. Having paid the toll charge, we received detailed written instructions. We were to go through the canal on Sunday 16 March, our pilot was to be Captain Robert Gray, who would join us at 1045 hr and our 'buddy ship' (the vessel we had to follow) would be the merchant vessel S.S. *Star Bay*.

In the meantime, and after having made all the necessary preparations on *Keramos* for the transit, Ken and I decided to stroll into Cristobal. We had not gone far, however, when we realized that we were being very closely followed by two well armed police. After about ten minutes they stopped us and asked where we were going. We told them that we wished to investigate the facilities in the Tax Free Zone, whereupon, they brusquely instructed us to go back to *Keramos*, saying that the district was exceedingly dangerous, as several murders were committed each day. We of course complied, but even so, they followed us all the way back, and waited until they were satisfied that we were safely on board again. Apparently, most of the trouble is connected with the flourishing drugs trade.

On the day fixed for the transit, Captain Gray arrived as arranged and briefed us regarding the *modus operandi*. He particularly stressed the precise action to be taken in the locks, where from his remarks, it was obvious that things could become rather exciting, if the crew failed to react appropriately. After weighing anchor, we went out into Limon Bay and soon saw the S.S. *Star Bay* approaching. Our pilot had a chat with her captain, over the radio, and then instructed us to station *Keramos* about 200 yards astern of our 'buddy ship'.

Through Limon Bay, the deep channel is marked by buoys, but we soon entered the canal, with dense forests on each side. After a short distance, we caught sight of the Colon to Panama City railway line, built in 1853 to replace 'the road to hell', along which the 'forty-niners' trudged on their way to the American gold fields.

We crossed the line of the old French canal, and then saw in the distance, the immense Gatun Locks. On the starboard hand was the Chagres river and the mile and a half long Gatun Dam, which had been built from earth excavated from the canal. All the locks had been constructed in pairs, one lock being for the 'up traffic' and the other for the 'down traffic'. They are 1,000 feet long and 110 feet wide; therefore as *Keramos* entered, she was completely dwarfed by the massive concrete walls. Men at the top of the walls threw down light lines (two from each side) to skilfully land on *Keramos* and to these, we attached our warps. The men then hauled in the warps and made them fast, so enabling us to quickly secure the warps on deck and hold *Keramos* centrally in the lock. While this was being done, the two huge gates were closed and water began to fill the lock from the seventy culverts built into the bottom of the lock chamber. As the water rushed in, *Keramos* was tossed about like a cork on a stormy sea, but even so, as we rapidly rose, it was imperative to carefully take in the warps and keep our fragile vessel well clear of the threatening walls.

Ken had previously told us that when, during the war, he had passed through the Gatun Locks, as a member of the crew on a warship (I hesitate to say he was in command), the vessel hit the wall and made a ten foot long gash. As we now passed through, he was surprised to find the mark was still visible.

Our pilot kept us entertained with a fund of reminiscences resulting from his long service on the canal. He pointed out where the roof of the control-house had been modified, to allow the *Queen Elizabeth II* to pass through the lock. She is the largest vessel to have made the transit and in 1975 paid the then record toll of $42,077. He told us that the lowest toll ever paid, was in respect of a man who swam, on successive days, along the entire length of the canal (including the locks); based on his weight of 140 lb, he was charged a toll of 36 cents.

As it took only a few minutes for the lock to fill, the gates at the other end were soon opened, allowing us to motor out and into the second lock, where the procedure was repeated. At Gatun, there is a flight of three locks, taking vessels up to the level of the large lake of Gatun, where we followed the buoyed channel for about 25 miles. During this easy part of the passage, Robert Gray joined us for lunch in the cockpit. He told us that his young son was having a birthday party and he was therefore, anxious to get home as soon as possible. He considered that we were being impeded by the *Star Bay*, so after giving the appropriate signal on the siren, *Keramos* swept past the large vessel and quickly drew ahead.

On leaving the lake, the waterway narrowed and soon we were again in a canal section, with dense forests on each side. However, we had not gone far, when an unexpected voice from loudspeakers in the forest, boomed out, "*Keramos* you are going much too fast – reduce your speed immediately". We complied, of course, but I asked what would happen if we should fail to do so. Robert Gray explained that officially he was in command of the yacht, and therefore, he would be held responsible; he could be heavily fined but in a really serious case, he could lose his pilot's licence.

After a while, we could see the high ground ahead through which the Culebra Cut had been driven and as we entered the Cut, it was impossible not to pay homage to those thousands of men who had toiled, and in particular, to those who had given their lives, in the great endeavour. On the port hand, we could see the site of the Culebra Slide, the gigantic landslide that had brought down millions of tons of sodden earth to bury excavators, railway trains and defenceless men. Farther on, we saw the place where the Cucaracha Slide had, many times, brought about the same kind of havoc and slaughter. The towering walls of this tremendous man-made canyon still seemed to threaten, and command every respect.

A further three miles brought us to the Pedro Miguel locks, where *Keramos* descended to the level of the Miraflores Lake, which had been formed by damming the waters of the Rio Grande. This lake is about two and a half miles long and at the dam, a flight of two more locks brought us down to the level of the Pacific Ocean.

From these locks to the end of the Naos Island breakwater, where the channel leads into the Pacific Ocean, is about eight miles, but our destination for the day was the Balboa Yacht Club. As we bid farewell to our able and friendly pilot, he looked at his watch and said it had been one of the fastest transits he had ever made. I suggested that perhaps we should put that down to the birthday party.

I had arranged to fly back to Britain via the Bahamas. While I was there, a man told me he had come to know that the exiled Shah of Iran was in hiding, on a small island off the coast of Panama, the location of which was a closely guarded secret. I became curious about this secret island and after a lot of geographical research, came to the conclusion that it must be one of the small islands in the group known as the Pearl Islands, which we would pass *en route* for Galápagos.

On my return to Panama, I tried to get a chart covering the Pearl Islands but found that the official publication had been withdrawn – a fact that appeared to support my assumption. So, in Panama City, I bought a post-card of every view of the islands that I could find and eventually came to the conclusion that the Shah was most likely on the island of Contadora – therefore, why not pay him a surprise visit?

In the absence of a proper chart, we cautiously approached the islands, with the aid of the post-cards. Soon we identified Contadora and decided to drop anchor close to a delightful little beach, overlooked by a magnificent villa. Ken, Nick and I went ashore in the tender, expecting to be accosted by armed guards, but nobody appeared until we arrived at the Holiday Inn, where we introduced ourselves. Having seen the luxurious swimming pool with a large bar in the middle, we could not wait to take a dip. Afterwards, we sat in the warm water on the submerged stools, before the bar, and relaxed with a cool refresher. While chatting with the barman, I said, "I suppose you get some interesting people staying here?" "Well of course", came the reply, "until two days ago, when he left for Egypt, to go into hospital, we had the Shah of Iran on the island". We were soon to learn, that the Shah had been residing in the villa overlooking the beach, where *Keramos* was anchored. One member of the crew, who was good at mixing metaphors, summed up the position by saying, "Although the bird had flown, we had scored a bull's-eye".

25

DARWIN'S GALAPAGOS ISLANDS

The voyage to the islands of Galápagos was mainly notable as a result of a frightening electrical storm, after dark, on 1 April, when I happened to be on watch. It started at about 2015 hr, with torrential rain and thunder, during which many seabirds landed on deck – a sure sign of impending foul weather. Within an hour, it was only too obvious, that we were at the centre of a very violent electrical storm. The lightning and crashes of thunder were simultaneous, with the vivid lightning continuously illuminating the sky.

It was, however, the electrical discharges that we found so terrifying. At the top of each mast was a dazzling blue-white light, similar to that produced by arc-welding, and from time to time, balls of shining light would run down the wire rigging, from the mastheads to the deck. From the various electrical instruments in the wheelhouse, there were heavy static discharges, so to save them from imminent destruction, I switched off as much as possible. This, however, seemed to make little difference, as the charges were apparently running along any available conductor. We endeavoured, as far as possible, to keep well away from the discharges and wore dark glasses to protect our eyes. While this was going on, the rain was sluicing down and the rising wind made it necessary to hand all sails, except for a small storm jib.

When we changed watch at midnight, we had a clear starry sky, a warm gentle wind, and the seabirds had decided they could manage without us. The most surprising outcome of that terrible storm, was that *Keramos* suffered no damage whatsoever.

The official port of entry for Galápagos was in Wreck Bay, on the island of San Cristobal, but Ken had learned that it was a very unfriendly place and several yachts had been impounded. Consequently, we decided to try our luck by making for Academy Bay on Santa Cruz. While in Panama, Ken and I had visited the Ecuadorean Embassy, with a view to obtaining authority to stay in the islands for longer than the prescribed 72 hours, but although we were able to obtain much useful information, the request for a longer stay was firmly rebuffed.

After anchoring in Academy Bay, the Port Captain soon came on board and he not only endorsed the 72 hour rule but in addition, read the 'riot act' regarding our fate, should we fail to comply.

The Galápagos consist of six main islands and about a dozen smaller ones. They lie on the equator, about 650 miles west of the coast of Ecuador and are the peaks of gigantic volcanoes, rising as much as 10,000 feet above the seabed – most of them still being active. As they are composed mainly of basalt and there is virtually no water supply on the islands, vegetation is extremely sparse. It is not surprising therefore, that until comparatively recent times, the islands have remained uninhabited. Consequently, the animals and endemic birds have no instinctive fear of man.

Because the archipelago has always been separated from the mainland, animals and plants have had to find their way there, across the open sea; exactly how this occurred, has led to much conjecture, but during the hundreds of thousands of years since their arrival, they have adapted to the local conditions, so that today, they bear little resemblance to the original continental species – hence most of them are unique. A quarter of the species of shore fish, half of the plants and almost all the reptiles are found nowhere else; in many cases distinct forms have evolved on the different islands.

This specialization within the archipelago attracted the attention of Charles Darwin, when he visited the islands on HMS *Beagle* in 1835. In particular, he noticed that there were thirteen species of finch, which although clearly related, differed in several respects. The greatest difference being in the shape and size of their beaks, which in the course of time, had adapted to the need to deal with a particular type of available food.

Some of the seed eating finches have a strong beak, like that of a parrot, in order to break the seeds, while other finches that eat insects, have a long thin beak in order to extract them from holes and crevices. The woodpecker finch has learned to use a piece of stick, to extract insects from where its beak cannot reach. This is the only bird in the world that has developed the skill of eating with a 'fork' and when it has found a really good one, the bird usually carries it around. Another finch is a vampire, using its beak to draw blood from the base of the booby's feathers – apparently without causing the booby any distress. It is an interesting and important fact, that none of these various species interbreed.

Following his visit to Galápagos, Darwin came to realize that species are not objects of divine creation but are subject to a continual process of evolution and this led to the publication of his famous work *The Origin of Species*. The Galápagos islands have, as a result, been called the birthplace of modern biology, but in addition, as the concept of evolution began to be applied to related branches of science, a real revolution in human thought was begun, which brought about a rational understanding of the true nature of the universe.

We made the best use of every available minute, to see as much as possible of this fascinating and unique domain. In particular, we were intriged by the flightless cormorants which have lost the ability to fly, due to the absence of predators and the ease with which they can catch fish, by using what remains of their wings to swim under water. Also by the only penguins that live in a tropical region; it would seem that they originated in Antarctica but made their way to Galápagos by following the cold Humbolt Current. And the waved albatross, the largest seabird found in the eastern Pacific; it is the size of a goose and has a wingspan of up to nine feet. Everywhere we could see the spectacular frigatebirds; the males are particularly conspicuous, because they have an enormous red bag under the beak, which is inflated to attract the female during courtship.

The word Galápagos is Spanish for tortoise and it was the giant tortoise that first attracted the attention of early visitors to the islands. During the nineteenth century, whaling fleets removed vast numbers of the reptiles for food and oil. In an age without refrigeration, their ability to live for a year or more in the holds of ships, without food or water, made them especially valuable.

At the Darwin Research Station in Academy Bay, several types of the giant tortoise are being bred, to supplement the depleted populations on most of the islands. Fully grown specimens can only be found in their natural habitat, in one or two remote places, which are not normally accessible to visitors. However, Murray met a man who offered to take us, in his old truck, to an isolated swamp where we could see a large number of them.

The offer was too good to refuse, so after piling into the dilapidated vehicle and mending a couple of punctures on the way, we eventually reached a place where the rough track terminated. From this point, our guide had arranged for the remainder of the journey to be made by pony. After traversing some very rough volcanic terrain, we came to a wooded glade, where we found a large number of the fascinating creatures wallowing in muddy pools. They were mostly of the type having a dome-shaped shell, which only permits feeding off lush vegetation at ground level.

In the business world, Murray had specialized in marketing and P.R. work and therefore, we tended to leave in his capable hands any difficult negotiations, and none could have been more difficult than trying to persuade the Port Captain to allow us to stay longer than the usual 72 hours.

The Captain told Murray that he was very interested in scuba-diving and would like to get a speargun, but they were unobtainable in

Ecuador. Murray told the Captain that we were very interested in staying in Galápagos for at least five days, and that we had on board a spare speargun. Murray would never disclose how the negotiations ended but as we enjoyed our extended stay, it was noticeable that the dire threats made on our arrival, were surprisingly not put into effect – and we never did discover what happened to that clapped-out speargun.

The Captain, however, insisted on our sailing right away from Galápagos, when we left Academy Bay. But Murray had learned that the patrol vessel had gone to Guayaquil, on the mainland and would be absent for about a week. In the circumstances we concluded that we could afford to take a few further liberties.

Accordingly, we made our departure from Santa Cruz on a westerly course, just before nightfall and then under the cover of darkness, changed course to take us into a sheltered bay (Bahia Elizabeth) off the island of Isabela. In the bay, there is a rocky islet and when we looked out, on the following morning, we could see that it was alive with many interesting birds and reptiles. Naturally, we just had to launch the tender and make our way over to the island, to explore and take photographs.

All the living creatures were so tame that we could walk among them, without causing them to move – or even to look at us. There were thousands of marine iguanas, which have evolved from the land iguanas. They are about three feet long, have a dark coloured rough skin and a row of spines, which run along the back from head to tail, making them look for all the world like diminutive dragons. These endemic reptiles drink sea water and possess glands to extract the excess salt. From time to time, the saline secretion is forcibly ejected from their nostrils, as a jet of fine spray, and this feature certainly adds to their dragon-like appearance. Equally interesting were the flightless cormorants, the blue-footed boobies, seals, pelicans and the penguins which actually came towards us, so that we were soon surrounded by a small circle of inquisitive onlookers.

Later in the day, we sailed into Caleta Tagus, a deep fiord-like inlet on Isabela, the steep sides of which are covered by the aromatic Palo Santo tree. This well sheltered creek was teeming with bird life, including pelicans, noddy terns, tropic birds with their long streaming tails, albatrosses and boobies.

The following morning we went over to the volcanic island of Fernandina and anchored off a sandy shore, sheltered by the Espinosa headland. We swam in the clear warm water and found the fur seals and sea lion pups so tame, that they nuzzled into us and playfully swam between our legs – they appeared, in fact, to enjoy our company. There were also many land iguanas, larger and more colourful than the marine variety but equally tame. We intended to climb up to the smoking crater, but after scrambling over the rough volcanic rock for a short distance, we found the going too strenuous – particularly as the temperature was well over 100°F.

It was exceedingly difficult to tear ourselves away from the magical islands, but we did feel that in spite of all the official restrictions, we had, by virtue of the unofficial liberties, seen much of what Galápagos has to offer. We therefore made our departure from Cabo Douglass, at 1600 hr on 15 April, and set course for the 3,010 nautical mile passage, across the Pacific to a small group of islands, known as the Marquesas.

26

THE MARQUESAS AND TUAMOTU ATOLLS

Soon after leaving Galápagos, we encountered many huge killer whales, some of which approached much too close for our peace of mind. In this vicinity, several yachts had been attacked and damaged by these powerful monsters, and a short time previously, a yacht was sunk and the crew – a family with two children – had spent over a month in an inflatable life-raft, before being rescued by a fishing boat.

We soon found the trade winds, which enabled us to enjoy some exhilarating sailing; under full sail with a boomed-out No 1 Yankee, we were surfing down the wave-fronts, in a surging mass of broken water, at speeds up to 16 knots. On 24 April, *Keramos* covered 252.6 sea miles in a 24 hour period. As we approached the Marquesas, however, conditions changed, and the sky became overcast, so preventing celestial navigation. It was necessary therefore, to up-date the last observed position, by feeding into the computer many course changes (due to the variable wind), the distances run and the drift due to the strong current. Nevertheless, just before midday on 2 May, the island of Nukuhiva was sighted, fine on the starboard bow and a couple of hours later, we anchored in the bay of Taiohae, close to the village of Vaitu.

We were immediately visited by a lone yachtsman who was known to everyone as 'Syd'. He had recently arrived after a 73 day passage fom Panama. He told us that when south of Galápagos, his yacht had been attacked by whales which destroyed his steering gear and part of the rudder. This elderly Englishman, after losing his wife, had sold his house and bought a small yacht – which he named the *Doreen Beatrice*. He then decided to sail round the world. We were to meet him again on several later occasions.

The owner of another yacht anchored nearby, had recently been in the news. While in Galápagos, he had contracted appendicitis and after requesting assistance by radio, an American warship had rushed to Tagus Cove, where the man was operated on by the ship's doctor.

Nukuhiva is the largest of the dozen or so islands in the Marquesas Group, which constitutes part of French Polynesia. White men first visited the islands at the close of the sixteenth century. The population of the Marquesas at the beginning of the nineteenth century was estimated to be around 80,000, but by 1842, when France took possession, there were only 6,000 inhabitants and within the next 50 years, the number was reduced to about 400. The white peoples with their alcohol and the Chinese with their opium, had virtually destroyed the native population, while the missionaries with their competing approaches to religious life, had succeeded in destroying their culture.

The island of Nukuhiva is mountainous, with heights rising up to 3,500 feet, while the rocky coastline is wooded and for the most part, carpeted by bright green undergrowth. In addition to the many palms, there are distinctive tropical trees such as the oil-bearing candlenut tree and the colourful mountain apple tree. The brightly hued tropical blossoms are to be found in profusion and they certainly augment the scenic appeal.

Ken was able to arrange for the use of a couple of sturdy mountain ponies, which enabled us to follow rough tracks up into the mountains, where spectacular waterfalls cascaded down the precipitous faces of thickly vegetated rocks. As the tracks twisted and turned, a succession of vistas opened up, which revealed in dramatic fashion the verdant beauty of the island.

In view of the anticipated heavy work programme in New Zealand and Australia, it was decided to increase the crew by engaging John Kemish to act as skipper. He had previously served in a similar capacity on Ken's yacht and had proved to be a very able seaman and a meticulous navigator. John travelled out by air to Tahiti and then by a variety of means to Nukuhiva. He arrived with much mail from England and a miscellaneous collection of equipment for *Keramos*. He was very soon to settle into life on board.

Before leaving Nukuhiva, we obtained a good supply of the local food items, including a wide variety of tropical fruits and half a pig. But the most surprising purchase was a box of salt bearing the words, 'Supreme Salt Co, Cobridge, Stoke-on-Trent'.

Our principal objective was Tahiti but on the way, I decided to call at the small island of Ua Pou, which is about 60 miles south of Nukuhiva. We anchored in Hakahetau Bay and on going ashore, found a picturesque village with a tiny chapel nestling among overhanging palm trees. It is quite impossible to adequately describe the scenic beauty of this island, with its indented mountain ranges and craggy pinnacles rising up into the clouds. Three of us climbed up the dried bed of a stream and from an elevated viewpoint, the panorama resembled a fairyland scene, as might be depicted on a highly imaginative pantomime backcloth.

About 500 miles to the south, lies the world's largest group of coral atolls – The Tuamotus – and on the chart, I noticed an oval-shaped atoll called Ahe, which I felt could be well worth a visit. It is about eleven miles long and five miles wide, with the rim varying in breadth from 100 to 600 yards. There is just one narrow pass through the coral rim, which leads into the sheltered lagoon. To gain access to the single village it is necessary to proceed cautiously through the pass and then find a way across the coral studded water to the other side of the lagoon.

So it was, that just before midday on 18 May, we were much occupied in searching for the *Passe de Reianvi*. Nick was perched high up on the mainmast with a walkie-talkie and binoculars. From the elevated position, he was able to estimate the depth of the water ahead from its colour, and by means of the walkie-talkie, keep those of us in the wheelhouse continuously informed regarding the best course to follow. John was at the wheel, Ken was monitoring the echo-sounder, while I was poring over the chart and keeping an eye on the radar. Once safely through the pass, we had to find a way between the many coral heads, most of which were just below the surface of the water. But after an anxious couple of hours, we eventually sighted the village huts, beneath the swaying palms and were soon safely at anchor.

The turquoise-blue water looked so inviting, that we could not resist a swim – that is, until we saw several huge yellow sharks approaching. It had not occurred to us, that they would find their way through the pass and across the lagoon.

On going ashore, we soon met the young village chief, and one of the first questions I put to him was, whether or not the sharks were dangerous. He replied in French, to the effect that he had never known anyone be attacked, but that was possibly because no sensible person would think of swimming in the lagoon!

The chief made us very welcome and everyone in the village was most helpful and friendly. Due to the isolation of their tiny world, they very rarely had the opportunity to meet visitors, and consequently, their simple way of life had changed very little during recent years. The chief told me that his authority and duties were exactly the same as those invested in his forefathers, who had been chiefs for countless generations. During one very interesting discussion with him, I asked what he would do if someone stole something, whereupon, he looked very puzzled and then said, "Why should anyone want to steal?" This confirmed my impression, that perhaps these simple, but good people, should send missionaries to the Western world.

The village community appeared to be healthy and supremely happy. They had a schoolroom, a chapel and a recreation area where they played volley-ball. In the evenings, they sang and danced to the accompaniment of ukulele type instruments. The only currency they have is coconuts, which, when the occasional small trading vessel calls, they exchange for things such as sugar, rice, flour, fats and coffee. It can therefore be truly said, that for them, wealth really does grow on trees.

The only sophisticated equipment they appeared to have was a diesel-generator, which was used to charge the batteries for their radio-telephone. The engine had recently broken down, but Nick was fortunately able to make a repair and get the telephone back in action. To mark their gratitude the villagers showered upon us gifts of all kinds – Ken was even offered a ukulele.

One morning Ken was looking over the bow of *Keramos*, to watch the shoals of brightly coloured fish, when his spectacles fell off and disappeared below the water. Murray was adamant that they would have to be recovered. He was an experienced scuba-diver, having qualified as an instructor, so he donned his equipment and prepared his under-water camera. Soon he was down on the sea-bed, where we could clearly see him searching for the spectacles and then as we feared, a shark appeared – and yet another. We naturally expected Murray to make a quick retreat, but he just swam forward and pointed his camera at them. We had the rifles handy, but they were not required, as very soon Murray safely surfaced. On handing the spectacles to Ken, he wished him 'happy returns' – as it was indeed his birthday.

When we asked Murray if he was not afraid the sharks might attack, he said, "As they only feed about once a month, I reckoned it was not likely that they had not eaten for such a long time". Nick reminded him that while that might be true, when they do eat, it is to enjoy a very big meal.

Our visit to Ahe was a wonderful experience and when the time came for us to leave, all the people of the village turned out to bid us farewell. As we sailed away, the sound of their lilting songs gradually faded, but I feel sure our treasured memories will remain with us for ever.

27

THE MAGIC OF TAHITI

After leaving Ahe, we sailed past many of the atolls in the Tuamotus, where the large number of wrecks bear witness to the navigational hazards. As we passed near to Raroia, we recalled that some years previous, the Kon-Tiki raft, after safely crossing the Pacific, had finally foundered on its outlying reefs. But it was hard to believe that from time to time, the serenity of these waters was shattered by the French atom-bomb tests taking place on Mururoa and Fangataufa.

During the late afternoon of 24 May, we sighted the high mountains of Tahiti, and soon after dark, we saw the flashes from the lighthouse on Pointe Venus. However, as we drew closer to the light, we were surprised to find that instead of the usual long and short, regular flashes, the periods of light were completely haphazard. A few days later, I visited the lighthouse and found that to seaward, there was a very tall palm tree swaying in the breeze and its branches were high enough to interrupt the beam of light; so obviously, this was the cause of the irregular flashes.

In the fine harbour of Papeete, *Keramos* went alongside the *Quai de Paquebots* to refuel (the first time since leaving Panama) and was then moored stern-to, on the *Quai Bir-Hakeim*.

Soon after our arrival, we learned that Syd, the lone yachtsman whom we met in Nukuhiva, had struck the Arue reef while approaching the Tahiti Yacht Club. His yacht was badly holed, but club members with the aid of a tug, had managed to pull the vessel clear and get it onto a slipway at the Yacht Club. Some of us went over to the Club and met Syd, to see if we could assist in any way with the repairs. But several of the members were already hard at work and well on the way to effecting a very competent restoration of the little *Doreen Beatrice*.

Tahiti conjures up the image of bare bosomed girls in grass skirts, living in palm-leaf huts, but Papeete (the capital of French Polynesia) is, an attractive modern town, with some very smart shops, cafés, restaurants and hotels. The post office, with its thickly carpeted floors, stylish furniture and contemporary lighting, is particularly impressive compared with British standards. Escalators connect with the first floor, where a philatelic department offers for sale a wide variety of large pictorial stamps, featuring the native fauna and flora.

The girls do occasionally wear grass skirts, but only when performing their traditional dances, to the frantic rhythm of the wooden drums. Normally, they wear fashionable European type clothes and with their strikingly beautiful features and trim figures, would not look out of place if strolling on the *Champs-Elysees*, in Paris.

▲21. Cook's Bay on the island of Moorea.

▼22. The Kia Ora Village Hotel, Moorea, with Tahiti in the far distance.

▲23. The Bora Bora lagoon, overshadowed by Mount Pahia.

▼24. Fijian *bure kalou* (pagan temple for human sacrifices).

▼25. Polynesian *tikis* (miniature pagan gods) and a cannibal fork.

▲26. Roberton Island, New Zealand. The Roberton's farm was just beyond the trees in the foreground. Jim Cottier's house can be seen at the far end of the beach.

▶27. One of the many Rotorua geysers, New Zealand. This one rises to a height of 120 feet.

▶28. The village of Rotorua amidst the steam from the geysers.

▶29. The roofs of the Sydney Opera House, covered by zircon glazed tiles.

▶30. The gardens and swimming pool at the Lindeman Island Hotel, Great Barrier Reef.

▼31. The lagoon on Stradbroke Island, Australia, from which zircon sand is dredged.

▲32. Ken arrives early at the open-air cinema on Christmas Island.

▼33. A coral beach on Direction Island, in the Cocos Group.

▲34. Guy and Nick get one more for the freezer.

▼35. Collecting rain water during the crossing of the Indian Ocean.

▲36. Nick makes a Seychellois flag.

▼37. The Vallée de Mai on the island of Praslin, Seychelles.

◄38. The busy market in Victoria, Seychelles.

▶39. The legendary love nut.

▼40. Typical Sardinian architecture as exemplified in the Aga Khan's Porto Cervo.

As the time had now come when Ken had to return to England, our daughter Diane and husband Roger joined us, to share our experiences on board *Keramos*, among some of the most beautiful and spectacular of the South Sea Islands.

The mountain scenery of Tahiti is unforgettable, but it is nevertheless, surpassed by that of Moorea (Tahiti's sister island) where we anchored in Cook's Bay. This sheltered creek penetrates deep inland up to a picturesque village, which is overshadowed by fantastic mountain peaks. The sunsets in this part of the world are famed, but when the sun sets behind the craggy pinnacles of Moorea, a constantly changing panorama of chimeric shapes and shades of every colour combine to produce images so fanciful, that even the French artist Gauguin, who spent ten years here, was not equal to the task of reproducing them on canvas.

Incidentally, it is interesting to note that Gauguin, had for a short time, been employed by the French Panama Canal Company and that he spent the last years of his life in the Marquesas – his tomb being on Hivaoa.

In addition to Cook's Bay, there is another deep inlet on the northern side of Moorea, which is called Opunohu Bay. The word 'bay' is very misleading, because it is really a narrow inlet, over two miles deep but only about 500 yards wide. To gain access, we had to coax *Keramos* through a small gap in the barrier reef, after which we sailed right up to the head of the creek, where we anchored in a secluded spot, only disturbed by the songs of the birds and the occasional 'plop', as a leaping fish fell back into the limpid water.

The coral sand shores are backed by vegetation, providing a riot of colour. There were masses of red, pink and white *hibiscus*, *bougainvillea*, *frangipane* and extravagant orchids, as well as the native flowers of Tahiti, the *pua* and the *tiare-tahiti*. Around the shores and high up to the skyline, rose the fantastically shaped peaks and pinnacles, while on the foothills were *pandanus*, wild bananas, Tahitian chestnut, *miki-miki*, fern trees and much more – but all combining to provide breath-taking views in every direction. Surely the scenic beauty of Moorea must be unrivalled anywhere in the world.

To get about on this wonderful island, and enjoy to the full, all it had to offer, we hired a mini-moke. One day four of us called at the very fine Kia-Ora hotel for lunch, and there we found a nice table-tennis room. The design was interesting because the thatched roof was supported by four stout columns made from the boles of big trees. As the table and all the necessary equipment was up to competition standard, we decided to make good use of the unexpected facility.

Murray hits the ball very hard and he soon had me retrieving balls well back from the table. As we approached the end of a game, I must have become over ambitious, because in a frantic effort to reach an angled drive, I collided with one of the timber roof supports; the result being a very severe pain in my chest, which made it necessary for me to return to *Keramos*.

The following morning, I was unable to get out of my bunk, and as a result, Diane and John decided that medical assistance was required. The Polynesian islands are served by a flying doctor and in no time at all, he flew over from Tahiti and came on board. He was French and proved to be a great character, with a perky sense of humour. After examining me, he diagnosed, "– – two ribs broken and two slightly bent". He asked how the accident had occurred and when I told him, he said, "Are you sure you were not playing chess?" When I asked if my ribs would have to be strapped, he commented, "Surely they don't still do that in England – we use the very latest treatments here". He happened to pick up a book that I had been reading and after noting the title, *The Fatal Impact*, he laughed, and then said, "Your impact must have been very severe, but I don't really believe it will prove fatal". Actually, Diane had brought the book on board and I found it most interesting. It described the fatal impact made by the white man on the Polynesians by, for example, introducing diseases to which they had no natural immunity.

The treatment administered by the doctor proved so effective, that during the following morning, I decided to take a gentle walk on shore. I was just strolling along a quite road, when suddenly, there was a screech of brakes and a Range-Rover skidded to a stop. It was the doctor, and as he approached, he thundered, "I am used to my patients doing what they are told, and I told you to stay in your bunk for at least two days".

ISLAND-HOPPING TO BORA-BORA

After leaving Moorea, we planned to sail to the lovely island of Bora-Bora, with short visits to some of the intermediate islands. Our departure from Moorea was made at 1730 hr on 26 June and as the island fell astern, the unforgettable mountains were bathed in the rosy glow of the setting sun.

The first port of call was Fare, lying at the foot of mount Turi, on one of the twin islands of Huahine. We found the Chinese stores on the waterfront very colourful, and most unusual due to the great variety of goods on offer being all jumbled together. Pharmaceuticals, for example, were being displayed inside several water closet pans.

We visited some of the *marae*, for which the island is famous. These are the ruins of stone structures, where in the distant past, the maori gods had their thrones, and where the people gathered to see the human sacrifices take place.

The next island was Raiatea, where *Keramos* went alongside the quay at Utura. On the lower slopes of the sacred mountain of Temechani, where it is said the spirits of the departed live, the unique *tiare apetahi* grows in profusion. The buds of this strange plant open at sunrise, with a loud resounding 'plop'. When many thousands of buds are opening, the sound is like that of distant machine-gun fire. The people believe the gods have ordained that the plant will only grow on the sacred mountain, and indeed, attempts to grow it elsewhere, have so far failed.

Then it was on to Tahaa, which shares the same lagoon as Raiatea. Here we sailed to the far end of Baie Hurepiti, which penetrates almost to the centre of the island and where we were surrounded by mountain jungle, with no sign of habitation. In the evening, we went onto the coral-sand shore and made a barbecue fire, over which we cooked, and much enjoyed steaks, kebabs and delicious Tahitian potatoes. The setting under the tall palms was completely magical, with the dark jagged peaks across the water, in silhouette – and above them, the brightly shining Southern Cross.

The following morning, on the way to Passe Raipai, we saw a large number of the local people, excitedly taking part in 'stone-fishing'. The method involves stretching a net across a narrow sheet of water and driving the fish into it. This is done by the people getting into the shallow water and advancing, in line abreast towards the net, while at the same time, picking up stones and throwing them forward. Whether or not the fish can can hear the frantic shouting, I do not know, but it appears to be an essential part of the ritual.

Once clear of the extensive reef, we hoisted the big spinnaker and made a very fast run to the southern tip of Bora-Bora. On the barrier reef the surf was thundering and breaking to give twenty foot high spray. But after entering the large lagoon, by the very narrow Passe Teavanui, we found tranquil blue water – and beyond, were the majestic mountains with mount Paia towering up into the clouds. We cautiously made our way across the lagoon to the tiny village of Farepiti, where we anchored in 15 fathoms.

We found there a small, but very hospitable yacht club, where we hired an old car. This enabled us to explore what has been called the most beautiful island in the world. The film *Hurricane* had recently been shot on the island and the club had managed to purchase the piano, which had featured in the film, and was now to feature in our evening singsongs.

The manager of the club told us that black-fin sharks could always be found off a particular coral shore, and for some inexplicable reason, Roger expressed a desire to see them. Accordingly, it was arranged that Murray, Nick and Roger would take the tender to the place indicated, and after donning diving equipment, Roger and Nick would enter the water, while Murray kept them covered with a speargun – just in case a shark decided to attack. When the expedition returned, I asked Roger if he had seen a shark. "Yes" he said, "and while Murray was aiming the speargun at it, I was quite happy, but when Nick pointed to a second shark coming up right behind me, I was petrified". I then asked Roger what happened next and he said, "Within three seconds I was back in the tender".

During World War II, the Americans had built an airstrip on the barrier reef, which later made it possible for light aricraft to provide a service to Tahiti. Therefore, when the time came for Diane and Roger to leave us, they flew to Tahiti, over the islands recently visited and then took a scheduled flight to London, with a stop-over in Los Angeles.

One day, Nick spotted Syd's *Doreen Beatrice* approaching the island, and as she was very close to the reef, he dashed off in the tender to guide the tiny yacht through the pass and into the lagoon. As a result, this most interesting character was soon on board *Keramos*, and relating further instalments from the continuing saga of his lone adventure on the high seas.

In the anchorage, there was another vessel that we had seen previously. This was the yacht *Shikama*, owned by Max and Shirley Vanderbent from Australia. Max was researching hypnotic regression, in which he would take his hypnotised subjects back in time, and then get them to relate in detail what they could see. I attended several of these sessions on his yacht, and found the experiences extremely thought provoking.

He always worked after dark, and by the flickering light of an oil-lamp, strategically placed before the volunteer subject. After seating his subject comfortably, Max would describe what he intended to do, stressing that the person would suffer no ill effects, either during or after the session and that all information given, would be strictly limited to that which the participant was freely willing to disclose. Before the session commenced, the subject was asked if, at the conclusion, he or she wished to remember all that had been said, or to forget everything – most people chose the first option.

Max would then ask his subject to relax completely, and with eyes half closed, to look at the flickering light. Speaking very slowly and quietly, Max would commence by saying something like this, "I want you to imagine that you are walking along a dark tunnel – at the far end you can see a faint light – and as you continue to walk – the light gets brighter – and brighter – and still brighter – until, as you reach the end – you find that you are on a white cloud – gently floating – drifting – higher and higher – – – ". Very soon the subject's eyes would close and Max would ask one or two questions, which would generally show that he or she was in a state of hypnosis.

Shirley, who was a qualified nurse, constantly kept the subject under close observation, because after a time, the person would slump down in the chair, with chin dug into the chest. She would then gently lift them into a more upright position.

Max had previously told me, that if he asked questions regarding things relating to a precise period, the answers would generally be remarkably accurate. For example, in Britain, a fork always had two prongs up to a certain well documented time, after which, the four-pronged fork came into vogue. Similarly, at fairly clear cut times, tableware changed from pewter to red-ware, and from red-ware to white-ware, while fashions in clothing have changed frequently and at well recorded times. Moreover, all such changes obviously related to location, as well as to time. After a session Max would check the given information against historical data, and then prepare a report on the correlation.

One evening, a girl was taken back four hundred years, in Egypt, and during the session she described a monument. Max asked her if she could see any inscription on it and she replied, "Yes, there is some strange lettering". Max then gave her a pencil and writing pad and asked her to write down what she could see. After the session, Max compared what she had written, with data in one of his reference books and found that the girl had correctly transposed some Egyptian hieroglyphics. He therefore asked her when she had been in Egypt. She maintained she had never visited Egypt. When he asked her how she had come to know about hieroglyphics, she laughed and said, "What on earth are hieroglyphics?"

Both Nick and Murray proved to be excellent hypnotic subjects. Nick described life as a crew member on a three-masted barque, at the beginning of the nineteenth century. His description of the tough captain's character and antics, were quite amusing. Murray gave a vivid account of his life on a farm, during the tenth century. Max asked him what he liked doing best and Murray said, he was always pleased when he could attend the local market, and added, "Tomorrow, I shall be taking apples to market". Max asked how much money he hoped to get for them, whereupon Murray replied. "I don't understand – what is money? I want to exchange them for some more ducks".

Some of the sessions were quite bizarre. One evening, Max took Murray back five hundred years, in North Africa, whereupon, he described life as a nomad in the desert, saying it was difficult to find enough food, while at night when the family slept in a tent, it could be extremely cold. Max took him forward in time to old age, and Murray said he could not expect to live much longer. He was then taken still further forward, to an hour before he died. Murray graphically described in a weak, faltering voice, exactly how he felt and concluded by saying, "I wish those people outside the tent would stop making so much noise – I would very much like to die in peace".

Max took one subject back in time, then forward to an hour after he had died and asked him what he could see. The subject said it was completely dark, and therefore he could not see anything. Max told me that he had done this many times, with people holding various beliefs and the result was always the same. He felt, however, that it would be quite wrong, to draw any definite conclusions from such experiments, as the working of the human mind, when under hypnosis, is far from being fully understood.

My own view is that during a lifetime, the brain stores a prodigious amount of information. If one considers all the places visited and things seen, all the conversations with different people, all the television programmes watched and all the books and newspapers, etc. that have been read, then it is obvious that the accumulated knowledge must be enormous. Unfortunately, with the passage of time, much of this is forgotten, or more precisely, the information stored in the brain cannot all be recalled. However, under hypnosis and with the appropriate stimulation, it would seem that subliminal information can be retrieved and incorporated in imaginative scenarios, with dreamlike mani-festation.

I asked Max if it is possible to hypnotise oneself, and during a later session, he demonstrated how this could be done. The person has to be a very good hypnotic subject and to have full confidence in the particular technique for terminating hypnosis at will. I discussed with Max, the possibility of self-hypnosis playing a part in voodoo and similar quasi religious performances, in which participants enter into a trance. He was firmly of the opinion that hypnosis – though not necessarily self-hypnosis – is a common feature of all such practices, as well as in those which depend on the suppression of pain, such as firewalking in Fiji and the strange feats of Indian fakirs.

As a result of the French influence in Polynesia, it is not surprising that 14 July should have a special significance and call for celebration. In Vaitape, many huts were constructed from timber and palm leaves, and then superbly decorated with a large number of beautiful flowers. The huts were used to accommodate small cafés, stalls for the sale of sweets and refreshments, and a wide variety of side-shows.

Competitions were organized for activities such as coconut husking, and javelin throwing where the target was a coconut at the top of a pole – at least 80 feet in height. For the children there was a slippery pole to climb, and it was amusing to see the youngsters rubbing coral-sand onto their knees and hands, in order to get a better grip.

In the evening, various competing troupes of dancing girls gave colourful displays, to the accompaniment of music and singing provided by the menfolk. The highly entertaining celebrations were finally brought to a close with fireworks, and the setting on fire of all the lovely palm-leaf huts.

Before leaving beautiful Bora-Bora, we took *Keramos* round to the Baie de Faanui, to take on stores and water at a village which serves as the centre for cock-fighting. We were shown the pit, with the terraced seating accommodation for spectators, and of course, the large number of cocks, all housed in separate cages. We stayed overnight, with *Keramos* moored alongside the tiny quay, and at 5 a.m. on the following morning, were awakened by a cacophonic dawn-chorus provided by over one hundred lusty fighting-cocks. The din had to be heard to be believed.

29

THE COOK ISLANDS TO FIJI

After the 560 mile voyage from Bora-Bora, we arrived at Rarotonga, in the Cook Islands, during the early hours of 19 July. Here we anchored off shore, with the intention of entering the tiny harbour of Avatiu in daylight. However, when we came to weigh anchor we found that it was badly fouled in the coral, and as a result, we decided to buoy the anchor chain, so that we could deal with the problem later, when the weather was more suitable for diving.

Most of the inhabitants of Rarotonga are to be found near the coast, because inland the island is mountainous and very thickly wooded. It is less developed than many of the islands lying to the north, but the people are extremely kind and friendly. One old man showed me how they used to make fire. Taking a sharp edged stone, he made a length-wise slit in a log taken from the peace tree. He then vigorously rubbed a pointed stick, to and fro, in the slit. When the stick began to glow, burning embers were knocked onto some coconut fibre, which he then waved in the air to produce a mass of flames.

Afterwards, the man told his very young grandson to show me how they climb the high palm trees. The child tied a short rope around a tree to form a loop and then, on stepping into the loop and lifting it waist high, he placed his bare feet against the tree, and with a swift double action, raised himself and quickly lifted the loop. By a rhythmic repetition of this movement, he simply glided up the tree, and in no time at all, was about 80 feet above ground. After the little fellow had descended, he invited me to climb the tree, but for obvious reasons, I declined – preferring instead to try the much safer enterprise of making fire.

The weather was noticeably cooler than we had recently experienced, but the most prevalent characteristic was the sudden squalls of very strong wind. Just before we arrived the sloop *Windward* had sought shelter, after being dismasted, and another yacht in the harbour had lost its wheelhouse on the way from Samoa. Near the harbour entrance, the large wreck of the brigantine *Yankee* is plainly visible; a recent hurricane having moved it from where it had struck the Avarua reef. The raft *Tahiti Nai II*, after its long voyage, also hit one of the local reefs and the leader of the expedition, Erik de Bisschop, lost his life.

One day, the owner of a large trimaran in the harbour, asked if I had a chart of Raoul island that he could borrow, and after studying it for some time, he said the island appeared to be well worth a visit. I therefore, suggested that he should take the chart, and copy the essential information to assist in laying off the courses through the outlying reefs. He assured me, however, that he had committed to memory all that was necessary. Two weeks later we heard, over the radio, that his yacht had been wrecked on the Raoul reef and he had been drowned.

When it was time for us to leave Rarotonga, the local people presented each of us, with the traditional farewell gift – a shell necklace. We were also given some excellent fishing tackle and many wonderful oranges. It is interesting to note, that the mutineer, Fletcher Christian, called at Rarotonga with HMS *Bounty* on his way from Tahiti to Pitcairn, and gave the inhabitants seeds for their first oranges.

After leaving the harbour, we had to recover our anchor from where we had left it on arrival. Murray dived to a depth of 12 fathoms and found that the chain had become entangled in several large coral heads. It took fully twenty minutes to get the chain clear, so that the anchor could be lifted by the windlass.

Our port of destination was now Pago Pago, on the island of Tutuila in the Samoan archipelago, about 755 miles away to the north-west. When we were about half-way, an exhausted tropic bird landed on deck and after Nick had nursed it for three days, it appeared to have recovered, but it was not to be. From time to time, hundreds of birds landed on *Keramos* but none of those that failed to leave within about two hours, ever survived.

As we approached Pago Pago, at about 2100 hr on 3 August, we expected to see flashes from the lighthouse at the harbour entrance, but there was nothing at all. Furthermore, there were no shore lights – the entire place was in complete darkness. On going ashore, we learned that the electricity generating station was out of action. Apparently, one of the maintenance engineers had put oil in the diesel engine where the water should have gone, and water where the oil should have gone – and the result was as might have been expected!

That was not all, as everyone we met had a tale of woe. There were no newspapers, because the only printing works on the island had been burned down. A cable railway that spanned the harbour and conveyed passengers to the summit of the Rainmaker mountain, had proved to be a great tourist attraction, but it had just been demolished.

It would seem that during some recent celebrations, arrangements had been made for a four-engined aircraft to fly low and pass under the cable. The stunt was accomplished successfully three times, but on the fourth attempt, the aircraft hit the cable, so destroying both the railway and the aircraft; the crew of course lost their lives. There was only one really good tourist hotel on the island and when the plane crashed, it landed on the hotel and put it out of business.

Keramos was anchored close to a small village community, where Sadie Thompson's boarding house – immortalised in Somerset Maughan's *Rain* – can still be seen.

Every evening, between six and six-thirty, there is a religious curfew, during which the people are in their houses at prayer and must not be disturbed. Green-uniformed guards are posted at each end of the village, to ensure strict compliance.

Alan Kirby, who had previously sailed on *Keramos* from Recife to Grenada, joined us here, together with his friend Paul Wilcox. Paul was engaged on scientific work in the United States, similar to that undertaken by Alan in Britain. On arrival, they made a comprehensive tour of the island and found much of interest – apart from the recent man-made destruction.

After a short overnight passage, we arrived at Apia in Western Samoa, just before midday on 15 August. We found the standard of living here much higher than in Pago Pago – and certainly less accident prone. There are good shops and an excellent market, while the hotels provide a first-class service.

One hotel in particular, is world famous – this is of course, Aggie's hotel. Many people had told us, that when in Samoa, we must visit 'Aggies'. As Alan, Paul and I walked along the harbour road and came up to the hotel, we were somewhat disappointed to find an unpretentious building, but on entering, we found ourselves in a completely different world. The service was impeccable and the various facilities provided all that could be desired. The real attraction and charm of the place, however, was not fully appreciated until we passed through the original part of the hotel and into the gardens, for here were wonderful tropical trees and flowers in profusion, surrounding a fine swimming pool, a bar and a number of exotic Polynesian huts accommodating luxuriously appointed suites for the guests.

We returned one evening for dinner, which was superb but it was the warm amiability engendered by the fabulous Aggie Grey, that made the occasion so memorable. Most evenings she could be seen dancing with the guests, in unrestrained abandon; she might just have been entertaining family friends. Anyone wishing to know more about the remarkable lady, should read *Aggie Grey of Samoa* by Nelson Eustis. Not long after our visit, I learned with great sadness of Aggie's death. I feel quite sure the place can never be the same again.

Murray, who had served us so well during the thousands of miles *Keramos* had sailed, since he joined us in Rio, decided that he would have to leave us, in order to pursue new business interests. Reluctantly therefore, we had to wave him farewell, as we sailed away from Apia, during the afternoon of 18 August, bound for Tonga.

Soon we were over the Tongan Trench, where the ocean bed falls steeply to 35,700 feet below the surface. This is very nearly the greatest ocean depth; only being exceeded by the Mariana Trench which has a depth of 36,198 feet. In the darkness of these great depths, strange creatures eke out a mysterious existence. We tossed into the water an empty Coca-Cola bottle and speculated as to how long it would take to reach the bottom.

At 0200 hr on Tuesday 19 August, *Keramos* crossed the International Dateline, so it immediately became 0200 hr on Wednesday 20 August. At the same time, the chronometer was changed from 11 hours behind Greenwich Mean time, to 13 hours ahead of G.M.T.

As we approached Tonga, *Keramos* was headed by strong winds which drove us too far to the west, so during the afternoon of 21 August we changed tack, and set course for Neiufu in the Vava'u Group. At that time, we happened to be very close to the spot, where in 1789, the crew of HMS *Bounty* mutinied.

Captain Bligh, together with the eighteen men who had remained loyal to him, were all put into an open boat, which was only 23 feet long, and then cast adrift, with few supplies and very little food. The feat of sailing against tremendous odds, the 3,900 miles to Timor in 41 days, must be regarded as one of the greatest achievements at sea, of all time. Anyone who saw the film, *Mutiny on the Bounty*, will no doubt, have formed a poor impression of Bligh's character – those who wish to know what he was really like, should read *Bligh* by Gavin Kennedy.

It was completely dark by the time we came up to the land, so we found the tortuous path around the many small islands and the six mile approach up the fiord-like entrance to Neiufu, quite exciting.

All the following morning was spent in receiving on board the endless procession of officials, who came to clear us for customs and immigration entry – and until this was complete, nobody was allowed to go ashore. Fortunately, the time was not without interest, as many traders in small canoes came alongside, to offer us a wide variety of goods, including wood carvings, raffia baskets, mats and shells.

Next day, we took *Keramos* farther up the estuary to Goodhope Beach, where there was to be a Tongan feast. On going ashore, after dark, we found the people preparing an *umu*, by placing stones over a hot fire. The food to be cooked was wrapped in banana leaves, and laid on the stones, after which, more leaves were piled on top to retain the heat. The food included a pig, many kinds of fish, with excellent lobsters and a variety of vegetables such as dalo, breadfruit and tapioca. Following the cooked food, which was served on leaves, we enjoyed delicious tropical fruits.

Then came the music, singing and communal merrymaking. The dancing girls rubbed coconut oil onto their skin to make it glisten in the amber light of the many oil lamps. Later, when it began to rain, the flickering scintillation from their gyrating bodies produced an effect similar to one only seen in firework displays.

The following morning, we attended a kava ceremony; the preparation of this traditional drink being the most honoured feature of Tongan life. The yanggona root is pounded to fine powder and then mixed with water to form a pulp, which after kneading, is diluted and strained through hibiscus fibres, to separate the precious juices.

I was particularly privileged to be nominated as the guest of honour and positioned at the head of the assembly. We all sat cross-legged on the floor of the small building during the ceremony, which was conducted with the utmost gravity according to sacramental ritual. To the cries of, "*Talo*", some of the juice was poured into a half-coconut shell and offered to me, whereupon, I was required to drain it at one go, and then spin the empty shell on the mat before me, while the assembly cried, "*A Matha*" (It is dry). The kava was then served to all present. The drink is non-alcoholic, tastes somewhat like menthol, and certainly produces a pronounced euphoric feeling.

Before leaving Tonga, we decided to take a look at some of the small islands, to the west of the Vava'u Group, that we had passed in darkness when we arrived. We had been told there were some spectacular caves, and that the possibilities for scuba-diving were excellent. We were not to be disappointed in either respect, but in addition, the superb tropical scenery must have cost the photographers on board a small fortune in film.

Swallows cave at the northern end of Kapa, was visited first, and found to be mainly of interest due to the intense blue of the water, and the range of colours on the sea-bed, when viewed from inside the cave.

To gain access to Mariners cave, it is necessary to swim under water for a distance of about five yards, at low tide. According to local legend, a young noble, fearing that a despotic king would steal his sweetheart, hid her in the secret cave and returned each night with food and water. Finally, the man built an outrigger canoe and spirited the girl away to safety in Fiji. This love story has been enshrined in ballads and in the works of many poets, including Byron.

We sailed for Fiji on 26 August, and two days later crossed the 180° meridian, so completing the first half of our intended circumnavigation. As we approached the Lau Group of islands, we were surrounded by a very large school of frolicsome, humpback whales – some coming within a few feet of *Keramos*. To avoid possible damage, we started the engine and did everything possible to frighten them away – short of endangering an endangered species.

On arrival in Suva, we were instructed over the radio, to make fast to the quarantine buoy and after being declared a healthy ship, we were permitted to go alongside the main quay for customs clearance. As all alcoholic drinks had to be sealed in our bonded locker, *Keramos* was for the first time, a 'dry' ship. We then sailed over to the lovely Bay of Islands and moored stern-to on the quay of the Tradewinds Hotel. In this position we were, when sitting in the cockpit, little more than twenty feet from the large open window of the hotel lounge. Every evening, while dining in the cockpit, we could see the spectacular cabarets presented in the lounge.

In this delightful haven, we were able to attend to some much needed maintenance on *Keramos* and as there was a plentiful supply of fresh water, we gave all the exterior surfaces a thorough scrubbing. When working below the waterline, however, we could never quite trust the many sea snakes that nosed around. They were up to seven feet in length and bright yellow in colour, with black bands. The turtles, on the other hand, although very inquisitive, were quite harmless.

We found the shops in Suva well stocked with a wide variety of goods, at very reasonable prices. In particular, we were able to buy Japanese photographic equipment at less than half the corresponding price asked in Britain. As a result, several new cameras and much auxiliary equipment appeared on board.

Occasionally the island's electricity supply would fail. We were told that a new power station had suffered a continuous series of breakdowns, until the mayor in desperation, had decided to get a witch-doctor to exorcise the evil spirits. Thereafter, for the following month or so, the plant was completely trouble free – and then one day, there was a catastrophic failure, which put the entire plant out of action. It was subsequently revealed, that at the precise time of the stoppage, the mayor had been thrown out of office.

We explored much of southern Viti Levu. Early one Sunday morning, Alan, Paul and I set off by local bus for the Tholoisuva National Park. The other passengers, being on their way to church, were dressed in their heavy black clothes, which contrasted greatly with their colourful and scanty, but essentially practical, week-day attire. The park is thickly forested with mahogany, and contains many cascading waterfalls and shimmering pools, which provided inviting subjects for a great deal of photography.

At one point on our walk, we had to cross a swiftly flowing stream by some very slippery stepping-stones, and Alan kindly offered to assist me, by taking across my new and much valued camera. When he was about half-way across, he slipped and in spite of valiant efforts to regain his balance, there came a moment when all that Paul and I could see above the water, was an extended arm and a hand tightly clutching a camera. After crossing without incident, and collecting my camera from its dripping guardian, I fully expected to hear from Alan an appropriate *bon mot* and I certainly did – but it would not look well in print!

The Fijian government had recently allocated a considerable sum of money to equip new schools, specifically for the teaching of pottery, with the aim of providing, in due course, employment for craft potters. Through introductions made by the British High Commission, I was able to meet the people concerned and co-operate in this worth-while project by setting up a sales agency in Suva, to facilitate the shipment from England of the necessary equipment and materials.

One day, Nick and I set out to visit the Governor's stately house. At the large entrance gates, were posted two armed sentries, resplendent in belted red tunics and scalloped white kilts. After marching to and fro several times, they would stand stiffly to attention, at each side of the elaborate entrance. I discussed with Nick, whether or not we should ask for permission to enter. He thought they would react like ceremonial guards in Britain and ignore all questions. I was not so sure and after approaching close to one of them, I said to Nick in a fairly loud voice, "I wonder if we are supposed to just walk through?" At this the guard performed a first rate ventriloquial act, as without moving a muscle of his body and without a quiver of the lips he muttered, "Yes – go straight in". I thanked him, while he continued to stand motionless, and stare into infinity.

We had hoped that Alan and Paul would be able to sail with us to New Zealand, but they both felt that the time had come, when duty would be calling in a pretty loud voice. So, after the kind of farewell party that had become customary on *Keramos*, they made their way to the airport at Nadi, from where they flew to Los Angeles.

Fiji was one of the last countries to abandon cannibalism, just over a hundred years ago. The practice was widespread, as prisoners taken in battle and shipwrecked mariners were invariably eaten. It is not surprising therefore that Fiji became known as the 'Cannibal Isles'. Among the Fijians, cannibalism was not simply a ritual or an act of vengeance, as there can be little doubt, that human flesh was enjoyed by all who ate it – and as with all meat, certain cuts were highly prized. One chief on Viti Levu, is said to have eaten 999 people, and to have marked the fact, by erecting a stone pillar on each occasion.

The flesh was wrapped in the leaves of a vegetable plant and cooked on heated stones in an *umu*. Wooden forks with carved handles were used when eating, because it was considered *tabu* to touch cooked human flesh with the fingers, as was the normal practice when consuming other meat.

Certain tribes of Fijians, such as the *Sawau* Tribe from the island of Beqa, still perform the firewalking ceremony and when we heard that such a ceremony was to be enacted not far from Suva, we decided this was something that should not be missed. When we arrived at the scene, we saw a number of large stones, on top of which was a pile of blazing logs, with flames rising to a height of eight feet or more.

At the appointed time, the *Bete* (Chief) and some of his men removed the remains of the burning logs and by the aid of long poles, moved the stones into position to form a bed about 20 feet long and 6 feet wide. A length of tree-fern called *Waqa-bala-bala*, said to contain the Spirit God, was next laid across the stones in all directions. Bundles of *sila* (swamp grass) were then placed around the bed of stones.

While the stones were being prepared, the firewalkers were in a nearby hut, from which loud exhortations and much chanting could be heard. When the *Bete* considered all was ready, he approached the hut and called out, "*Vuto-o*", whereupon, the men came out and advanced in single file toward the stones. The *Bete* then slowly led the bare-footed firewalkers six times round the bed of stones. After loudly intoning a brief incantation, with arms outstretched, the *Bete* stepped onto the stones and slowly made his way, from end to end. The firewalkers, about twenty in all, then one by one, repeated the performance, without apparent distress.

At the conclusion of the ceremony, the spectators were ushered away, without having an opportunity to inspect the site. But after a few minutes, I was able to return and carefully examine the stones. I found that most were still very hot – certainly too hot to touch – but those over which the men had walked, which were marked by white footprints, were noticeably cooler. Moreover the footprints showed that all the men had followed the same path.

Around the bed of stones was a considerable quantity of white wood-ash, which had been wetted by water from the swamp grass, so that when the men were walking around the bed, their feet would have been coated by a protective layer of the heat insulating ash. I rubbed my hand in some of the wood-ash paste, which strongly adhered and enabled me to momentarily touch the stones on which the men had walked.

I collected samples of the stones and when later examined, found that the rock was of volcanic origin and had low specific heat and thermal conductivity, while the rough dark coloured surface facilitated rapid radiation of heat. The rock was therefore, ideally suited to this particular purpose.

To what extent the 'goings-on' inside the hut induced a pain resisting state of hypnosis, I do not know, but I do believe there were sufficient physical factors to account for the apparently mysterious performance, among which is the fact that these men never wear shoes, so the soles of their feet must become leather hard.

I do not wish to give the impression that the entire show was one big confidence trick. It is quite possible that during the course of time, these people, by trial and error, have discovered what works and what does not, and this accumulated knowledge has been passed on, from one generation to the next, until today, they are able to put on a quite remarkable performance. One thing is very certain – not for all the tea in China, would I have walked across those stones.

As the time for our departure approached, we were urged to extend our stay, in order to witness the rising of the *mbalolo*. This is a segmented worm, about eighteen inches long, which is highly esteemed as a culinary delicacy. It lives in the fissures of coral, from which it emerges only on two days in the year, to propagate and die. The timing for this emergence is quite remarkable, as it only takes place before sunrise, on the day when the moon enters the third quarter in October and November. Within recorded memory, the rising of the *mbalolo* has always occurred on these precise days, and at no other time. How the worms, while hidden away in the coral, can know what the moon is doing, must remain one of the world's great mysteries.

We would very much have liked to see this strange phenomenon of nature, and possibly to have feasted on the clever worms, but we on *Keramos*, also had to have regard to the calendar and in particular, to the fast approaching hurricane season in Fiji. So, on 26 September, we set sail for the Bay of Islands in New Zealand, 1210 miles to the south of Fiji.

30

KERAMOS II IN NEW ZEALAND

Before leaving England, I had received an interesting introduction to Captain Jim Cottier, who is the warden of the Wildlife Sanctuary on Roberton Island – one of the many lovely islands in the Bay of Islands. So, after clearing customs in Opua, I decided to sail over to Jim's small island. As we approached, only one house could be seen, and that was overlooking the beach in Lagoon Bay; accordingly we dropped anchor there and made for the shore in the tender. As we did so, a man left the house and called out, "Hello Henry Podmore, and welcome". It was to be a welcome in more than mere words, because nobody could have been more hospitable.

We were all invited to his charming house, where he wined and dined us right royally. At that time, Jim was living alone, as his wife Jenny, had recently sailed to England on a tall-mast sailing ship.

Jim told us about James Cook's visit to the island in November 1768, when he was captain of HM Barque *Endeavour*. The vessel was then anchored where *Keramos* was now lying. Unfortunately, when Cook came to leave the island, *Endeavour* struck Whale Rock, but as the wind was light, no serious damage was sustained.

Jim took us on a walk round the island and it was then, that the dramatic history of the place began to unfold. He showed us where in 1839, the first owner of the island – John Roberton – had built his house and farm buildings. To illustrate subsequent events, Jim produced a book entitled, *Motuarohia – An island in the Bay of Islands – sometimes known as Roberton's Island*, which had been written by Maurice Lennard. In the book is a copy of a letter, written sometime during 1840, by Roberton's wife, to her mother and father-in-law, who were living in Edinburgh. The following extracts have been taken from the letter:

"My dear father and mother.
Almost a lunatic, I sit down to advise you which I can assure you is a task such a one that I cannot describe. Not only that I am very ill but also to tell you most melancholy news that is to say that your only son and my dear affectionate husband died on the 17th day of last month. He was unfortunately drowned opposite our house and island. He was sailing merely for his own amusement in a new boat that has just come from the builder. It was very large and having only one small boy with him in the boat, they were caught in a sudden gust of wind and in

195

one moment they disappeared and drowned. I have had 3 boats employed for the last fortnight searching for their poor bodies but with little success. A few days ago a small part of my poor Roberton's breast with fishes teeth marks in it, Oh the sight of this has thrown me into a bed of illness. I hope it will please God to restore me again to health if it only be for the sake of my poor dear children. - - - On account of our building taking so much cash at the time of my poor Roberton's death I had only ten pounds in the house. I have spent thirty since in one way and another, I have been compelled to borrow. What to do I cannot tell. I am here on an inhospitable island in a cannibal country with only one servant in the house. I cannot keep servants without keeping them well and paying them. - - - "

After the tragedy, Mrs Roberton bravely continued with the farming and to assist her, engaged a white man, Thomas Bull, and a sixteen year old Maori boy, named Maketu. Also living on the island with her, in addition to her son and daughter, was a young girl, Isabella Brind.

From all accounts, Bull was a brutal character, who made life for the young Maketu exceedingly uncomfortable. As a result, Maketu awaited an opportunity to seek revenge. So it was, that during the night of Sunday 30 November 1841, while Bull lay asleep, Maketu crept upon him, and split his head open with an axe.

According to Maori custom, Maketu felt fully justified in his action and immediately reported the matter to Mrs Roberton, who told the boy that now the community had agreed to abide by English law, he would no doubt be tried, and hanged for murder. This it would seem, further enraged Maketu; so much so, that in a fit of uncontrolled temper, he killed and horribly mutilated the woman and the two little girls. The young son escaped from the house and fled to the top of Pa Hill, which overlooks the northern cliffs; here Maketu caught the little boy and threw him two hundred feet down, to his death on the rocks below.

After much resistance from the powerful Maori community, Maketu was eventually handed over to stand trial for murder, in accordance with English law, to which they had recently subscribed by the Treaty of Waitangi. This being the first such trial in New Zealand, it was to be expected that it would be followed with much interest by the Maoris. Apparently, they were impressed by the fairness of the trial, and even accepted the sentence of death, but the procedure of hanging was new to them, and as a result, some let it be known that they would seek retribution upon anyone who took part in the hanging. It was not surprising therefore, that no official hangman was appointed.

Keramos II In New Zealand

The gallows was set up before the Auckland Court-house, in Queen Street. The platform was said to merely consist of a rough door, having hinges on one side and a bolt on the other. A strong guard surrounded the scaffold to keep back the large crowd, which consisted mainly of Maoris. At the appointed time, Maketu was surreptitiously pushed through an opening in the wall of the Court-house and onto the platform. From behind a screen, someone threw the noose loosly over the prisoner's head and with his own hands, it was carefully adjusted into postion – then, before anyone could release the bolt, he stumbled off the edge of the small platform.

It was reported that, "The platform only allowed a short drop and as he slowly strangled, his body revolved with the slow unravelling of the rope and his blue blanket, which was his only covering, fell away". It was not surprising that the Maoris strongly disapproved of this form of execution and sought to have restored, the right to despatch murderers by their traditional method, which consisted of a swift blow to the head, by a heavy wooden club.

Jim joined us on *Keramos* for dinner, followed by an extremely convivial evening. The animated conversation continued well into the small hours of the following day, before we eventually saw him safely back on shore. It was not surprising therefore, that in spite of Jim's horrific stories, all on board should sleep later than usual, with the result that our intended early departure was somewhat delayed. When I went over to my desk, I was surprised to find a note which read:

"Jove, you fellows sleep soundly. Thanks again for a
wonderful evening. The weather forecast is not good
– so watch out for Whale Rock.

Bon voyage. Jim."

By the desk was a large basket containing hen and duck eggs, and several jars of honey from Jim's apiary. As *Keramos* sailed away, we signalled "*Au revoir*" on the siren, while Jim waved fervently, from his little beach.

That evening was spent at Whangarei and the following day, we continued sailing south to Bon Accord harbour. Here we met two wardens, who had been shooting wallabies. They said it was necessary to shoot about 300 each year, to prevent them becoming a pest – they are rated of little value except for their fur.

The approach to Auckland, past the many off-shore islands, was very attractive and as *Keramos* neared the harbour, we were instructed to go alongside in Cook's Wharf. The principal of our New Zealand agency – Ray Browning – was soon on board and together, we compiled an itinery of works visits, which was to keep me busy for the following couple of weeks.

I then flew back to England. The flight was exceptionally comfortable, with excellent service, and menus such as I had never seen before, on an aircraft – perhaps the fact that Princess Anne and Captain Mark Phillips were on board, had something to do with it. They had recently been staying at the Tradewinds Hotel in Suva, to attend the tenth anniversary of Fiji's independence.

While I was away, John arranged for Keramos to be hauled out of the water, in order to get the barnacles removed and to have anti-fouling paint applied to the hull. The paint for this work was that which had arrived too late for use in Grenada, and after crossing the Atlantic by air on three occasions, had subsequently been carried on *Keramos* for over 13,000 miles.

I returned to Auckland on 6 November, after a short visit to Hong Kong, and a week later, Ken Isted rejoined us. Together with Ray Browning, I visited more of the potteries on the North Island, and combined this work, with much sightseeing in this interesting and wholly delightful country.

Keramos left Auckland on 23 November, to sail over to the Coromandel peninsula. Here, I visited a number of small potteries, including one run by Barry Bicknell, which was particularly interesting because the required clay and the wood for firing the kilns is transported from deep within the dense kauri forest by a small gauge railway. The track crosses deep ravines by spectacular bridges, designed and built by the versatile Barry.

We called next at Great Barrier Island, where a narrow entrance leads to a large expanse of water, surrounded by forested mountains. As the island is now a protected nature reserve, we were able to see much of the indigenous wildlife, including kiwis, wallabies and opossums; in addition to a wide variety of sea and land birds.

Our next port of call was Tauranga, situated in a beautiful and well sheltered estuary. Nearby, there are several places of interest, including a quaint Maori village and the famous caves at Waitomo, which are illuminated solely by the light emitted from millions of glow-worms. When entering the series of caves, which is normally done by boat, it is imperative to preserve complete silence, otherwise all the lights go out.

There is also the community at Rotorua, where people live close to the fires of the earth's molten interior. The district is actually inside the caldera of an active volcano, so it is not surprising that there should be gurgling pools of boiling mud and dozens of thermal geysers ejecting jets of steaming water, which rise to over 100 feet. A Maori village is located amidst all this thermal activity, and where at times, the smell of sulphurous fumes is quite overpowering. The villagers wash clothes in the boiling water and even use it for cooking. There is a chapel and a graveyard – to see clouds of steam rising from the graves, certainly makes one stand and stare.

From Tauranga, we sailed across the Bay of Plenty (so named by Captain Cook, because he was able to find in the vicinity, a liberal supply of excellent food), past the very active volcano on White Island, and then to Gisborne, where there is a colony of highly esteemed craft potters. We were invited into many homes, and entertained some very interesting people on board, including the immense figure of Ian Fitzpatrick, the captain of the 'All Blacks'. Typically, his mother was at pains to assure me that, "He is really a very gentle lad".

During the evening of 7 December, as we were sailing across Hawke Bay, bound for Wellington, we heard a storm warning given over the Gisborne Fishermen's Radio Service. By the following morning, it had become very cold, visibility had deteriorated, it was raining heavily and the continual increases in wind strength, were demanding corresponding reductions in sail.

That night, as *Keramos* was approaching the Cook Strait, the full force of the storm was experienced during Ken's watch (midnight to 0400 hr) and John's watch (0400 to 0800 hr). But from time to time, during the course of that dreadful night, the entire crew was called upon to assist in safeguarding the yacht. Nevertheless, structural damage was sustained and the reefed mainsail was rent in two. It therefore became expedient to hand all sails and allow our stricken vessel to drift to the east, under bare poles.

When I took over at 0800 hr, Wellington radio was still warning of hurricane force winds and advising all shipping in the Strait to seek shelter immediately. It announced that the Wellington to Picton ferry service had been cancelled, due to the dangerous conditions. However, the weather soon began to improve and by the aid of storm sails, we were able to make very slow progress against the tremendous seas. From time to time, we had encountered higher waves, but here, there was a wave front advancing from the north-east, which was meeting another wave front coming through the Strait, and the interaction between the two, was resulting in a very violently confused sea, with much broken water.

I have often been asked what it is like to be at sea, in a sailing yacht, during really bad weather. The two factors that combine to produce the most discomfort are the violent motion and the fearful noise. The wind screeches through the rigging, the sails clatter, waves crash on deck and to all this general racket, is added the intermittent, shattering thuds, as the vessel drops off the top of a breaking wave. On deck, flying spray so reduces visibility, that one might just as well keep the eyes closed. It becomes essential to wear protective clothing, life-jacket and safety-harness, with the latter securely attached to a strong point, because the chances of going back and finding anyone who was washed overboard, would be extremely remote.

Due to the violent motion, it can be almost as dangerous when below deck. Irrespective of the task at the time, it is essential to keep one hand free to grasp something secure. On the approach of bad weather, we always stretched ropes across the saloon to assist and safeguard movement. The dining table could be folded and lowered to a secure position by means of a central steel column, while all the chairs were held on rails, to which they could be made fast. The doors of lockers and all drawers were self-locking. In the galley, there was a specially designed stowage position for evey article – nevertheless, some items always seemed to take wing. Each bunk was fitted with a canvas cover, which could be tightly fastened to prevent the occupant being forcibly ejected.

It is said that the most secure vessel at sea, in a storm, is a well corked bottle. Accordingly, all hatches and openings on *Keramos* could be made completely watertight. The cockpit was self-draining and the hatchway, between the cockpit and the saloon, could be rendered watertight by a pair of rising doors composed of armour-plate glass and steel-sheet. It is also said, that the best way to get water out of a boat, is to give a frightened man a bucket; in that case, we only employed the second best method, which was to use a variety of powerful pumps.

At about 0830 hr on that eventful day, I spotted Cape Palliser on the radar. It was then just over 24 miles away to the north and by gradually closing the land, we were able to gain some shelter from the wind that was then funnelling through the Strait. Even so, the anemometer was registering over 70 mph and in the gusts, the needle was going right off the scale. Strangely, at that time and for over two hours, about 60 dolphins continued to swim around *Keramos*; whether we were assisting them in some way, or they were just being friendly, I do not know.

By mid-afternoon, we were cautiously creeping across Palliser Bay and approaching Baring Head. An hour later we rounded Pencarrow Head and then took great care to keep well clear of Barrett Reef, where a few years previous, one of the large ferries foundered, with the loss of almost all on board.

Eventually, on reaching the harbour at Wellington, we selected the most sheltered spot we could find and secured *Keramos* with all the anchors at our disposal. Nevertheless, we considered it prudent to maintain an anchor watch throughout the night, with the engine on stand-by, in case the anchors should drag.

The following day, Ray Browning joined us, so that after crossing the Strait to South Island, visits could be made to the various potteries in the vicinity of Nelson. We decided that our base for this work should be Picton, at the head of Queen Charlotte Sound, which is just one of the many interconnecting sounds, penetrating deep inland. The locality, known as the Marlborough Sounds is, by virtue of the large sheets of water and the surrounding mountains, famed for its scenic beauty.

I found much interest at all the potteries we visited. Most of them produce general utility ware, but the decoration often incorporates Maori designs to very good effect. In one factory, I was surprised to see two of father's dead-weight pumps, bearing 1912 patent numbers, and by all accounts, still giving excellent service. Wherever we went, we were received with great kindness; invariably entertained to a delightful meal in someone's home and after each tour inland, I would return to *Keramos*, laden with gifts such as strawberries, boysenberries, honey, nuts, pickles, cakes, wines and even wonderful New Zealand lamb. I much enjoyed working with Ray, but on the approach of the holiday period, we regretfully had to bid him farewell, when he flew back to Auckland to spend Christmas with his family.

Just outside Picton, there is a large sheep abattoir, which we were invited to visit. It handles 5,000 sheep each day, but its sister factory can process 15,000 daily. No part of the sheep is wasted: hormones are extracted from the gall; tallow and neatsfoot oil obtained from the bones; excellent fertilisers prepared from the blood and certain other parts of the animal, while the wool and skins are fully processed. From the time a sheep leaves the reception pen, to the time when the meat is placed in the freezer, is just 24 minutes. On arrival, the sheep are washed and thoroughly inspected, after which they are led in batches of about thirty, to the killing point, by a specially trained sheep called 'Judas', which scuttles, to and fro, all day long, leading its fellows to the slaughter – but taking great care not to get embroiled itself.

On Christmas Eve, Ken and Nick decided to join the people making their way to the nearby church for the midnight service. Ken said the sermon placed much emphasis on the 'fire and brimstone' aspect, while the qualifications for entry to Paradise were pitched at such a high level, that in his opinion, very few people would make it. He confided that when the collection bag was passed round, it was difficult to decide whether to accept the inevitable and keep his money, or attempt to buy his way out of the impending predicament.

Although it was of course mid-summer, we spent a festive Christmas Day on *Keramos*, entertaining business friends in the traditional English manner. At our various ports of call in New Zealand, friends had left parcels on board marked, "Not to be opened until Christmas", so we all had a busy and exciting time opening presents. Before we left Auckland, Ray's wife Doreen, had put on board several packages for Christmas, which we found to contain home made mince pies, Christmas cake and a wide variety of pastries; all of which were much appreciated – particularly, when we were later battling across the Tasman Sea.

During the morning of 29 December, we refuelled *Keramos* and then sailed from Queen Charlotte Sound into several other connecting sounds, where the scenery is equally superb, before emerging into Cook Strait. Soon we had on our port hand, the aptly named Farewell Spit. This narrow sandbank extends out to sea, for over twelve miles and attracts large numbers of migrating birds of varied species, including the godwit, dotterel, wrybill, tattler and the turnstone. On the water around *Keramos* were flocks of storm-petrels (Mother Carey's chickens) and many penguins rounding-up the fish.

Away to the north, and fully 90 miles away, we could see the volcanic cone of Mount Egmont, in the hazy glow of the setting sun. Astern were the mountains of the Marlborough Sounds, and of course, the many friends who had made our short stay so memorable – ahead lay the unpredictable Tasman Sea.

31

TO SYDNEY AND A RUDE AWAKENING

The Tasman has a bad reputation for sudden squalls, called Southerly Busters, and soon after leaving the Cook Strait, we were introduced to one of them. Fortunately their approach is heralded by an isolated black cloud, which makes it possible to reduce sail before the onslaught commences. On this particular occasion the blow was soon over, and as the sun returned, we noticed a lone albatross circling around *Keramos*. This kind of thing is not unusual in these parts, but we were surprised to find that it was still with us at daybreak, on the following morning. After it had been there for two days, we really began to wish it would go away. We knew the seamen of old believed that albatrosses embodied the souls of departed mariners, and that they would follow ships to warn of impending danger. Of course, we did not believe such things – it was noticeable, however, that passing ships were given a much wider berth than usual. After the bird had been with us for five days, we were relieved to make a safe landfall, and to see our guardian disappear over the horizon.

We arrived in Sydney harbour – the world's largest natural harbour – just before midnight, on 5 January, 1981, and proceeded to Watsons Bay for customs clearance, which kept some of us up for most of the night. The following morning, we moved *Keramos* nearer to the city centre and were accorded a warm reception at the Cruisng Yacht Club of Australia. The Club provides excellent facilities and has extensive private moorings in a secluded creek. A very nice pier extends from the premises out to the deep water, and at the end, *Keramos* was permitted to lie alongside.

I was soon in touch with Geof. Cowan, the principal of our Australian agency, who ensured that the following days were fully occupied, but nevertheless, with some time for sightseeing in the fine city. The locals refer to the imposing harbour bridge, as the 'coathanger' and to the magnificent opera house, as the 'a$350 million view'.

I found the spectacular arched roofs of the opera house particularly interesting, because the vast shining surfaces are covered by ceramic tiles. Moreover, the weather resistant glaze on the tiles owes it opaque whiteness to zircon, which had been shipped from Brisbane to Britain, for ultra-fine grinding by the Vibro-Energy mills, in Stoke.

Ken, Nick and I attended a performance of Brittens, *Midsummer Night's Dream*, in the opera house. During the interval, the audience left the auditorium and made its way to the large balconies overlooking the harbour. These provide wonderful views of the illuminated bridge and the many ships, as their lights delineate a web of criss-crossing paths, against the dark background of the water.

After the performance, we made our way back to *Keramos* and for once, we all decided to retire early to our bunks. Shortly after midnight, we were awakened by a devastating crash, as *Keramos* was rammed violently against the pier. John was the first up on deck – closely followed by the rest of us. We were amazed to see a large ferryboat, close alongside, and slowly going astern. Fearing a further collision, I called on her crew to stop the boat, but they said they were unable to do so, because the engine controls had failed. We endeavoured to get fendoffs down between the two vessels, to minimse further damage, while the crew on the ferryboat leaned on the rails, and watched our efforts with sublime indifference.

After what seemed an eternity, the intruder disappeared into the darkness. It was not until John returned to his cabin, that we discovered the true extent of the damage, for we then saw a great hole in the hull, just above the waterline and very close to where John's head must have been, as he lay asleep in his bunk – no wonder he was the first up on deck!

While Nick took the appropriate action to safeguard *Keramos*, John went over to the ferryboat to obtain all necessary information for insurance purposes, etc. He found the offending vessel was the *John Cadman* and that since discontinuing service as a ferry, she had been rebuilt in order to provide passengers with a first-class meal, while cruising round the extensive waters of the harbour.

That evening, after the diners had disembarked, the crew had taken their meal and then commenced to move the vessel away from the quay and out to its mooring buoy, in the commercial part of the harbour. It was then that the engine controls, between the wheelhouse and the engine room, had apparently failed, with the result that she finished up roaming among the yachts in the private harbour and inevitably damaging several, in addition to *Keramos*.

A complete change in our plans was now imperative. Consequently, it was arranged that Nick would carry out temporary repairs, to enable *Keramos* to be moved to a boatyard, while John and Ken would attend to the insurance survey and organize the essential repair work. As *Keramos* would obviously be out of commission for some time, I decided to return to Britain.

After I had discussed the nature of the unfortunate incident with our insurers, it was agreed that a claim for damages due to negligence, should be made against the owners of the *John Cadman*, with the action being contested through the Australian Courts in Sydney. As the evidence in our favour was so overwhelming, our advisers believed the outcome would be a foregone conclusion, but to our utter amazement, the Court rejected the claim, on the grounds that the damage was the result of an accident.

It was obviously necessary to lodge an appeal against this strange decision and to ensure that the court be comprehensively apprised on the various points that we had wrongly assumed to be axiomatic. Among these, was the action the crew of the *John Cadman* should have taken to avoid collision with other vessels, such as controlling the engine from the engine room. If for some extraordinary reason that was not possible, then the engine should have been stopped. No attempt was made to anchor the vessel or to sound the mandatory warning signals.

Needless to say, there was little difficulty in winning the appeal, but seven years were to elapse, before the claim for damages and the substantial costs could be quantified and agreed.

Back in Sydney, John was finding it difficult to locate a boatyard capable of making an effective repair. Eventually, however he arranged for the necessary work to be carried out, by a yard adjoining the Royal King Alfred Yacht Club, at Pittwater – some twenty miles to the north of Sydney.

We often wondered, what had led the seafarers of old, to believe that an albatross would follow a ship for days, in order to warn of portentous danger!

32

THE GREAT BARRIER REEF

I returned to *Keramos* on 13 March 1981, to find her fully restored and looking very smart once again. During the following week, I was able to call upon various business associates, several of whom we entertained on board, while the crew were making final arrangements for our much delayed departure.

When *Keramos* left Pittwater, I had on board John Kemish, Ken Isted, Nick Allen, Guy Merison and Peter Langford. Guy had previously gone out to Australia with the under 21 England Rugby Team, then worked for a year on a sheep farm as a jackaroo, and sailed in the Sydney to Hobart yacht race. Whereas Peter had travelled around quite a bit, to gain experience in the restaurant business, before joining us as a cook/deckhand.

We were bound for North Stradbroke Island, 450 miles to the north, where Consolidated Rutile Ltd dredge mineral sands from the lagoon, in order to separate the zircon, rutile and ilmenite. Since World War II, many thousand tons of zircon sand from this deposit had been shipped to England, for ultra-fine grinding in the Vibro-Energy Mills. I was therefore, very interested to learn something about the origin of the material and the method of processing.

We arrived at the island on 27 March and straightaway Al Taylor, the mine manager, took Ken and I on a tour of the plant and the extensive workings. The suspension of sand in water is sucked up, at the rate of 3,500 tons per hour, by the world's largest mineral dredger, and then pumped to a processing plant, where the required minerals are extracted. The remaining sand is transported to various parts of the island, for use in conjunction with a big development and rehabilitation scheme. The various minerals are subsequently transported to Brisbane, where they are subjected to sophisticated purification processes, before being shipped to many parts of the world, but mainly to Europe. Ken and I went over to Brisbane, to see this interesting plant and to explore a little of the fine city.

Then we were away once again, up the east coast, for a short visit to the attractive seaside resort of Mooloolaba. Soon after leaving there, and while approaching Sandy Cape, Guy noticed a red distress flare towards the land, and this was quickly followed by further flares. Over the radio, we learned that a ship had gone to the assistance of a motor yacht with engine trouble, and a tow had been requested. We were then asked to stand by the yacht, until the tug arrived. Accordingly, we made our way over to the stated position, which was about six miles away, and soon sighted a motor yacht called *New Moon*.

On going alongside, as it had no radio, we learned that it was bound for Bundaberg and could only proceed at about five knots, due to a gearbox problem. The crew told us that if we could accompany them to the Breaksea Spit buoy, which was about 35 miles distant, they would be able to manage the short remaining distance to their intended destination. John reported the situation to the duty officer at the Sea Rescue Authority, who then cancelled the tow and asked us to escort the vessel as requested. Accordingly, we set off together, at about 0100 hr, during Ken's watch.

The navigation hereabouts is quite tricky, due to the close proximity of many dangerous reefs, which demand accurate course changes, and the fact that there are no navigational aids, until Breaksea Spit is reached. At 0750 hr, John located the buoy right ahead on radar, and forty minutes later, we bid farewell to the *New Moon*, as she bore away to port, while we changed course for Lady Elliot island.

Apparently, the crew had only recently taken over the yacht and we strongly suspected that they were not equal to the task of navigating through the hazardous waters. This view was supported by the fact that when we increased speed to well above five knots, they had no difficulty in keeping up with us. Throughout the operation, John maintained continuous radio watch with the Rescue Authority, which finally voiced unstinted praise for the manner in which the 'rescue' had been carried out.

On 5 April, we called at Middle Island, in the Percy Group, where the lone inhabitant has erected, in West Bay, a rough shed and installed a telephone. This enables visiting yachtsmen to communicate with his house, where they can be assured of a warm welcome. The shed now contains many mementos and interesting messages left by yachtsmen. Close by is a sparsely equipped shelter, with a sign at the entrance reading, 'The Percy Hilton'. We were now back in the tropics and at the southern end of the Great Barrier Reef, so the scuba diving was providing much interest. Besides the usual brightly coloured fish, we were able to see many turtles, seahorses and large yellow seasnakes. When going on shore, it was usually advisable to carry a paddle from the tender, to ward off inquisitive emus.

The following day, we threaded our way among the 74 small islands in the Whitsunday Passage, famed for outstanding scenic interest and made a stop at Lindeman Island. Here there is a very fine hotel, with a lovely swimming pool where we were able to relax, without fear of the many nasties that one can encounter on the coral reefs.

Our next anchorage was in the Nara Inlet, which penetrates almost two miles into the middle of Hook Island. On the shores we could see many wild goats, and in the trees flocks of white cockatoos. Surprisingly, the air was thick with swarms of very colourful butterflies.

We put into Townsville to take on board a large quantity of stores and then into the rapidly developing tourist resort of Cairns. Here we, all found considerable interest in the theme park called 'Reef World', where in giant, glass-sided tanks were displayed many varieties of coral, and the spectacular fish that are to be found on the reefs. A large section was devoted to the dangerous species, such as stonefish, giant gropers, sharks, moray eels and stingrays. A highly dramatic commentary described the dangers and serious risk to life, if the necessary precautions are not taken. It was stressed, in no uncertain manner, that stonefish can cause human paralysis within two minutes and stingrays have often been known to cause death.

After leaving Cairns, we sailed to Low Islets, where we found a sheltered spot for an overnight stop in the lighthouse anchorage. The keeper and his family were very pleased to see us and have a chat, as they very rarely had visitors. Earlier in the day, their provisions for the month had been delivered. These included two large cases of beer and I noticed that already several tins were missing. Moreover, the supply continued to dwindle, as the keeper's stories became wilder and wilder.

As darkness approached, he said he would have to attend to his duties and invited us to accompany him. With some assistance from behind, he mounted the circular staircase and commenced to demonstrate his nightly routine; the shutters were opened and the rotating mirrors set in motion.

He then told us that each evening, he had to send a weather report to the meteorological office and proceeded to show how he obtained the required information from his various instruments. Ken asked him how he determined 'the further outlook' to which he replied, "If the crabs come out of the water and onto the beach, I know it is going to be stormy and the farther they come from the water, the worse it is going to be".

After an entertaining half hour, we descended the steps together, and as he extracted another tin from the case, he reminded us that we should hear his report on the radio, following the late news bulletin. We routinely monitored the weather forecasts, because the cyclone season for the area was not then over, and when later that evening, we listened to the shipping reports from coastal stations, the announcer concluded by saying, "No report has been received from Low Islets" – we wondered why!

From Low Islets northward, along the barrier reef, there are no further navigation aids until the Torres Strait is reached, and as navigation is much easier when the colour of the water can be seen, it is not advisable to sail at night. As a result, towards the end of each day, we would seek a suitable overnight anchorage.

Stops were made at Cape Flattery, where Guy went over to a fishing boat and obtained a large quantity of wonderful prawns, which Peter cooked for dinner; Lizard Island where the chart was marked 'Incompletely surveyed'; Flinders Island, memorable because of the colourful and noisy parrots; Night Island where the water was teeming with large fish, which leaped as high as ten feet in the air; Portland Road, notable on account of the many twelve foot high termite ant-hills, with their strange tower and turreted embellishments, the pervasive crocodiles and kangeroos, and the woman who was complaining bitterly because a 15 foot long python had just taken all her chickens – and Hannibal Island, where Guy caught three nice sea-perch with the speargun.

On reaching the Torres Strait, we anchored off Mount Adolphus Island and as there was still about an hour of daylight remaining, Nick and Guy decided to go ashore, to pursue their respective interests, with Nick exploring the coral and Guy searching for rare shells. After a while, they had become well separated and while Guy was wading in muddy water, his foot was bitten by a stingray. Recalling the horrific commentary at Reef World in Cairns, he naturally assumed urgent treatment was called for, and as he could not then see Nick, he jumped into the tender and dashed over to *Keramos*.

On board, we carried comprehensive first-aid and medical equipment, together with a good supply of drugs. Fortunately, I knew where to find information on the appropriate treatment, which was immediately applied. Nevertheless, by this time, Guy's foot and leg up to the knee, had swelled to twice the normal size and it was obvious that he was in much pain. He was very concerned about having abandoned Nick, and stressed that as it was beginning to go dark, he would have to go back to the island, because only he knew precisely where Nick could be found. Accordingly, with Peter at the helm and Guy holding a powerful torch, they were just about to set off, when we heard a shout from the water – it was Nick, and he had swum at least half-a-mile through water infested with sharks, crocodiles, moray eels and very definitely stingrays.

Nick had seen Guy mysteriously disappear with the tender, and when nobody returned for him, he assumed there must be a problem of some kind. As he did not fancy the prospect of spending a night on the island, with the crocodiles, he had decided that the least of all evils was to swim for it.

Guy's leg continued to swell up the thigh, and by the following morning, it looked a sorry sight. The pain killers had proved effective but I do believe, that with the dramatics of Reef World still very much in mind, he was agreeably surprised to find he was still alive.

My stand-by reference book on such occasions is *The Ship Captain's Medical Guide*. Most medical books for the layman only outline the symptoms, and then invariably advise the patient to see a doctor. This book, however, is quite different, as the content is essentially practical – even if it is a fractured spine or childbirth, the appropriate action to be taken is fully explained. And if all else fails, you only have to turn to the final chapter, which details the precise procedure for burial at sea, including the form of burial service to be conducted by the master of the vessel.

Later in the day, we went over to Port Kennedy on Thursday Island, where many Japanese people live. Most are employed in the pearling industry and due to the great depths at which the divers have to work, the occupation is extremely hazardous. This may be judged by noting the names of over 300 divers on the memorial, in the town centre.

The very fine cathedral was built by public subscription (mostly from England), in memory of the 137 people who lost their lives, when the liner *Quetta* from Glasgow, foundered on the nearby Albany Reef, when bound from Brisbane to London. I visited a potter, who showed me an interesting collection of pottery that had been recovered from the wreck. This included Royal Doulton china, in excellent condition and several stoneware, ginger-beer bottles, made by Moira Pottery at their works, near to Burton-on-Trent.

33

ACROSS THE TIMOR SEA AND INDIAN OCEAN

We made our departure from Thursday Island at midday, on 28 April, bound for the Seychelles, 5,445 miles away, but with short stops planned at Christmas Island and the Cocos (Keeling) Islands. We soon fell into our usual ship routine for long ocean passages, with four hour watches viz:

Ken and Nick   2400 to 0400 hr and 1200 to 1600 hr.
John and Peter   0400 to 0800 hr and 1600 to 2000 hr.
Guy and myself   0800 to 1200 hr and 2000 to 2400 hr.

People have often asked what we found to do, on these long voyages and implied that life must be very boring. Actually, there is always a great deal to do, in working and maintaining the yacht – even when not on watch. Moreover, as we all had hobbies or personal interests that could be pursued at sea, there was never a dull moment. Of course the life would not suit everyone, but for those who love the sea it is unmitigated joy.

By 5 May, we were passing between the Hibernia Reef on the port hand and the coast of Timor, which was about twenty miles away. Many pirates operate in this locality, so we pressed on as quickly as possible. We did see a few local craft, but they were too slow to catch us.

Whenever the wind was sufficiently light, Guy would get out his steel fishing line, which had a breaking strength of 135 pounds, and troll for big ones. In these waters they were so plentiful that there was never any difficulty in keeping the freezer full. We had many excellent fish recipes but Nick's fish pie was always billed as, 'Todays Special'.

As we approached Christmas Island, we began to see some of the wonderful sea-birds for which the island is renowned. Most breed only on this island and these include Abbott's booby (the world's rarest booby), the Christmas Island frigate-bird which is a large black and white bird and the magnificent golden bosun-bird, with its yard long golden tail streamers.

An hour before we anchored, at midday on 11 May, in Flying Fish Cove, our imminent arrival had been announced over the island's radio. The announcer assured us of a friendly welcome and said that *Keramos* was the first yacht to visit the island during 1981.

Within a few minutes of going ashore, the harbour master, Jim McMasters, was taking four of us on a tour of the island. The principal industry is the mining of phosphate, which is shipped to all parts of the world, for use as a fertiliser; the rich deposit having been formed from the droppings of myriads of birds, during past ages. Jim took us to see the extensive workings, and also showed us how well the excavations had been rehabilitated by landscaping and afforestation.

In the rain-forests we saw thousands of the giant, red land-crabs, which are an endemic species. The mass migration of these crabs, from the forests to the sea, for breeding, must be one of the world's most amazing spectacles of nature. The migration commences with the first monsoonal rains in November, when the males make their way to the seashore; the females arrive soon after and are mated. The spawn is subsequently cast into the sea, from where the pea-sized crabs emerge about a month later, and begin their progression *en masse*, along well defined migration routes, to the high ground in the forests. At its peak, the migration takes on the appearance of a seething pink carpet, covering the foreshore, roads, gardens and indeed everything that lies in its path.

We left Christmas Island on 14 May, accompanied by many of the wonderful sea-birds. At nightfall, a booby succeeded in alighting on the top of the swaying mizzen mast, and then to our surprise, the bird tucked its head under its wing and went to sleep. Soon, another booby arrived and endeavoured to perch on top of the first one and finding this impossible transferred its attention to the 98 foot high mainmast. The top must have been swinging through an arc of at least 35 feet and the bird spent about twenty minutes trying to get the timing just right. Eventually, it discovered that it was best to alight when the mast came to the end of a swing, but it still had to make an allowance for the forward speed of the boat; it was therefore, a remarkable gymnastic feat. How the boobies manage to balance under such difficult conditions is hard to understand, but to do so while asleep, was to us at least, a complete mystery.

During the run to the Cocos Islands, Guy on two occasions had long and hard fights with big fish, but at the end of each tussle, all that he had on the hook was the head of a large fish. Obviously, a still larger fish – possibly a shark – must have struck, but somehow managed to avoid taking the hook. It was Guy's great ambition to catch a shark, but he never succeeded. He would see a shark alongside and dash down to the galley, to get a piece of juicy red meat, which the shark would eagerly snap up, but when he put some of the same meat onto a hook and trailed it in the water, the shark would look at it disdainfully, and then slowly glide away.

We were up to the Cocos Islands by 0300 hr, on 17 May, so decided to heave to, until after sunrise, when it would be possible to estimate the depth of water over the coral.

After anchoring between Prison Island and Direction Island, we relaxed in the cockpit over breakfast and unanimously agreed that this was certainly one of the most striking places we had yet found. Many factors, no doubt, contributed to that impression, but certainly, the intensity of the breathtaking colours must have been dominant. The water varied in colour from the deepest mazarine blue, near to *Keramos*, and then through sky blue, azure blue and opaque turquoise, as the eye ranged towards the dazzling white of the coral-sand shore; beyond which were the brilliant greens and yellows of the majestic palms – and all shimmering under the scorching light of the sun, as it steadily rose into a sky of the richest cobalt.

We could hardly wait to get on shore and when we did, it was to find a 'paradise island'. There were tropical fruits, coconuts and even fresh water; the most colourful birds and fish; fantastic coral and shells –but surprisingly, we had the island all to ourselves. Whenever I have read about paradise islands, there has always been much mention of beautiful dusky maidens – unfortunately, Direction Island is lacking in just this one respect.

Later in the day, we went over to West Island, for the usual entry clearance. This was effected by two customs officers, two immigration officers, a doctor and a nurse – such is bureaucracy, when a tiny group of islands becomes nationalised. Near to the quay there is a settlement store, where a limited range of goods can be purchased, but for visitors, a purchase tax of 150% was payable. Fortunately, Guy was able to use his manly charm to inveigle a young native lady to make tax-free purchases on our behalf.

Before leaving Cocos, we returned to Direction Island, so that we could spend a memorable night under its magic spell. Then early the following morning, and all too soon, it was up with the anchor and off on the 2,625 mile voyage to the island of Mahé, in the Seychelles.

For the first half of the passage, I decided to keep about 150 miles south of the great circle track, where more favourable winds could be expected. As by 28 May, we were less than 1,000 miles from our destination, we changed to a more northerly course, but from then on, the wind became progressively lighter, until we were only covering about 130 miles each day.

We had not been able to refuel since leaving Cairns, and by this time, the tanks were almost empty. Each day we had to use some fuel to run the generator, in order to provide electricity for cooking and charging the batteries, which supplied the refrigerator and freezer, etc. As a result, we had insufficient fuel to run the main engine for propulsion.

Moreover, as the waste heat from the engine was used to operate the distillation plant that converted sea water into drinking water, we were getting quite low on water.

An extract from the ship's log for 31 May, reads:

"We have now exceeded our estimated time for the voyage by two days and still have 870 miles to go. For the past two days, we have experienced a flat calm, with the sails hanging limp. We only have 90 gallons of fuel remaining and this is required for the generator and as a main engine reserve for manoeuvering into port. During the rainstorms, we have large waterproof sheets suspended over the decks to catch water, which is being piped into the tanks. Providing we get more rain, we do not expect to have a water problem; stocks of food are satisfactory. However, if we don't get some wind soon, the validity period of our visas may prove inadequate. Nick has gathered together pieces of coloured cloth and is now sewing them on the machine, to make a Seychellois flag".

Fortunately, two days later, we were blessed with a good sailing breeze, which stayed with us until midday on 5 June, when we arrived at Port Victoria. We were instructed to anchor by the lighthouse and were soon boarded by several officials, who, while being quite helpful, insisted on taking away our firearms and ammunition, because they had just recently quelled a revolution. After being cleared for entry, we were permitted to refuel and take on water, before proceeding to the yacht club moorings.

There is an excellent open market in the town, where we were able to purchase provisions to replenish our much depleted stocks, while the shops were the best we had seen since leaving Cairns. Some of the hotels provide very good facilities, but the service can be somewhat lackadaisical. Most of them have large swimming pools which we put to good use.

One day, Guy had been gathering shells on the fabulous Grande Anse beach and as usual, had tucked them into a large pocket in his swimming trunks. Later, we went to the Mahé Beach Hotel for refreshments and a swim. When Guy dived into the water, the shells fell out of his pocket and were strewn about the bottom of the pool. As he retrieved them, the onlookers could not understand how it was possible to find such wonderful shells at the bottom of a swimming pool. Typically, Guy made the most of the opportunity to spin some yarn, which resulted in the more credulous swimmers searching over the entire bottom of the pool for shells.

Mahé is a very beautiful island which provides a great deal of interest, but as we were by this time several days behind schedule and the yacht harbour was not suitable for carrying out underwater maintenance, we decided to sail over to the neighbouring island of Praslin – but first, we had to recover our guns. When we enquired as to the procedure, we were informed that we would have to retrieve them from the barracks, which were on the other side of town. Accordingly, Nick, Guy and Peter duly collected the guns, together with the speargun, Very-pistol and a large quantity of ammunition. Putting the guns on their shoulders, they marched off down the main street and as might have been expected, in view of the recent fracas, everyone thought another revolution had started. Very soon they were accosted by men in uniform, and after the three had been subjected to a lot of questioning, they were eventually escorted back to *Keramos* by an armed guard.

On the island of Praslin, we found a delightful, sheltered anchorage in the Anse Petit Coeur, at the head of which is a fine restaurant – La Reserve. The owner, who was then the Minister of Finance, made us welcome and invited us to avail ourselves of the many interesting facilities. We were also loaned the use of a small car, with which to explore the lovely island.

Praslin is world renowned, due to the 46 acre primaeval forest in the Vallée de Mai. Here can be seen many intriguing birds, such as the garrulous bulbul and the very rare black parrot, but the greatest interest is undoubtedly provided by the wonderful trees, and in particular, by the *coco-de-mer* palms. These graceful trees reach a height of 150 feet and take almost a millennium to reach maturity. Some of the present trees must therefore, have started growing well before the battle of Hastings.

There are male and female *coco-de-mer* palms, growing side by side, but the male trees are taller by some twenty feet and tend to overshadow the females. It is perhaps, this 'protective semblance' and the form of the male inflorescence, which is as long and thick as a man's arm and shaped like the male organ; together with the nut, which resembles the female human pelvis, which have given rise to the fascinating Seychellois love legend. This tells of the male palms walking over to unite with the waiting female palms, in the darkness of tempestuous nights – but that it is fatal for anyone to witness this amorous encounter.

The love nuts, as they came to be known, are really like two large coconuts, side-by-side and joined together at the upper part. The width can be as much as two feet and they can weigh up to fifty pounds, so making them the largest seeds in the vegetable kingdom. The nuts first became known when they were washed up on the shores of the

Maldive Islands, where they were highly prized. Like ambergris, they became by right the sole property of the kings of the islands, and any other person found to be in possession of a *coco-de-mer* nut, was liable to have the hands chopped off. The people believed that the nuts grew on trees, under the sea, and hence the name.

It is believed that originally, the islands of the Seychelles formed part of Asia, before Africa and Asia separated, due to continental drift. This has led some people to suggest, that the Vallée de Mai was the biblical site of the Garden of Eden, and over the years, this has stimulated a great deal of imaginative thought. Thus the *coco-de-mer* has been referred to as 'The Tree of Knowledge' and the breadfruit tree as 'The Tree of Life'.

The shape of the nut has provoked much speculation but perhaps none more so, than that by General Gordon, who appears to have not only been intrigued by the suggestive shape but also by the fact that it is enclosed in a heart-shaped fruit, and this led him to write ". . . . I have already alluded to the temptation of Eve and surely if curiosity could be excited by any tree, it would be this . . . . I have also stated that the heart is said by the Scripture, to be the seat of desires."

About 3,000 *coco-de-mer* nuts are produced each year. The delicately flavoured jelly, which they yield, is often mixed with liqueur and served to tourists and others, who wish to indulge in the thrill of consuming the 'Forbidden Fruit'.

To walk through the forest of the Vallée de Mai, as the sun begins to set, is an unforgettable experience. The light filters through the fan-shaped branches of the tall palms, to give twinkling green and yellow tints, against the roseate background of the sky, and if there happens to be a slight breeze, the haunting sound of the rustling leaves adds to the dramatic atmosphere; but one should heed the warning given in the Seychellois love legend – and refrain from lingering into the impassioned night.

After dragging ourselves away from the seductive charm of the Anse Petit Coeur, at 0700 hr on 15 June, we arrived off Bird Island by mid-afternoon. Almost every square inch of land on this small island is occupied by breeding terns. There is only one property, which serves as a honeymoon hotel. The young couples who stay there, no doubt leave with fond memories of the place, but their sweet billing and cooing will most certainly have been drowned, by the never ceasing cacophony produced by the millions of loudly squawking terns.

Before nightfall, we were away again on a course directed towards a position about 150 miles south of Raz Azir, in Somalia – this being the first leg of a tortuous 3,510 mile voyage to the port of Suez, in Egypt.

34

TO THE LAND OF THE PHARAOHS

At 0805 hr on 17 June, we crossed the equator and were then back in the Northern Hemisphere for the first time since leaving Galápagos. The following day, the weather began to deteriorate and soon we were battling against a full gale in a very rough sea. At times the wind was gusting up to Force 10 and we were getting quite a lot of water into the cockpit. When Peter was taking a dish of hot food out of the microwave oven, he was thrown across the galley and sustained a badly scalded leg.

The routing chart for June, shows that between Raz Azir and the island of Socotra in the Arabian Sea, the winds for 30% of the time, are between Force 7 and 12, while the Pilot Book states that the Horn of Africa experiences many more gales than does Cape Horn – so, it must be just about the windiest place in the world.

After rounding the Horn, shortly after midday on 21 June, we set a course along the coast of Somalia and towards Bab el Mandeb, at the entrance to the Red Sea, which was then 400 miles away. The gales slowly subsided and as a result, we were able to open the hatches – the first time this had been possible for almost three days. The temperature rapidly soared to around 112°F, which was not surprising, as we were now sailing along the hottest coastline in the world.

Through the heat haze, we could just make out the barren white cliffs backing the shoreline, but soon, they were to disappear from view altogether, as a duststorm suddenly arose, which restricted visibility to about 100 yards – and made it necessary to close the hatches once again. As we were wearing the absolute minimum of clothing, the foul grey dust adhered to our perspiring bodies, with the result that we quickly assumed the unbecoming colour of donkeys. Below deck, it was unbearably hot, even with the air-conditioning working to maintain the lowest possible temperature. Showers at very frequent intervals, were therefore, the order of the day, to both remove the dust and provide a temporary respite from the oppressive heat.

At 1930 hr on 24 June, we entered the Abu Ali Channel in the Red Sea and now the dust was a bright red, which rapidly transformed the donkeys into Red Indians. The dust floats on the water and imparts the colour, from which the name of the Sea was derived. At night, the dust makes it very difficult to determine the colour of ship's navigation lights and this, together with the fact that the local ships don't respect the normal rules of the sea, made for some hair-raising encounters.

Listening to Channel 16 on the VHF radio, often proved highly entertaining, as here again, the rule prohibiting the use of bad language, apparently does not apply in this locality. One evening, we heard a very irate helmsman communicating with another – not with us, I hasten to add – and his lengthy diatribe finished with, ". . . . you steer ship damn bad, you a bloody f...ing bastard " – but that was nothing compared with the reply! This was certainly the place to increase one's vocabulary, with regard to imprecations and blasphemy.

Previous mention has been made to the lone yachtsman – Syd – whom we first met at Vaitu, in the Marquesa islands and subsequently came across on several other occasions. Sometime after my return to England, I learned that his tiny yacht had hit a reef at the southern end of the Red Sea and as a result, the propeller was badly damaged. The wind happened to be light at the time, so he was able to get the boat off the reef and sail into a small port, where he managed to get a replacement propeller – but unfortunately, not of the correct type. Soon after leaving port, he was caught in a severe squall and due to the poor performance of the propeller, he was unable to prevent his yacht from again hitting the reef, and this time, the little *Doreen Beatrice* became a total wreck. Providentially, the crew of a passing boat saw the elderly man in the water and were able to snatch him to safety.

Very often *Keramos* would be accompanied by dolphins, which would swim in the bow-wave for an hour or more. Why they do this, nobody seems to know, but some years ago, there was in the Red Sea, a very well known dolphin which seamen called 'Pelorus Jack', because it would meet up with a ship and then swim ahead, to guide it through the dangerous reefs off Raz Abu Shagara. It would then leave, to render the same service to another ship sailing in the opposite direction. The pelorus is an instrument carried on ships to lay a required compass course. When Pelorus Jack eventually died, the loss was mourned by mariners all over the world.

One day, Guy was playing a big fish, when he somehow managed to get the steel trace wrapped around the propeller. He immediately went overboard with a hacksaw, to cut the trace away, but soon, the largest shark we had yet seen, made a rapid approach. John, who had been supervising the operation, yanked Guy back on board so vigorously, that Guy's arm was quite badly sprained. Peter sarcastically suggested that most likely, the shark would have done less damage than John had managed to do, but he did concede that the threatening vultures, which had suddenly appeared, were already departing.

On 3 July, we approached the coast of Egypt and were somewhat surprised to see a magnificent range of mountains, with peaks rising up up to 6,000 feet. Later in the day and just before entering the Gulf of Suez, a sudden squall blew out the head panel of the mainsail. As it was by now, too much covered in dust to take below, Nick and Guy took the sewing machine on deck and within an hour, the sail was back in action.

In the congested shipping lanes of the Gulf, we encountered many oil rigs and large platforms, which made navigation very difficult – particularly at night, when their powerful working lights made identification of the navigation lights almost impossible.

In due course, we came up to the entrance to the Suez Canal and were instructed over the radio, to anchor at a position about three miles from the port of Suez, and then await the arrival of a port agent. After a considerable delay, a man arrived and piloted us to an anchorage close to the town. He then offered to negotiate on our behalf, the necessary arrangements for the canal transit and in addition, assist in refuelling and the purchase of stores and provisions – including a good supply of hashish. When we told him we were not into drugs, he said, "Then what about nice French girls?" In the circumstances, I decided it would be better to go on shore and find a reputable agent – as a result, we engaged the services of 'The International Shipping Agency'.

We expected to take on water and fuel, sometime during the following morning, but were informed that this could not be arranged before early evening. Ken therefore hired a car with driver, to take the two of us and Peter to Cairo. We were surprised to find that before we could make the trip, it was necessary to get special visas in addition to those previously obtained in Australia, but after this frustrating delay, we were away at a furious speed to visit the large and richly adorned Mosque of Mohammed Ali. From the Mosque, it was only a short distance to Cairo, where the noise and traffic was quite unbelievable. Here we visited the City Museum, to see the magnificient treasures from the tombs. It was already becoming apparent, that Ken, either by luck or good judgement, had engaged a most helpful man who was not only a capable driver, but also a very knowledgeable guide, for he next whizzed us off to the pleasant town of Giza and soon after he had related the history of the Pyramids – there they were!

I found the construction of the stupendous Pyramids of particular interest, as I had just finished reading a remarkable book entitled, *The Secret of the Pyramids*, which amongst other revelations, describes the manner in which the huge stones were transported from Luxor and how the early constructions collapsed, until after much experiment, the builders developed the technique of making the courses of stonework slope inwards.

The entire locality around the Pyramids is now highly commercialised, with a wide range of articles and services being offered, by very persuasive salesmen. It was not altogether surprising therefore, that Peter should be inveigled into hiring a camel. We watched him mount the frisky animal, with some concern for his safety, but were totally unprepared to see the pair take off at tremendous speed and soon disappear beyond the distant, desert horizon. We were quite sure, at the time, that it would be necessary to engage a new cook, but fortunately, the camel at least, knew the way back.

On the return journey to Suez, our driver stopped at a typical Egyptian café in a small village, where we ordered cool drinks. We were interested to see the locals passing from one to the other, a very potent hookah and in due course, it was passed to Peter. Now as readers may have already guessed, Peter was not the kind of person who would miss the opportunity to participate in a new experience – but he did insist on having a new mouthpiece.

By the time we returned to *Keramos*, she was being refuelled from a barge lying alongside. We learned that our provisions were to be delivered later in the day, while the pilot for the canal transit was due to join us at 0300 hr, on the following day. The provisions were eventually delivered on board around midnight, after which, there was a great deal of haggling regarding the charge for so-called extras.

By the time the provisions had been stowed away, the pilot arrived and almost immediately, we were away along the canal, at nine knots. The fee for the pilot had been agreed with the agents and paid in full, but from the outset, the wretched man began to make all kinds of outrageous demands, which we tended to resist or ignore, apart from providing him with good food and refreshment. However, just before reaching Ismalia, at about 0840 hr, he instructed us to anchor at the side of the canal, while he went to a control office to obtain further instructions. This I resolutely refused to do, as the proximity of the passing ships, would have exposed *Keramos* to an unacceptable risk of collision. At the cost of a bottle of whiskey and other miscellaneous inducements, he eventually agreed that we could anchor in the lake at Ismalia, and after this had been done, he departed.

About an hour later, we were very surprised but relieved to see him return. The bartering, however, was by no means over, because he then told us that when he went home at the end of the day, his children always asked what he had brought for them – consequently, he could not return empty handed. When I asked how many children he had, he said, "Nine". Now it is not easy to find on a yacht, things that might be of interest to children, and particularly for nine children of widely differing ages. Peter therefore started to make a lot of fudge, while Nick concocted a sweetmeat consisting of cornflakes, treacle, desiccated coconut, and goodness knows what else. In due course, we put the terrible man ashore with his loot, and cleared customs at Port Said.

We then heaved a deep sigh of relief, in the belief that our brushes with officialdom were now over, but that was not to be, because on approaching the open sea, we realised that we were being followed by a police patrol boat, and the crew obviously wanted us to stop. Some of us were by now getting rather tired of the Suez 'powers that be' and were in favour of ignoring this latest intervention – particularly as their boat was obviously not fast enough to catch us. My curiosity, however, got the better of me, as I could not think what they could be wanting – we therefore stopped.

As soon as the patrol boat came alongside, a police officer jumped aboard *Keramos* and demanded cigarettes. We told him we did not have any, as none of us smoked. Thereupon he adopted a threatening attitude, saying that all boats carried cigarettes and he did not believe we were any different. He then went on to say that he had the necessary authority to search the yacht – but while the argument continued, John surreptitiously slipped the engine into gear and slowly increased the revs. Suddenly, the officer looked around to find that we were surging forward into the open sea, while the police boat was being left way behind. At this point, he appeared to lose interest in cigarettes, and very politely requested us to put him back on his boat. Having done just that, we were now free, at last, to continue our voyage in familiar waters and set a course for the friendly island of Rhodes.

35

THE FINAL LAP

On approaching the island of Rhodes, on 11 July, we were informed that there was no room for *Keramos* in the Mandraki yacht harbour, so we were obliged to moor in the outer harbour. Having anchored, Nick and Guy took a warp to the shore and were just about to make it fast, when they heard a voice say, "Do you want any help?" It was our daughter Diane and husband Roger, who were on holiday – that is until we found them some work to do on *Keramos*.

It had been previously arranged, that when we reached the Mediterranean, John and Guy would leave us; John in order to take up management in the yacht brokerage business and Guy to pursue a career in the City. Both had served *Keramos* well, not only in the day to day routine, but more importantly, in helping to foster a fine team spirit which is so imperative, when a small group of people are never more than a few feet apart, for every minute of the day and for periods of several weeks – as was the case on the long ocean passages.

The objective now was to sail to Cannes, on the French Riviera, in easy stages, with a view to visiting *en route* business friends, and entertaining some of them on board. During this period, my crew would be Ken, Nick and Peter but in addition, various members of the family would assist over certain stages of the cruise.

Before leaving Rhodes, we took *Keramos* into the Mandraki harbour, in order to take on water. In doing so, we passed between the two columns, which mark the positions occupied by the feet of the Colossus of Rhodes, as its legs spanned the entrance to the harbour. This mighty statue was, of course, one of the seven wonders of the world, before it was sadly demolished by an earthquake.

A short sail took us to the magnificent harbour of Lindos and while there, some of us found sufficient energy to climb up to the acropolis. Then on to the island of Karpathos, before crossing over to Crete, where we moored in the picturesque but tiny harbour of Ayios Nikolaos. Diane and Roger knew this place well, as a result of previous visits and were therefore able to introduce us to the best cafés and restaurants.

I had visited Iraklion with the first *Keramos* and so, having already navigated from Iraklion to England, it was contended that when I reached Iraklion again, I would have completed a circumnavigation of the world – in any case it provided Diane and Roger with a good excuse to arrange a champagne celebration. In due course, *Keramos* completed a voyage round the world, when she crossed longitude one degree West, off the south coast of Spain and soon after that, she crossed her outward track to Rio, at a point to the west of Cape St Vincent.

While in Crete, we could not resist making a further visit to the ruined Minoan palace at Knossos, where the painstaking work of restoration now enables visitors to gain a very good impression of the advanced nature of the Minoan civilisation, during the period 2600 to 1450 BC. Indeed, when compared with life in Britain during the Bronze Age, life in Crete must have provided an earthly paradise. That it was terminated in such a dramatic manner, without doubt, greatly retarded the development of civilisation as we now know it.

The cataclysmic end came in 1450 BC, when an earthquake shattered the cone of the volcano on the nearby island of Santorini, so allowing the sea to flood into the white-hot core and produce what is believed to have been the greatest explosion of all time. A succession of tremendous tidal waves resulted, which completely destroyed the Minoan fleet and submerged all the towns on the northern coast of Crete.

Before leaving Crete, we had to bid farewell to Roger, who returned to London, but on our arrival in Malta, we were joined by our son Ian and his wife Patricia. On 29 July, the girls dressed *Keramos* overall, to celebrate the royal wedding. We were able to see the ceremony, as broadcast on television, from a station in Italy.

On arrival at Empedocle, in southern Sicily, a customs officer and his assistant came aboard. When I presented the officer with the customary crew list, he said, "There are only two ladies included on this list – we have seen three ladies on the yacht". I endeavoured to convince him that the list was correct and that they must have been mistaken, but he continued to insist that they had seen three ladies, and in the circumstances, it was necessary for him to search the yacht. So, while his assistant stayed in the cockpit to ensure nobody slipped ashore, the officer went below and carried out a very thorough search. Of course, he failed 'to find the lady' and after a great deal of agitated muttering between the two officials, they eventually accepted the list as correct. I could never make up my mind, whether they had been genuinely mistaken, or had deliberately created the issue, to provide an excuse for carrying out the search. Of one thing I am quite sure, not one of the men on board could possibly have been mistaken for a lady!

While at Empedocle, we took advantage of the opportunity to visit the famous Valley of the Temples, at Agrigento. Here, there are a large number of ruined Roman temples and in some of them, the beautiful mosaics are in an excellent state of preservation.

Not Without Incident

The call at Marsala will best be remembered for the ability to buy exceptionally good wine at the equivalent price of 55 pence a bottle. Ian bought a cask of sherry at an equally ridiculous price.

We just had to call once again at the Aga Kahn's magnificent Porto Cervo, in Sardinia and to moor stern-to on the magnificent quay, with its row of illuminated, polished brass bollards. Each time we have visited this attractive development, it has in the meantime, grown in size and the five star facilities have been still further improved. The hotels, villas, restaurants and boutiques have all been designed by the estate's architects, who have taken great care to preserve the distinctive style, typical of northern Sardinia, and skilfully sited the various buildings within the attractive landscape, to create a village which manifests a charcteristic charm.

Further calls were made at historic Bonifacio and the modern town of Ajaccio, in Corsica, before eventually arriving on 22 August, at Cannes, where *Keramos* was moored stern-to in the stylishly equipped Porto Canto.

During the world cruise, our good ship had sailed 37,403 nautical miles, equivalent to 43,077 statute miles and had called at no less than 175 different places. Although she had been in many hazardous situations, she had never at any time let the crew down.

After *Keramos* had been completely overhauled and Nick and Peter had returned, subsequent to extended home vacation, she resumed voyaging in European waters.

During the summer of 1982, however, I retired from executive business, but continued to work in a consultative capacity. Although this inevitably changed the pattern of my life, it has nevertheless continued to be 'not entirely without incident'.

ACKNOWLEDGEMENTS

Much of the material herein is based on information culled from my personal diaries and documents, including ship's journals and log books, but I am greatly indebted to all who have shared my experiences, for their helpful co-operation. Additionally, I have to thank my cousin, H. John Podmore, who throughout the preparation of this work has provided a steadfast source of creative advice, as well as giving me the benefit of his photographic expertise.

For their kind permission to reproduce photographs, I wish to thank the following: Murray Aitkin (Plates 7,13,17); Michael Clarke (Plate 9); Jack Cockroft (Plate 15); Denis Fahey (Plate 8) and H. John Podmore (Plate 1, which is a copy of a portrait by Philemon Swift and plate 14). The remaining photographs were taken by myself.

The cover design is by David Frith, who also prepared the maps and designed the layout for the illustrations.

Finally, I have to thank our son Andrew, and his wife Carole, for their valued assistance with regard to typesetting, illustrating and printing, under the auspices of the publishers Catchrose Ltd.

I have drawn freely from many of the authors listed in the bibliography, and my dependence on them is considerable. However, any errors of fact or interpretation are mine alone.

BIBLIOGRAPHY

Bagnis, Raymond. *Fishes of Polynesia*. Editions du Pacific. 1972
Belfield, E. & Essame H. *The Battle for Normandy*. B.T.Batsford Ltd. 1965
Board of Trade. *Ship Captain's Medical Guide*. H.M.Stationery Office. 1967
Brookes, John. *South American Handbook*. Trade & Travel Publications. 1977
Curry, Dr. Manfred. *Yacht Racing*. G. Bell & Sons Ltd. 1935
Dalton, B. & Stanley, D. *South Pacific Handbook*. Moon Publications. 1979
Dodd, Edward. *Polynesian Seafaring*. Dodd Mead & Co. 1972
Dousset, R. & Taillemite, E. *The Great Book of the Pacific*. Edita Lausanne
Eustis, Nelson. *Aggie Grey of Samoa*. Hobby Investments Pty. Ltd. 1978
Fayon, Maxime. *Seychelles*. Kina Italià SpA. 1981
Gaisford, John. *Atlas of Man*. Marshall Cavendish Editions. 1978
Hargreaves, D. & B. *Tropical Blossoms of the Pacific*. Hargreaves & Co. 1970
Hargreaves, D. & B. *Tropical Trees of the Pacific*. Hargreaves & Co. 1970
Hart, J.C. & Stone, W.T. *Cruising Guide to the Caribbean*. Dodd Mead & Co. 1979
Holman, Gordon. *Stand By To Beach!* Hodder & Stoughton Ltd. 1944
Howarth, David. *Dawn of D-Day*. Collins. 1959
Hunte, George. *The West Indian Islands*. B.T. Batsford Ltd. 1972
Jacobs, C. & B. *South Pacific Travel Digest*. Paul Richmond & Co. 1978
Kennedy, Gavin. *Bligh*. Gerald Duckworth & Co. Ltd. 1978
King, Michael. *New Zealand*. A.H. & A.W. Reed. 1979
Lennard, M. *Motuarohia (Roberton's Island)*. The Pelorus Press Ltd. 1959
Maldonado, Father Victor. *Galápagos*. Charles Darwin Scientific Stn. 1978
McCullough, David. *The Path Between the Seas*. Simon & Schuster N.Y. 1977
Montgomery, Field Marshall. *Normandy to the Baltic*. Hutchinson & Co. 1947
Montgomery, Field Marshall. *Memoirs*. Collins. 1958
Murray, K.W.J & Kohorn, R.S.von. *Marlborough Sounds*. Steven William Pbn. 1979
Neuhoff, Sonia di. *The Minoan Civilisation & the Knossos Palace*. Apollon Pbn.
Phillips-Birt, Douglas. *A History of Seamanship*. Doubleday & Co. Inc. 1971
Pope, D. & J. *North Island*. A.H. & A.W. Reed. 1980
Power, Allan. *The Great Barrier Reef*. Paul Hamlyn Pty. Ltd. 1974
Putigny, Bob. *Tahiti and its Islands*. Les Editions du Pacifique. 1980
Reed, A.H. & A.W. *Capt. Cook in New Zealand*. Halstead Press. 1951
Rudder, C. & C. *Focus on Fiji*. Investment Service Ltd. 1973
Salmon, J.T. *The Native Trees of New Zealand*. A.H. & A.W. Reed Ltd. 1980
Thornton, Ian. *Darwin's Islands*. The Natural History Press. 1971
Tuck, G. & Heinzel, H. *Seabirds*. William Collins Sons & Co. Ltd. 1978
White, A. & Epler, B. *Galápagos Guide*. Libri Mundi. 1972